D1527317

The History of
American Education

EDUCATION INFORMATION GUIDE SERIES

Series Editor: Francesco Cordasco, Professor of Education, Montclair State College, Upper Montclair, New Jersey

Also in this series:

BILINGUAL EDUCATION IN AMERICAN SCHOOLS—*Edited by Francesco Cordasco and George Bernstein*

HIGHER EDUCATION IN AMERICA—*Edited by Franklin Parker**

MEDICAL EDUCATION IN THE UNITED STATES—*Edited by Francesco Cordasco and David N. Alloway**

MUSIC EDUCATION—*Edited by Ernest E. Harris*

THE PHILOSOPHY OF EDUCATION—*Edited by Charles Albert Baatz**

PSYCHOLOGICAL FOUNDATIONS—*Edited by Charles Albert Baatz and Olga K. Baatz**

READING IN AMERICAN SCHOOLS—*Edited by Maria E. Schantz and Joseph F. Brunner**

SOCIOLOGY OF EDUCATION—*Edited by Francesco Cordasco and David N. Alloway*

WOMEN'S EDUCATION IN THE UNITED STATES—*Edited by Kay S. Wilkins*

*in preparation

The above series is part of the
GALE INFORMATION GUIDE LIBRARY

The Library consists of a number of separate series of guides covering major areas in the social sciences, humanities, and current affairs.

General Editor: Paul Wasserman, Professor and former Dean, School of Library and Information Services, University of Maryland

Managing Editor: Denise Allard Adzigian, Gale Research Company

The History of American Education

A GUIDE TO INFORMATION SOURCES

Volume 7 in the Education Information Guide Series

Francesco Cordasco

Professor of Education
Montclair State College
Upper Montclair, New Jersey

With

David N. Alloway

Professor of Sociology
Montclair State College
Upper Montclair, New Jersey

Marjorie Scilken Friedman

Former Instructor, History of Education
New York University
New York

AUG   1997

Gale Research Company
Book Tower, Detroit, Michigan 48226

016.370973
H673

Library of Congress Cataloging in Publication Data
Main entry under title:

The History of American education.

(Education information guide series ; v. 7) (Gale
information guide library)
Includes indexes.
1. Education—United States—History—Indexes.
I. Cordasco, Francesco, 1920-   II. Alloway,
David Nelson. III. Friedman, Marjorie Scilken.
IV. Series.
LA212.H57   016.37′0973   79-23010
ISBN 0-8103-1382-0

In Memory Of
A.W. Littlefield
Publisher, Scholar, Friend

VITAE

Francesco Cordasco, a cultural historian and sociologist, is a professor of education at Montclair State College, and has taught at New York University, the City University of New York, Long Island University, and the University of Puerto Rico. Cordasco has served as a consultant to the Migration Division, Commonwealth of Puerto Rico, to the U.S. Office of Education, and to federal, state, and community antipoverty programs. He is the author of books on ethnic communities in the United States, immigrant children, urban education, and educational sociology.

David N. Alloway, an urban sociologist, is a professor of sociology at Montclair State College, and has taught at Western Illinois University, Indiana State, University of Pennsylvania, Seton Hall University, and Fairleigh Dickinson University. Alloway has conducted community surveys, social stratification studies, and has contributed articles to the ENCYCLOPEDIA BRITANNICA and to a wide range of professional and academic journals. He is coauthor of MINORITIES AND THE AMERICAN CITY and coeditor of "Poverty in America," a special issue of the JOURNAL OF HUMAN RELATIONS.

Marjorie Scilken Friedman has been an instructor at New York University, City University of New York's Brooklyn, Hunter and City Colleges, and the Adelphi Urban Center. She has also taught at the University of Puerto Rico and the University of Tel-Aviv in Israel. She received her Ph.D. in history and philosophy of education from New York University, and her M.A. from Columbia University. Her current and continuing interest is in minority education and in pluralism in education.

CONTENTS

INTRODUCTION

The history of American education has received a commanding attention as a result of the social criticism which enveloped the United States during the 1960s and the 1970s. If American education has enjoyed considerable popular support during the last two centuries (its dramatic expansion is an attestation of the support), the last two decades have witnessed new appraisals which have attempted to challenge the optimistic liberalism concerning the values of education delineated by earlier historians, of whom Ellwood P. Cubberley and Paul Monroe were most representative. The whole ideological terrain of American educational history has been and is continuing to be reexamined.

Diane Ravitch (who has been characterized as a chastened liberal) has acerbically examined the new emerging social historiography, and joining the ranks of other contemporary historians (particularly, Bernard Bailyn and Lawrence Cremin), she has subjected the works of the new radical revisionists to a penetrating scrutiny. Professor Ravitch has argued that the revisionists assert that "the schools are themselves oppressive institutions which regiment, indoctrinate, and sort children, either brutally or subtly crushing their individuality and processing them to take their place in an unjust social order."[1] And the objects of her disenchantment are the works of a wide range of historians and social critics among whom are included Michael B. Katz, Clarence Karier, Joel Spring, Colin Greer, Walter Feinberg, Samuel Bowles, and Herbert Gintis. In a larger frame of reference, the doyen of American educational historians, R. Freeman Butts, has perceptively observed:

> Recent research undertaken by scores of scholars in U.S. history in general and in the history of education in particular now enable us to formulate a new interpretative synthesis to replace the one embedded in the 1919 introductory textbook by Ellwood P. Cubberley, PUBLIC EDUCATION IN THE UNITED STATES, which dominated the field from the 1920s to the 1940s. We need to modify Cubberley's essentially optimistic and naive image of the "public school triumphant," and we need a more balanced conception of the dynamics of social change than that portrayed in the pessimistic and narrowly class-oriented framework promoted by radical historians during the past decade. I do not believe that either the culturalist approach or the radical approach will appropriately revise Cubberley or produce the conceptual framework that is necessary.

Introduction

> I believe that the best hope for a critical reassessment of the history of public education is within a framework that views public education as an essential ingredient of the persistent tensions created by three basic themes in American civilization: the cohesive value claims of a democratic political community summed up in the constitutional ideals of liberty, equality, justice, and obligation for the public good; the pluralistic loyalties that give particular identity and coherence to the different segments of society that arise from diversities of religion, language, culture, ethnicity, race, and locality; and the long-term worldwide modernization process that has been pushing all Western societies for more than 200 years toward national centralization, popular participation, industrialization, urbanization, and secularization.[2]

Essentially, this is a reasoned judgment and one which would invite wide agreement; yet, it is not unanticipated that a continuing examination of American educational history will attest that the history of American public education (however interpreted) is of commanding significance in the evolving formation of American society, and that the field deserves special study in its own right.

It is against this background that THE HISTORY OF AMERICAN EDUCATION: A GUIDE TO INFORMATION SOURCES has been prepared. It is intended as a reference bibliography addressed to the many constituences which will, hopefully, find it useful. Its coverage is comprehensive, but it is not intended as definitive or complete: clearly, a definitively complete register of titles would be impracticable. However, the volume's dimensionally comprehensive plan affords a convenient bibliographical register which will adequately serve the needs to which it is addressed. The articulation and arrangement of the entries have been structured to provide overviews of the resources available in bibliographies, reference works, and source collections; separate sections have been allocated to historiography, and to the American college and university; and to the history of textbooks, teaching, teachers, and curriculum. A series of sectional chronological tableaux have permitted the management of related entries; and a separate division has allowed a flexible handling of miscellaneous titles which have a generalized referential significance. At best, the format is convenient, and the indexes facilitate the search for specific areas and fields of interest.

I am deeply indebted to David N. Alloway and Marjorie Scilken Friedman, who provided assistance in this venture, but defects in design or errors which have crept into the text should be solely assigned to me.

F.C.

NOTES

1. Diane Ravitch, THE REVISIONISTS REVISED: A CRITIQUE OF THE RADI-
CAL ATTACK ON THE SCHOOLS (New York: Basic Books, 1977), p. 3.
See, also, Peter Clecak, "An Ideological Battle Over School History," THE
CHRONICLE OF HIGHER EDUCATION 17 (October 16, 1978): 14-15. In
noting Ravitch's charges, Clecak observes: "Although hardly novel, these
charges against radical critics of American education are serious. . . . [Ra-
vitch] uses the present neo-conservative mood to advantage, salvaging the considerable residue of the liberal vision of American education, discarding its im-
plausible dimensions, and hinting at future paths for research and reformist politics that may yield modest, though solid, returns."

2. R. Freeman Butts, PUBLIC EDUCATION IN THE UNITED STATES: FROM
REVOLUTION TO REFORM (New York: Holt, Rinehart and Winston, 1978),
p. vi. See, also, Butts's "Public Education in a Pluralistic Society," EDUCA-
TIONAL THEORY 27 (Winter 1977); and his "The Search for Purpose in American Education," COLLEGE BOARD REVIEW, no. 98, Winter 1975-76, pp. 3-
19.

Chapter 1

BASIC REFERENCE WORKS AND PERIODICALS

1. GENERAL

1 Adams, James Truslow, ed. DICTIONARY OF AMERICAN HISTORY.
   7 vols. 2d ed. New York: Charles Scribner's Sons, 1940.

2 Adams, James Truslow, and Coleman, R.V., eds. ATLAS OF AMERICAN
   HISTORY. New York: Charles Scribner's Sons, 1943. 360 p.

3 Andrews, Wayne, ed. CONCISE DICTIONARY OF AMERICAN HISTORY.
   New York: Charles Scribner's Sons, 1962. 1,164 p.

4 Baum, Willa K. ORAL HISTORY FOR THE LOCAL HISTORY SOCIETY.
   Stockton, Calif.: Conference of California Historical Societies, 1969.
   44 p.

5 Bemis, Samuel Flagg, and Griffin, Grace G. GUIDE TO THE DIPLO-
   MATIC HISTORY OF THE UNITED STATES, 1775-1921. Washington,
   D.C.: Government Printing Office, 1935. 996 p.

6 Bergman, Peter M., ed. THE CHRONOLOGICAL HISTORY OF THE
   NEGRO IN AMERICA. New York: Harper and Row, 1969. 698 p.

7 Boatner, Mary Mayo III. THE CIVIL WAR DICTIONARY. New York:
   David McKay, 1959. 990 p.

8 Diaz, Albert James, ed. GUIDE TO MICROFORMS IN PRINT. Washington, D.C.: NCR-Microcard Editions, 1961-- .

9 _____. SUBJECT GUIDE TO MICROFORMS IN PRINT. Washington,
   D.C.: NCR-Microcard Editions, 1962-63-- .

10 DIRECTORY OF AMERICAN SCHOLARS. 6th ed. Vol. 1: HISTORY.
    New York: R.R. Bowker, 1974. 772 p.

Reference Works and Periodicals

11   Dixon, Elizabeth I., and Mink, James V. ORAL HISTORY AT ARROW-
      HEAD: PROCEEDINGS. Los Angeles: First National Colloquium on
      Oral History, Oral History Association, 1967. 135 p.

12   Edward, Paul, et al., eds. THE ENCYCLOPEDIA OF PHILOSOPHY.
      4 vols. New York: Macmillan, 1972.

      A reprint of the original 8 volumes into 4.

13   Elliott, Stephen P., ed. ENCYCLOPEDIA OF AMERICAN HISTORY.
      Guilford, Conn.: Dushkin Publishing Group, 1973. 413 p.

14   Filler, Louis. A DICTIONARY OF AMERICAN SOCIAL REFORM. New
      York: Philosophical Library, 1963. 859 p.

15   Freidel, Frank, ed. HARVARD GUIDE TO AMERICAN HISTORY. Rev.
      ed. 2 vols. Cambridge, Mass.: Harvard University Press, 1974.

16   Gould, Julius, and Kolb, William L., eds. DICTIONARY OF THE SO-
      CIAL SCIENCES. New York: Free Press of Glencoe, 1964. 777 p.

17   Greene, Evarts B., and Harrington, Virginia D. AMERICAN POPULA-
      TION BEFORE THE FEDERAL CENSUS OF 1790. 1932. Reprint. Glou-
      cester, Mass.: Peter Smith, 1966. 228 p.

18   Hart, James D. THE OXFORD COMPANION TO AMERICAN LITERA-
      TURE. 4th ed. New York: Oxford University Press, 1965. 1,004 p.

19   Hodge, Frederick Webb, ed. HANDBOOK OF AMERICAN INDIANS
      NORTH OF MEXICO. 2 vols. 1905. Reprint. New York: Pageant
      Books, 1959.

20   Howe, George F., et al., eds. GUIDE TO HISTORICAL LITERATURE.
      New York: Macmillan, 1961. 997 p.

      Prepared for the American Historical Association.

21   Hurwitz, Howard L. AN ENCYCLOPEDIC DICTIONARY OF AMERICAN
      HISTORY. New York: Washington Square Press, 1968. 894 p.

22   Johnson, Thomas, ed. THE OXFORD COMPANION TO AMERICAN
      HISTORY. New York: Oxford University Press, 1966. 912 p.

23   Jones, H.G. THE RECORDS OF A NATION: THEIR MANAGEMENT,
      PRESERVATION, AND USE. New York: Atheneum, 1969. 326 p.

24   Jones, Howard M., and Ludwig, Richard M. GUIDE TO AMERICAN LITERATURE AND ITS BACKGROUNDS SINCE 1890. 4th ed., rev. and enl. Cambridge, Mass.: Harvard University Press, 1972. 278 p.

25   Kagan, Hilde Heun. THE AMERICAN HERITAGE PICTORIAL ATLAS OF UNITED STATES HISTORY. New York: American Heritage Publishing, 1966. 424 p.

26   Lord, Clifford L., and Lord, Elizabeth H. HISTORICAL ATLAS OF THE UNITED STATES. Rev. ed. 1953. Reprint. New York: Johnson Reprint, 1969. 253 p.

27   Lossing, Benson John, ed. HARPER'S ENCYCLOPEDIA OF UNITED STATES HISTORY. 10 vols. New York: Harper and Bros., 1901.

28   McDonald, Donna, ed. DIRECTORY OF HISTORICAL SOCIETIES AND AGENCIES IN THE UNITED STATES AND CANADA, 1973-1974. Nashville: American Association for State and Local History, 1972. 378 p.

29   Morris, Richard B., ed. ENCYCLOPEDIA OF AMERICAN HISTORY. Enl. and updated. New York: Harper and Row, 1970. 864 p.

30   Sheehy, Eugene P. GUIDE TO REFERENCE BOOKS. 9th ed. Chicago: American Library Association, 1976. 1,015 p.

31   Shumway, Gary L. ORAL HISTORY IN THE UNITED STATES: A DIRECTORY. New York: Oral History Association, 1971. 120 p.

32   Sills, David L., ed. INTERNATIONAL ENCYCLOPEDIA OF THE SOCIAL SCIENCES. 17 vols. New York: Macmillan, 1968.

33   Smith, James W., and Jamison, A. Leland, eds. RELIGION IN AMERICAN LIFE. 4 vols. Princeton, N.J.: Princeton University Press, 1961.

34   THE STATISTICAL HISTORY OF THE UNITED STATES FROM COLONIAL TIMES TO THE PRESENT. Stamford, Conn.: Fairfield Publishers, 1965. 1,015 p.

35   U.S. Department of the Interior. BIOGRAPHICAL AND HISTORICAL INDEX OF AMERICAN INDIANS AND PERSONS INVOLVED IN INDIAN AFFAIRS. 8 vols. Boston: G.K. Hall, 1966.

36   U.S. Department of the Interior. Geological Survey. THE NATIONAL ATLAS OF THE UNITED STATES OF AMERICA. Washington, D.C.: Government Printing Office, 1970. 430 p.

37   U.S. Library of Congress. A GUIDE TO THE STUDY OF THE UNITED
      STATES OF AMERICA: REPRESENTATIVE BOOKS REFLECTING THE DE-
      VELOPMENT OF AMERICAN LIFE AND THOUGHT. Washington, D.C.:
      Government Printing Office, 1960. 1,208 p.

38   U.S. National Archives and Records Service. General Services Adminis-
      tration. GUIDE TO THE NATIONAL ARCHIVES OF THE UNITED STATES.
      Washington, D.C.: Government Printing Office, 1974. 909 p.

           Describes the history and function of each agency and lists
           available records.

39   U.S. National Historical Publications Commission. GUIDE TO ARCHIVES
      AND MANUSCRIPTS IN THE UNITED STATES. New Haven, Conn.: Yale
      University Press, 1961. 798 p.

40   Van Doren, Charles, and McHenry, Robert, eds. WEBSTER'S GUIDE TO
      AMERICAN HISTORY: A CHRONOLOGICAL, GEOGRAPHICAL, AND
      BIOGRAPHICAL SURVEY AND COMPENDIUM. Springfield, Mass.: Mer-
      riam Co., 1971. 1,441 p.

41   Wesley, Charles H., et al. INTERNATIONAL LIBRARY OF NEGRO LIFE
      AND HISTORY. 10 vols. New York: Publishers Co., 1967-68.

42   Whitehill, Walter Muir. INDEPENDENT HISTORICAL SOCIETIES: AN
      ENQUIRY INTO THEIR RESEARCH AND PUBLICATION FUNCTIONS AND
      THEIR FINANCIAL FUTURE. Boston: Boston Athenaeum, 1962. 611 p.

43   Wynar, Lubomyr R. AMERICAN POLITICAL PARTIES: A SELECTIVE
      GUIDE TO PARTIES AND MOVEMENTS OF THE 20TH CENTURY. Little-
      ton, Colo.: Libraries Unlimited, 1969. 427 p.

44   Young, Margaret Labash, et al., eds. DIRECTORY OF SPECIAL LIBRARIES
      AND INFORMATION CENTERS. 3 vols. 3d ed. Detroit: Gale Re-
      search, 1974.

2. BIBLIOGRAPHIES

45   American Bibliographical Center. AMERICA: HISTORY AND LIFE: A
      GUIDE TO PERIODICAL LITERATURE. Santa Barbara, Calif.: Clio Press,
      1964-- . Quarterly.

           An index beginning with periodical literature in 1964. In-
           cludes precis of individual articles. Five-year indexes.

46   American Historical Association. BIBLIOGRAPHIES. Washington, D.C.:
      1960-- .

(a) Berwick, Keith B. THE FEDERAL AGE, 1789-1829. (1961) 42 p.

(b) Blum, Albert B. A HISTORY OF THE AMERICAN LABOR MOVEMENT. (1972) 41 p.

(c) Bridges, Hal. CIVIL WAR AND RECONSTRUCTION. 2d ed. (1962) 25 p.

(d) Carter, Harvey L. FAR WESTERN FRONTIERS. (1972) 64 p.

(e) De Conde, Alexander. NEW INTERPRETATIONS IN AMERICAN FOREIGN POLICY. 2d ed. (1961) 43 p.

(f) Elkins, Stanley, and McKitrick, Eric. THE FOUNDING FATHERS: YOUNG MEN OF THE REVOLUTION. (1962) 30 p.

(g) Fite, Gilbert C. AMERICAN AGRICULTURE AND FARM POLICY SINCE 1900. (1964) 30 p.

(h) Freidel, Frank. THE NEW DEAL IN HISTORICAL PER-SPECTIVE. 2d ed. (1965) 25 p.

(i) Galambos, Louis. AMERICAN BUSINESS HISTORY. (1967) 34 p.

(j) Gaustad, Edwin S. RELIGION IN AMERICA: HISTORY AND HISTORIOGRAPHY. (1973) 59 p.

(k) Grantham, Dewey W., Jr. CONTEMPORARY AMERICAN HISTORY: THE UNITED STATES SINCE 1945. (1975) 46 p.

(l) Greene, Jack P. THE REAPPRAISAL OF THE AMERICAN REVOLUTION IN RECENT HISTORICAL LITERATURE. (1967) 84 p.

(m) Hagan, William T. THE INDIAN IN AMERICAN HISTO-RY. (1971) 34 p.

(n) Harlan, Louis R. THE NEGRO IN AMERICAN HISTORY. (1965) 29 p.

(o) Hicks, John D. NORMALCY AND REACTION, 1921-1933: AN AGE OF DISILLUSIONMENT. (1960) 23 p.

(p) May, Ernest R. AMERICAN INTERVENTION: 1917 AND 1941. 2d ed. (1969) 28 p.

(q) Morgan, Edmund S. THE AMERICAN REVOLUTION: A REVIEW OF CHANGING INTERPRETATIONS. (1958) 22 p.

(r) Mowry, George E. THE PROGRESSIVE ERA, 1900-20: THE REFORM PERSUASION. (1972) 39 p.

(s) Scott, Franklin D. THE PEOPLING OF AMERICA: PER-SPECTIVES ON IMMIGRATION. (1972) 75 p.

(t) Sellers, Charles Grier. JACKSONIAN DEMOCRACY. (1958) 20 p.

(u) Singletary, Otis A., and Bailey, Kenneth K. THE SOUTH IN AMERICAN HISTORY. 2d ed. (1965) 31 p.

(v) Stevens, Harry R. THE MIDDLE WEST. 2d ed. (1965) 28 p.

(w) Stover, John F. TRANSPORTATION IN AMERICAN HISTORY. (1970) 40 p.

(x) Wright, Louis B. NEW INTERPRETATIONS OF AMERICAN COLONIAL HISTORY. 3d ed. (1969) 32 p.

47   _____. WRITINGS ON AMERICAN HISTORY. Washington, D.C.: American Historical Association, 1904-- . Annual.

An annotated compilation of emerged historical works.

48   Beers, Henry P. BIBLIOGRAPHIES IN AMERICAN HISTORY: GUIDE TO MATERIALS FOR RESEARCH. 2d ed. New York: H.W. Wilson, 1942. 503 p.

49   Cassara, Ernest. HISTORY OF THE UNITED STATES OF AMERICA: A GUIDE TO INFORMATION SOURCES. Detroit: Gale Research, 1977. 459 p.

A selective guide to some two thousand titles on all aspects of the American experience.

50   Cohen, Hennig, ed. ARTICLES IN AMERICAN STUDIES, 1954-1968: A CUMULATION OF THE ANNUAL BIBLIOGRAPHIES FROM "AMERICAN QUARTERLY." 2 vols. Ann Arbor, Mich.: Pierian Press, 1972.

Bibliographies, usually briefly annotated.

51   Dougherty, James J., et al. WRITINGS ON AMERICAN HISTORY, 1973-74: A SUBJECT BIBLIOGRAPHY OF ARTICLES. Washington, D.C.: American Historical Association, 1974. 276 p.

52   Dumond, Dwight L. A BIBLIOGRAPHY OF ANTISLAVERY IN AMERICA. Ann Arbor: University of Michigan Press, 1961. 119 p.

53   GOLDENTREE BIBLIOGRAPHIES IN AMERICAN HISTORY. New York: Appleton-Century-Crofts; Northbrook, Ill.: AHM Publishing, 1970-- .

(a) Bremmer, Robert H. AMERICAN SOCIAL HISTORY SINCE 1860. (1971) 144 p.

(b) Burr, Nelson R. RELIGION IN AMERICAN LIFE. (1971) 192 p.

(c) DeSantis, Vincent P. THE GILDED AGE: 1877-1896. (1973) 168 p.

(d) Donald, David. THE NATION IN CRISIS, 1861-1877. (1969) 112 p.

(e) Fehrenbacher, Don E. MANIFEST DESTINY AND THE COMING OF THE CIVIL WAR. (1970) 144 p.

(f) Ferguson, E. James. CONFEDERATION, CONSTITUTION, AND EARLY NATIONAL PERIOD, 1781-1815. (1975) 168 p.

(g) Fowler, Wilton B. AMERICAN DIPLOMATIC HISTORY SINCE 1890. (1975) 176 p.

(h) Greene, Jack P. THE AMERICAN COLONIES IN THE EIGHTEENTH CENTURY, 1689-1763. (1969) 160 p.

(i) Grob, Gerald N. AMERICAN SOCIAL HISTORY BEFORE 1860. (1970) 160 p.

(j) Herbst, Jurgen. THE HISTORY OF AMERICAN EDUCATION. (1973) 172 p.

(k) Kirkland, Edward C. AMERICAN ECONOMIC HISTORY SINCE 1860. (1971) 96 p.

(l) Link, Arthur S., and Leary, William M., Jr. THE PROGRESSIVE ERA AND THE GREAT WAR, 1896-1920. (1969) 96 p.

(m) Shy, John. THE AMERICAN REVOLUTION. (1973) 152 p.

(n) Taylor, George Rogers. AMERICAN ECONOMIC HISTORY BEFORE 1860. (1969) 128 p.

(o) Vaughan, Alden T. THE AMERICAN COLONIES IN THE SEVENTEENTH CENTURY. (1971) 144 p.

54   Hasse, Adelaide R. MATERIALS FOR A BIBLIOGRAPHY OF THE PUBLIC ARCHIVES OF THE THIRTEEN ORIGINAL STATES: COVERING THE COLONIAL PERIOD AND STATE PERIOD TO 1789, 1906. Reprint. New York: Argonaut Press, 1966. 339 p.

55   INDEX TO LITERATURE ON THE AMERICAN INDIAN. San Francisco: Indian History Press, 1972-- .

56   Kaplan, Louis, et al. A BIBLIOGRAPHY OF AMERICAN AUTOBIOGRAPHIES. Madison: University of Wisconsin Press, 1961. 384 p.

57   Nevins, Allan, et al. CIVIL WAR BOOKS: A CRITICAL BIBLIOGRAPHY. 2 vols. Baton Rouge: Louisiana State University Press, 1967-69.

58   REVIEWS IN AMERICAN HISTORY. Westport, Conn.: Redgrave Information Resources, 1973-- .

59 Trask, David F., et al. A BIBLIOGRAPHY OF UNITED STATES--LATIN
    AMERICAN RELATIONS SINCE 1810: A SELECTED LIST OF ELEVEN
    THOUSAND PUBLISHED REFERENCES. Lincoln: University of Nebraska
    Press, 1968. 472 p.

60 U.S. Library of Congress. THE NEGRO IN THE UNITED STATES: A
    SELECTED BIBLIOGRAPHY. Washington, D.C.: Government Printing
    Office, 1970. 325 p.

61 Waseman, Manfred J., ed. BIBLIOGRAPHY ON ORAL HISTORY. New
    York: Oral History Association, 1971. 48 p.

62 White, Carl M., ed. SOURCES OF INFORMATION IN THE SOCIAL
    SCIENCES. 2d ed. Chicago: American Library Association, 1973.
    702 p.

3. BIOGRAPHIES

63 [Cattell, Jacques]. LEADERS IN EDUCATION. 5th ed. New York:
    R.R. Bowker, 1974. 1,309 p. See also: John F. Ohlers, BIOGRAPHI-
    CAL DICTIONARY OF AMERICAN EDUCATORS. 3 vols. Westport,
    Conn.: Greenwood Press, 1978.

64 CONTEMPORARY AUTHORS: A BIO-BIBLIOGRAPHICAL GUIDE TO CUR-
    RENT AUTHORS AND THEIR WORKS. 64 vols. Edited by Chris Nasso.
    Detroit: Gale Research, 1962-- . Biennial.

65 Hopkins, Joseph G.E. CONCISE DICTIONARY OF AMERICAN BIOG-
    RAPHY. 2d ed. New York: Charles Scribner's Sons, 1977. 1,229 p.

66 James, Edward T. NOTABLE AMERICAN WOMEN, 1607-1950. 3 vols.
    Cambridge, Mass.: Harvard University Press, 1971.

67 Johnson, Allen, et al., eds. DICTIONARY OF AMERICAN BIOGRAPHY.
    21 vols. New York: Charles Scribner's Sons, 1928-- .

        Supplements, 1-4, 1944-74.

68 THE NATIONAL CYCLOPAEDIA OF AMERICAN BIOGRAPHY: BEING
    THE HISTORY OF THE UNITED STATES ILLUSTRATED IN THE LIVES OF
    THE FOUNDERS, BUILDERS, AND DEFENDERS OF THE REPUBLIC, AND
    OF THE MEN AND WOMEN WHO ARE DOING THE WORK AND
    MOULDING THE THOUGHT OF THE PRESENT TIME. 53 vols. and 12
    supplements. Clifton, N.J.: James T. White, 1892-- .

        Edited by "Distinguished Biographers."

69   U.S. Congress. The House. BIOGRAPHICAL DIRECTORY OF THE
      AMERICAN CONGRESS, 1774-1961. 85th Congress, 2d session. House
      Document 442. Washington, D.C.: Government Printing Office, 1961.
      1,863 p.

70   WHO'S WHO IN AMERICA, 1978-1979. 2 vols. 40th ed. Chicago:
      Marquis Publishing, 1978.

71   WHO'S WHO OF AMERICAN WOMEN, 1974-1975. 8th ed. Chicago:
      Marquis Publishing, 1973.

72   WHO WAS WHO IN AMERICA. 6 vols. Chicago: Marquis Publishing,
      1942-- .

4. PERIODICALS

73   Camp, William L., and Schwark, Bryan L. GUIDE TO PERIODICALS IN
      EDUCATION AND ITS ACADEMIC DISCIPLINES. 2d ed. Metuchen,
      N.J.: Scarecrow Press, 1975. 552 p.

      Lists some six hundred periodicals issued in the United States.
      Entries are arranged within fifty-seven general and subject
      categories.

74   Davis, Sheldon E. EDUCATIONAL PERIODICALS DURING THE NINE-
      TEENTH CENTURY. Washington, D.C.: U.S. Bureau of Education,
      1919. 125 p.

      Originally issued as U.S. BUREAU OF EDUCATION BULLETIN
      1919. No. 28.

75   A LIST OF SELECTED PERIODICALS AND JOURNALS

      (a) AFRO: AMERICAN STUDIES: AN INTERDISCIPLINARY
      JOURNAL. New York: Gordon and Breach, Science Publish-
      ers. Quarterly.

      (b) AGRICULTURAL HISTORY. Agricultural History Society
      and the University of California Press. Quarterly.

      (c) AMERICAN ANTHROPOLOGIST. American Anthropologi-
      cal Association. Quarterly.

      (d) AMERICAN ANTIQUITY: JOURNAL OF THE SOCIETY
      FOR AMERICAN ARCHAEOLOGY. Quarterly. Society for
      American Archaeology.

      (e) AMERICAN ARCHIVIST. Society of American Archivists.
      Quarterly.

      (f) AMERICAN ECONOMIC REVIEW. American Economic
      Association. Quarterly.

(g) AMERICAN HERITAGE. American Heritage Publishing Co. Bimonthly.

(h) AMERICAN HISTORICAL REVIEW. American Historical Association. Quarterly.

(i) AMERICAN JEWISH ARCHIVES. Hebrew Union College, Jewish Institute of Religion. Semiannually.

(j) AMERICAN JEWISH HISTORICAL QUARTERLY. American Jewish Historical Society. Quarterly.

(k) AMERICAN JOURNAL OF ECONOMICS AND SOCIOL-OGY. American Journal of Economics and Sociology. Quarterly.

(l) AMERICAN JOURNAL OF EDUCATION. 32 vols. Hartford, Conn.: Henry Barnard, 1855-1882. Also edited by publishers.

(m) AMERICAN JOURNAL OF INTERNATIONAL LAW. American Society of International Law. Five times annually.

(n) AMERICAN JOURNAL OF LEGAL HISTORY. American Society for Legal History. Quarterly.

(o) AMERICAN JOURNAL OF SOCIOLOGY. University of Chicago. Bimonthly.

(p) AMERICAN LITERATURE: A JOURNAL OF LITERARY HISTORY, CRITICISM, AND BIBLIOGRAPHY. Duke University Press. Quarterly.

(q) AMERICAN NEPTUNE: A QUARTERLY JOURNAL OF MARITIME HISTORY. Peabody Museum of Salem. (Mass.). Quarterly.

(r) AMERICAN POLITICAL SCIENCE REVIEW. American Political Science Association. Quarterly.

(s) AMERICAN QUARTERLY. American Studies Association and the University of Pennsylvania. Quarterly.

(t) AMERICAN SOCIOLOGICAL REVIEW. American Sociological Association. Bimonthly.

(u) AMERICAN SOCIOLOGIST. American Sociological Association. Quarterly.

(v) AMERICAN STUDIES. Midcontinent American Studies Association, the University of Kansas, and the University of Missouri at Kansas City. Occasional.

(w) AMERICAN WEST. American West Publishing Co. Bimonthly.

(x) AMERIKASTUDIEN/AMERICAN STUDIES. Formerly JAHRBUCH FUR AMERIKASTUDIEN. Deutsche Gesellschaft for Amerikastudien. Semiannually.

(y) ANNALS OF THE AMERICAN ACADEMY OF POLITICAL AND SOCIAL SCIENCE. American Academy of Political and Social Science. Bimonthly.

(z) ANNALS OF THE ASSOCIATION OF AMERICAN GEOG-RAPHERS. Association of American Geographers. Quarterly.

(aa) BUSINESS HISTORY REVIEW. Harvard Graduate School of Business Administration. Quarterly.

(bb) CANADIAN REVIEW OF AMERICAN STUDIES. Canadian Association for American Studies. Semiannually.

(cc) CATHOLIC HISTORICAL REVIEW. American Catholic Historical Association. Quarterly.

(dd) CHURCH HISTORY. American Society of Church History. Quarterly.

(ee) CIVIL WAR HISTORY: A JOURNAL OF THE MIDDLE PERIOD. Quarterly.

(ff) CLA JOURNAL. College Language Association. (Specializes in black literature). Quarterly.

(gg) DEMOGRAPHY. Population Association of America. Quarterly.

(hh) EARLY AMERICAN LITERATURE. Modern Language Association: Early American Literature Group. Thrice annually.

(ii) ECONOMIC GEOGRAPHY. Clark University. Quarterly.

(jj) ETHNOHISTORY. American Society for Ethnohistory (formerly known as the Ohio Valley Historical Indian Conference). Quarterly.

(kk) EXPLORATIONS IN ECONOMIC HISTORY. Formerly EXPLORATIONS IN ENTREPRENEURIAL HISTORY. Kent State University Press. Quarterly.

(ll) FOREIGN AFFAIRS. Council on Foreign Relations. Quarterly.

(mm) GEOGRAPHICAL REVIEW. American Geographical Society. Quarterly.

(nn) HISTORIAN. Phi Alpha Theta, International Honor Society in History. Quarterly.

(oo) HISTORIC PRESERVATION. National Trust for Historic Preservation. Quarterly.

(pp) HISTORY AND THEORY: STUDIES IN THE PHILOSOPHY OF HISTORY. Wesleyan University Press. Occasionally.

(qq) HISTORY OF EDUCATION QUARTERLY. History of Education Society. Quarterly.

(rr) HISTORY NEWS. American Association for State and Local History. Monthly.

(ss) HISTORY OF POLITICAL ECONOMY. Duke University Press. Quarterly.

(tt) HISTORY: REVIEW OF NEW BOOKS. Washington, D.C.: Heldref Publications, 1971-- . (Books are reviewed within a few months of their initial publication). Ten times annually.

(uu) HISTORY TODAY. London: History Today. Monthly.

(vv) HUNTINGTON LIBRARY QUARTERLY: A JOURNAL FOR THE HISTORY AND INTERPRETATION OF ENGLISH AND AMERICAN CIVILIZATION. Huntington Library. Quarterly.

(ww) INDIAN JOURNAL OF AMERICAN STUDIES. American Studies Research Center, Hyderabad (India). Semiannually.

(xx) ISIS: INTERNATIONAL REVIEW DEVOTED TO THE HISTORY OF SCIENCE AND ITS CULTURAL INFLUENCES. History of Science Society. Five times annually.

(yy) JOURNAL OF AMERICAN FOLKLORE. American Folklore Society. Quarterly.

(zz) JOURNAL OF AMERICAN HISTORY. Organization of American Historians. Quarterly.

(aaa) JOURNAL OF AMERICAN STUDIES. British Association for American Studies and the Cambridge University Press. Thrice yearly.

(bbb) JOURNAL OF CHURCH AND STATE. J.M. Dawson Studies in Church and State, Baylor University. Thrice yearly.

(ccc) JOURNAL OF ECONOMIC HISTORY. Economic History Association. Quarterly.

(ddd) JOURNAL OF ECONOMIC LITERATURE. American Economic Association. Quarterly.

(eee) JOURNAL OF INTERDISCIPLINARY HISTORY. MIT School of Humanities and Social Science. Quarterly.

(fff) JOURNAL OF LIBRARY HISTORY, PHILOSOPHY AND COMPARATIVE LIBRARIANSHIP. School of Library Science, Florida State University. Quarterly.

(ggg) JOURNAL OF NEGRO HISTORY. Association for the Study of Negro Life and History. Quarterly.

(hhh) JOURNAL OF POLITICAL ECONOMY. University of Chicago Press. Bimonthly.

(iii) JOURNAL OF POLITICS. Southern Political Science Association. Quarterly.

(jjj) JOURNAL OF POPULAR CULTURE. Popular Culture Section, Popular Literature Section of the Modern Language Association of America, and the Popular Culture Section of the Midwest Modern Language Association. Quarterly.

(kkk) JOURNAL OF SOCIAL HISTORY. Rutgers University. Quarterly.

(lll) JOURNAL OF SOUTHERN HISTORY. Southern Historical Association. Quarterly.

(mmm) JOURNAL OF THE HISTORY OF THE BEHAVIORAL SCIENCES. Brandon, Vt.: Clinical Psychology Publishing Co. Quarterly.

(nnn) JOURNAL OF THE HISTORY OF IDEAS. City University of New York. Quarterly.

(ooo) JOURNAL OF THE HISTORY OF PHILOSOPHY. Journal of the History of Philosophy. Quarterly.

(ppp) LABOR HISTORY. Tamiment Institute. Quarterly.

(qqq) MILITARY AFFAIRS. American Military Institute. Quarterly.

(rrr) NEW ENGLAND QUARTERLY: A HISTORICAL REVIEW OF NEW ENGLAND LIFE AND LETTERS. Colonial Society of Massachusetts and the New England Quarterly. Quarterly.

(sss) PACIFIC HISTORICAL REVIEW. Pacific Coast Branch, American Historical Association. Quarterly.

(ttt) PAPERS OF THE BIBLIOGRAPHICAL SOCIETY OF AMERICA. Bibliographical Society of America. Quarterly.

(uuu) PERSPECTIVES IN AMERICAN HISTORY. Harvard University: Charles Warren Center for Studies in American History. Annually.

(vvv) PMLA: PUBLICATIONS OF THE MODERN LANGUAGE ASSOCIATION OF AMERICA. Modern Language Association. Six times yearly.

(www) POLITICAL SCIENCE QUARTERLY. Academy of Political Science. Quarterly.

(xxx) PROCEEDINGS OF THE AMERICAN ANTIQUARIAN SOCIETY. American Antiquarian Society. Semiannually.

(yyy) PROCEEDINGS OF THE AMERICAN PHILOSOPHICAL SOCIETY HELD AT PHILADELPHIA FOR PROMOTING USEFUL KNOWLEDGE. American Philosophical Society. Bimonthly.

(zzz) PROLOGUE: JOURNAL OF THE NATIONAL ARCHIVES. National Archives and Records Service of the General Services Administration, United States. Quarterly.

(aaaa) REVIEW OF POLITICS. University of Notre Dame. Quarterly.

(bbbb) SOUTHERN FOLKLORE QUARTERLY: A PUBLICATION DEVOTED TO THE HISTORICAL AND DESCRIPTIVE STUDY OF FOLKLORE AND TO THE DISCUSSION OF FOLK MATERIAL AS A LIVING TRADITION. South Atlantic Modern Language Association and the University of Florida. Quarterly.

(cccc) TECHNOLOGY AND CULTURE. Society for the History of Technology. Quarterly.

(dddd) WESTERN HISTORICAL QUARTERLY. Western Historical Association and Utah State University. Quarterly.

(eeee) WILLIAM AND MARY QUARTERLY. Institute of Early American History and Culture, College of William and Mary. Quarterly.

Chapter 2

BIBLIOGRAPHIES, ENCYCLOPEDIC WORKS, INDEXES, AND CATALOGS

76 Altbach, Philip G. A SELECT BIBLIOGRAPHY ON STUDENTS, POLI-
   TICS, AND HIGHER EDUCATION. 2d rev. ed. Cambridge, Mass.:
   United Ministries in Higher Education, Center for International Affairs,
   Harvard University, 1970. 65 p.

77 Beach, Mark. A BIBLIOGRAPHIC GUIDE TO AMERICAN COLLEGES
   AND UNIVERSITIES: FROM COLONIAL TIMES TO THE PRESENT.
   Westport, Conn.: Greenwood Press, 1975. 314 p.

   Contains 2,806 unannotated entries which describe the development of such institutions.

78 Bellack, Arno A. "History of Curriculum Thought and Practice." RE-
   VIEW OF EDUCATIONAL RESEARCH 39 (1969): 283-920.

   Covers writings published between 1964 and 1968 on the current situation in curriculum theory and related sectors.

79 Blessing, James H. GRADUATE EDUCATION: AN ANNOTATED BIB-
   LIOGRAPHY. Washington, D.C.: Government Printing Office, 1961.
   151 p.

   Covers the period 1957 to 1960 but also includes many earlier
   publications "of exceptional interest and importance." Lists
   882 entries.

80 Blishen, Edward, ed. ENCYCLOPEDIA OF EDUCATION. New York:
   Philosophical Library, 1970. 882 p.

81 Boydston, Jo Ann, and Andresen, Robert L., eds. JOHN DEWEY: A
   CHECKLIST OF TRANSLATIONS, 1900-1967. Carbondale: Southern Illinois University Press, 1969. 210 p.

   Contains an extensive listing of the translations of Dewey's
   writings into other languages.

82   Boydston, Jo Ann, and Poulos, Kathleen. CHECKLIST OF WRITINGS ABOUT JOHN DEWEY. 2d ed. Carbondale: Southern Illinois University Press, 1978. 488 p.

83   Brickman, William W. "Educational History of the United States." SCHOOL AND SOCIETY 72 (1950): 436-440.

        A bibliographical critique essay on thirty-one works of major importance published during 1947-50.

84   _____. "A Bibliographical Introduction to History of the U.S. Higher Education." In A CENTURY OF HIGHER EDUCATION: CLASSICAL CITADEL TO COLLEGIATE COLLOSUS, edited by William W. Brickman and Stanley Lehrer, pp. 257-85. New York: Society for the Advancement of Education, 1962.

85   _____. "An Historical Survey of Foreign Writings on American Educational History." PAEDAGOGICA HISTORICA 2, no. 1 (1962): 1-21.

        Contains essay on treatment of education in the United States in French, German, Dutch, and other languages.

86   _____. "Selected Bibliography of the History of Education in the United States." PAEDAGOGICA HISTORICA 10, no. 3 (1972): 622-30.

87   _____. BIBLIOGRAPHICAL ESSAYS ON THE HISTORY AND PHILOSOPHY OF EDUCATION. Norwood, Pa.: Norwood Editions, 1975. 185 p.

88   _____. RESEARCH IN EDUCATIONAL HISTORY. Folcroft, Pa.: Folcroft Library Editions, 1975. 254 p.

        Initially appeared as: GUIDE TO RESEARCH IN EDUCATIONAL HISTORY (New York: New York University Bookstore, 1949).

89   Brown, Elmer E. "The History of Secondary Education in the United States--Bibliography." SCHOOL REVIEW 5 (1897): 84-94, 139-47.

90   Butler, Nicholas M., ed. EDUCATIONAL REVIEW: ANALYTICAL INDEX TO VOLUMES 26-60: JUNE, 1903, TO DECEMBER, 1915. Easton, Pa.: Educational Review Publishing, 1916.

91   California, University of. Department of Pedagogy. CATALOGUE OF BOOKS IN THE PEDAGOGICAL SECTION OF THE UNIVERSITY LIBRARY. Rev. ed. Berkeley, Calif.: Regents of the University, 1895.

92   Caliver, Ambrose. EDUCATION OF NEGROES: A FIVE YEAR BIBLI-

OGRAPHY, 1931-1935. U.S. Office of Education Bulletin no. 8, 1937. Washington, D.C.: Government Printing Office, 1937. 63 p.

93 Carrell, William D. "Biographical List of American College Professors to 1800." HISTORY OF EDUCATION QUARTERLY 8 (1968): 358-74.

A compilation of the lives and works of 142 early American college faculty members.

94 Chambers, Merritt M. "A Brief Bibliography of Higher Education in the Middle Nineteen Sixties." BULLETIN, SCHOOL OF EDUCATION, INDIANA UNIVERSITY 42 (1966): 1-52.

95 Columbia University. Teachers College Library. DICTIONARY CATALOG OF TEACHERS COLLEGE LIBRARY. 36 vols. Boston: G.K. Hall, 1970.

96 Cordasco, Francesco. "Academic Freedom in the Last Decade: A Preliminary Annotated Bibliography." PEABODY JOURNAL OF EDUCATION 36 (1958): 166-69.

97 _____. "Reference Books in Education: A Bibliographical Commentary." (STECHERT-HAFNER) BOOK NEWS 17 (1963): 81-83.

98 _____. THE EQUALITY OF EDUCATIONAL OPPORTUNITY: A BIBLIOGRAPHY OF SELECTED REFERENCES. Totowa, N.J.: Rowman and Littlefield, 1973. 139 p.

99 _____. "The School and the Children of the Poor: A Bibliography of Selected References." BULLETIN OF BIBLIOGRAPHY 30 (1973): 93-101.

100 _____. IMMIGRANT CHILDREN IN AMERICAN SCHOOLS: A CLASSIFIED AND ANNOTATED BIBLIOGRAPHY WITH SELECTED SOURCE DOCUMENTS. Fairfield, N.J.: Augustus M. Kelley, 1976. 381 p.

101 _____. "Social Reform in American Education: A Bibliography of Selected References." BULLETIN OF BIBLIOGRAPHY 33 (1976): 105-10.

102 _____. A BIBLIOGRAPHY OF VOCATIONAL EDUCATION: AN ANNOTATED GUIDE. New York: AMS Press, 1977. 245 p.

Includes three thousand entries covering the past seventy-five years in industrial, vocational, trade, manual, and career education.

103 _____. "Bilingual and Bicultural Education in American Schools: A Bibliography of Selected References." BULLETIN OF BIBLIOGRAPHY 35 (1978): 53-72.

Encyclopedias, Indexes, and Catalogs

104 Cordasco, Francesco, and Brickman, William W., eds. A BIBLIOGRAPHY OF AMERICAN EDUCATIONAL HISTORY: AN ANNOTATED AND CLASSIFIED GUIDE. New York: AMS Press, 1975. 394 p.

105 Cordasco, Francesco, and Covello, Leonard. STUDIES OF PUERTO RI-CAN CHILDREN IN AMERICAN SCHOOLS: A PRELIMINARY BIBLIOG-RAPHY. New York: Department of Labor, Migration Division, Common-wealth of Puerto Rico, 1967. 33 p.

> Also available in: EDUCATION LIBRARIES BULLETIN, Insti-tute of Education, University of London 31 (1968): 7-33; and JOURNAL OF HUMAN RELATIONS 16 (1968): 264-85.

106 Davis, Sheldon E. EDUCATIONAL PERIODICALS DURING THE NINE-TEENTH CENTURY. Washington, D.C.: Government Printing Office, 1919. 125 p. Reprint. New York: Scarecrow Press, 1970.

> Contains an introductory note by Francesco Cordasco. The principal source for nineteenth-century educational periodicals.

107 DeBoer, Peter P., and McCaul, Robert L. "Annotated List of CHICAGO TRIBUNE Editorials on Elementary and Secondary Education in the U.S." HISTORY OF EDUCATION QUARTERLY 3 (1973): 201-14.

> Covers the period 1875 to 1885.

108 _____. "Annotated List of CHICAGO TRIBUNE Editorials on Elementary and Secondary Education in the U.S., 1852-1900." HISTORY OF EDU-CATION QUARTERLY 13 (1973): 97-107.

> The first part covers public opinion on educational affairs for the period 1852-74.

109 _____. "Annotated List of CHICAGO TRIBUNE Editorials on Elementary and Secondary Education in the U.S., 1886-1900." HISTORY OF EDU-CATION QUARTERLY 13 (1973): 457-85.

> Includes editorials on Dewey in 1899.

110 Deighton, Lee C., ed. ENCYCLOPEDIA OF EDUCATION. 10 vols. New York: Macmillan, 1971.

> Annually supplemented by the EDUCATION YEARBOOK, 1972-1973-- . (New York: Macmillan).

111 Dressel, Paul L., and Pratt, Sally B. THE WORLD OF HIGHER EDUCA-TION: AN ANNOTATED GUIDE TO THE MAJOR EDUCATION. San Francisco: Jossey-Bass, 1971. 238 p.

> Deals with research and scholarly commentary.

112 Eells, Walter C. BIBLIOGRAPHY ON JUNIOR COLLEGES. U.S. Office of Education Bulletin no. 2. 1930. Washington, D.C.: Government Printing Office, 1930. 120 p.

113 _____. COLLEGE TEACHERS AND COLLEGE TEACHING: AN ANNOTATED BIBLIOGRAPHY ON COLLEGE AND UNIVERSITY FACULTY MEMBERS AND INSTRUCTIONAL METHODS. Atlanta: Southern Regional Educational Board, 1957. 282 p.

   Supplements: 1-2, 1959, 1962. 134 p., 192 p.

   Includes 2,700 entries published since 1945, arranged by subject with author index.

114 Eells, Walter C., and Hollis, Ernest V. THE COLLEGE PRESIDENCY, 1900-1960: AN ANNOTATED BIBLIOGRAPHY. U.S. Office of Education Bulletin no. 45, 1961. Washington, D.C.: Government Printing Office, 1961. 143 p.

   Covers 695 publications that appeared in the period.

115 Federal Writer's Project, WPA, Massachusetts. SELECTIVE AND CRITICAL BIBLIOGRAPHY OF HORACE MANN. Boston: State Department of Education, 1937.

116 Finkelstein, Barbara J. "Schooling and Schoolteachers: Selected Bibliography of Autobiographies in the Nineteenth Century." HISTORY OF EDUCATION QUARTERLY 14 (1974): 293-300.

117 Gersman, Elinor M. "A Bibliography for Historians of Education." HISTORY OF EDUCATION QUARTERLY 12 (Spring 1972): 81-88; 12 (Winter 1972): 531-41.

118 _____. "A Bibliography for Historians of Education." HISTORY OF EDUCATION QUARTERLY 13 (1973): 447-55.

119 _____. "A Bibliography of Current Periodical Literature in Educational History." HISTORY OF EDUCATION QUARTERLY 13 (1973): 91-96.

120 _____. "Textbooks in American Educational History." HISTORY OF EDUCATION QUARTERLY 13 (1973): 41-51.

121 _____. "A Bibliography for Historians of Education." HISTORY OF EDUCATION QUARTERLY 14 (1974): 279-92.

122 _____. "A Selected Bibliography of Periodicals in Educational History." HISTORY OF EDUCATION QUARTERLY 15 (1975): 227-49.

123 _____. "A Selected Bibliography of Periodicals in Educational History." HISTORY OF EDUCATION QUARTERLY 17 (1977): 275-96.

124 Good, H.G. "History of Education in the United States: Higher Education." REVIEW OF EDUCATIONAL RESEARCH 9 (1939): 347-51, 415-70.

125 Gougher, Ronald L. "Comparison of English and American Views of the German University, 1840-1865: A Bibliography." HISTORY OF EDUCATION QUARTERLY 9 (1969): 477-91.

126 Gray, Ruth A. DOCTORS THESES IN EDUCATION: A LIST OF 797 THESES DEPOSITED WITH THE OFFICE OF EDUCATION AND AVAILABLE FOR LOAN. U.S. Office of Education Pamphlet no. 60. 1935. Washington, D.C.: Government Printing Office, 1935. 69 p.

Includes theses thru 1934.

127 Green, Paul G. AN ANNOTATED BIBLIOGRAPHY OF THE HISTORY OF EDUCATION IN KANSAS. Emporia: Kansas State Teachers College, 1935. 140 p.

128 Hall, G. Stanley, and Mansfield, John M. HINTS TOWARD A SELECT AND DESCRIPTIVE BIBLIOGRAPHY OF EDUCATION. Boston: Heath, 1886. 310 p. Reprint. Detroit: Gale Research, 1973. With a new foreword by Francesco Cordasco.

129 Harvard University Library. EDUCATION AND EDUCATION PERIODICALS. 2 vols. Cambridge, Mass.: Harvard University Library, 1968. (Widener Library Shelflist, 16-17).

Lists some thirty thousand works in the Widener Library. Vol. 1: classification schedule, classified listing call numbers. Vol. 2: alphabetical by author or title, chronological listing.

130 Herbst, Jurgen, comp. THE HISTORY OF AMERICAN EDUCATION. Northbrook, Ill.: AHM Publishing Corp., 1973. 153 p.

131 Jorgenson, Lloyd P. "Materials on the History of Education in State Historical Journals." HISTORY OF EDUCATION QUARTERLY 7 (1967): 234-54; 8 (1968): 510-27; 9 (1969): 73-87.

132 Karpinski, Louis C. BIBLIOGRAPHY OF MATHEMATICAL WORKS PUBLISHED IN AMERICA THROUGH 1850. Ann Arbor: University of Michigan Press, 1940. 697 p.

Covers over one thousand books in three thousand editions in North America thru 1850, and in South America through 1800.

133 Kelsey, Roger R. BIBLIOGRAPHY ON HIGHER EDUCATION. Washington, D.C.: American Association for Higher Education, 1972. 60 p.

134 King, Clyde S. HORACE MANN, 1796-1859.: A BIBLIOGRAPHY. Dobbs Ferry, N.Y.: Oceana Publications, 1966. 453 p.

135 Knowles, Asa A., ed. THE INTERNATIONAL ENCYCLOPEDIA OF HIGHER EDUCATION. 10 vols. San Francisco: Jossey-Bass, 1977.

   Contents grouped under eight broad categories: (1) national systems of higher education; (2) topical essays; (3) fields of study; (4) educational associations; (5) centers and institutes of higher educational research; (6) reports on higher education; (7) an international directory of documentation and of information centers; and (8) acronyms, a glossary and an index.

136 Leidecker, Kurt F. "Bibliography: William Torrey Harris in Literature." In WILLIAM TORREY HARRIS, 1835-1935, edited by Edward F. Schaub, pp. 125-36. Chicago: Open Court Publishing, 1936.

137 McCarthy, Joseph M. AN INTERNATIONAL LIST OF ARTICLES ON THE HISTORY OF EDUCATION PUBLISHED IN NON-EDUCATIONAL SERIES, 1965-1974. New York: Garland Publishing, 1977. 228 p.

138 Mann, B. Pickman. "Bibliography of Horace Mann." In REPORT OF THE COMMISSIONER OF EDUCATION FOR THE YEAR 1896-1897, pp. 897-927. Vol. 1. Washington, D.C.: Government Printing Office, 1898.

139 Marks, Barbara S., ed. THE NEW YORK UNIVERSITY LIST OF BOOKS IN EDUCATION. New York: Citation Press, 1968. 527 p.

140 Mayhew, Lewis B. "The Literature of Higher Education." EDUCATIONAL RECORD 46 (1965): 5-32.

141 _____. THE LITERATURE OF HIGHER EDUCATION, 1971. San Francisco: Jossey-Bass, 1971-- . 162 p.

   Intended as an annual. Irregular.

142 Meeth, Louis R. SELECTED ISSUES IN HIGHER EDUCATION: AN ANNOTATED BIBLIOGRAPHY. New York: Institute for Higher Education, 1965. 212 p.

   Contains references to "readings on various subjects related to the establishment of policy in, and the operation of, colleges and universities."

143 Monroe, Paul, ed. A CYCLOPEDIA OF EDUCATION. 5 vols. New York: Macmillan, 1911-1913. Reprint. Detroit: Gale Research, 1968.

Also see: Francesco Cordasco," The 50th Anniversary of Monroe's Cyclopedia of Education," SCHOOL AND SOCIETY 91 (1963): 123-24; and William W. Brickman and Francesco Cordasco, "Paul Monroe's CYCLOPEDIA OF EDUCATION with Notices of Educational Encyclopedias Past and Present," HISTORY OF EDUCATION QUARTERLY 10 (1970): 324-37.

144 Monroe, Walter S., and Asher, Ollie. A BIBLIOGRAPHY OF BIBLIOGRAPHIES. Bulletin no. 36. Urbana, Ill.: Bureau of Educational Research, College of Education, University of Illinois, 1927. 218 p.

145 Monroe, Walter S., and Shores, Louis. BIBLIOGRAPHIES AND SUMMARIES IN EDUCATION TO JULY, 1935. New York: Wilson, 1936. 470 p.

146 Monroe, Will S. BIBLIOGRAPHY OF EDUCATION. New York: Appleton, 1897. 202 p. Reprint. Detroit: Gale Research, 1968. 202 p.

New introduction by Francesco Cordasco. Includes list of reports of the U.S. Commissioner of Education, and notices of educational journals.

147 _____. BIBLIOGRAPHY OF HENRY BARNARD. Boston: New England Publishing, 1897.

148 Nelson, Charles A., ed. EDUCATIONAL REVIEW: ANALYTICAL INDEX TO VOLUMES 1-25: JANUARY, 1891, TO MAY, 1903. Easton, Pa.: Educational Review Publishing, 1904.

149 Nelson, Martha F., comp. INDEX BY AUTHORS, TITLES, AND SUBJECTS TO THE PUBLICATIONS OF THE NATIONAL EDUCATIONAL ASSOCIATION FOR ITS FIRST FIFTY YEARS, 1857 TO 1906. Winona, Minn.: National Educational Association, 1907.

150 Noble, Stuart G. "State Histories of Education." REVIEW OF EDUCATIONAL RESEARCH 6 (1936): 372-77, 429-31.

151 Park, Joe, ed. THE RISE OF AMERICAN EDUCATION: AN ANNOTATED BIBLIOGRAPHY. Evanston, Ill.: Northwestern University Press, 1965. 216 p.

152 Porter, Dorothy B., and Ellis, Ethel M., comps. THE JOURNAL OF NEGRO EDUCATION: INDEX TO VOLUMES 1-31, 1932-1962. Washington, D.C.: Howard University Press, 1963.

153 "Publications from 1898 to 1940 by E.L. Thorndike." TEACHERS COL-
LEGE RECORD 41 (1940): 699-725.

154 Quay, Richard H. RESEARCH IN HIGHER EDUCATION: A GUIDE TO
SOURCE BIBLIOGRAPHIES. New York: Entrance Examination Board,
1976. 60 p.

155 _____. IN PURSUIT OF EQUALITY OF EDUCATIONAL OPPORTUNITY:
A SELECTIVE BIBLIOGRAPHY AND GUIDE TO RESEARCH LITERATURE.
New York: Garland Publishing, 1977. 183 p.

156 _____. INDEX TO ANTHOLOGIES ON POSTSECONDARY EDUCATION,
1950-1977. Westport, Conn.: Greenwood Press, 1978. 387 p.

157 Reddick, L.D. "Select Bibliography," JOURNAL OF EDUCATIONAL
SOCIOLOGY 19 (1946): 512-16.

158 Reisner, Edward H., and Butts, R. Freeman. "History of American Education During the Colonial Period." REVIEW OF EDUCATIONAL RE-
SEARCH 6 (1936): 357-63, 417-22.

159 Richey, Herman G. "History of American Education Since the Beginning
of the National Period." REVIEW OF EDUCATIONAL RESEARCH 6 (1936):
363-77, 422-29.

160 _____. "History of Education in the United States: Adult Education."
REVIEW OF EDUCATIONAL RESEARCH 9 (1939): 352-56, 417-19.

161 Richmond, W. Kenneth. THE LITERATURE OF EDUCATION: A CRITICAL
BIBLIOGRAPHY, 1945-1970. London: Methuen Press, 1972. 206 p.

162 Ryan, W. Carson, Jr. THE LITERATURE OF AMERICAN SCHOOL AND
COLLEGE ATHLETICS. New York: Carnegie Foundation for the Advancement of Teaching, 1929. 247 p.

> Includes 1,030 annotated entries, including notices of the his-
> tory of American collegiate athletics.

163 Sheldon, Henry D. A CRITICAL AND DESCRIPTIVE BIBLIOGRAPHY OF
THE HISTORY OF EDUCATION IN THE STATE OF OREGON. Eugene:
University of Oregon Press, 1929. 110 p.

164 Shereshewsky, Murray S., ed. HISTORY OF EDUCATION QUARTERLY
INDEX. New York: History of Education Society, 1973. 72 p.

> A ten-year index (Vols. 1-10) by title, subject, and author.

165   Simpson, Benjamin R., et al. "Annotated Chronological Bibliography of Publications by E.L. Thorndike." TEACHERS COLLEGE RECORD 27 (1926): 466-515.

     Covers the period 1898-1925.

166   Soper, Wayne W. "History of Education in the United States: Secondary Education." REVIEW OF EDUCATIONAL RESEARCH 9 (1939): 342-46, 413-14.

167   Stayer, George D., Jr. "History of Education in the United States: Elementary Education." REVIEW OF EDUCATIONAL RESEARCH 9 (1939): 340-41, 413.

168   Thomas, Milton H. JOHN DEWEY: A CENTENNIAL BIBLIOGRAPHY. Chicago: University of Chicago Press, 1962.

169   U.S. Bureau of Education. ANALYTICAL INDEX TO BARNARD'S AMERICAN JOURNAL OF EDUCATION. Washington, D.C.: Government Printing Office, 1892. 128 p.

     The only index to Barnard's AMERICAN JOURNAL OF EDUCATION (31 vols., 1855-81).

170   _____. INDEX TO REPORTS OF THE COMMISSIONER OF EDUCATION. Washington, D.C.: Government Printing Office, 1909. Reprint. Totowa, N.J.: Rowman and Littlefield, 1970.

     With a new introduction by Francesco Cordasco.

171   U.S. Department of Health, Education and Welfare. SUBJECT CATALOG OF THE DEPARTMENT LIBRARY. 20 vols. Boston: G.K. Hall and Co., 1965.

172   U.S. Educational Research Information Center. CATALOG OF SELECTED DOCUMENTS ON THE DISADVANTAGED. 2 vols. Washington, D.C.: Office of Education, Bureau of Research, 1966.

     Includes 1,740 selected documents. Citations are given in numerical sequence with author and subject indexes.

173   U.S. Office of Education. BIBLIOGRAPHY OF PUBLICATIONS OF THE UNITED STATES OFFICE OF EDUCATION, 1867-1959. Totowa, N.J.: Rowman and Littlefield, 1971. 57 p., 158 p., 157 p.

     A reprint of three compilations: LIST OF PUBLICATIONS OF THE UNITED STATES BUREAU OF EDUCATION, 1867-1910; LIST OF PUBLICATIONS OF THE OFFICE OF EDUCATION, 1910-1936; and 1937-1959 PUBLICATIONS: OFFICE OF EDUCATION. Thoroughly indexed. Introductory note by Francesco Cordasco.

174 U.S. Office of Education. Library. BIBLIOGRAPHY OF RESEARCH
STUDIES IN EDUCATION: 1928-41. 4 vols. Reprint. Detroit: Gale
Research, 1974.

A facsimile reprint. Covers 47,866 entries, many of which
are annotated. Introduction by Francesco Cordasco.

175 Vivola, Robert. A GUIDE TO INFORMATION ON EQUAL EDUCATION-
AL OPPORTUNITY. New York: Institute for Urban and Minority Education, Teachers College, Columbia University, 1977. 85 p.

176 Walch, Timothy. "Archival Research Opportunities in American Educational History." HISTORY OF EDUCATION QUARTERLY 16 (1976): 479-
86.

Includes a bibliography of education collections accessioned
recently.

177 Weinberg, Meyer, ed. SCHOOL INTEGRATION: A COMPREHENSIVE
CLASSIFIED BIBLIOGRAPHY OF 3100 REFERENCES. Chicago: Integrated
Education Associates, 1967. 137 p.

178 _____, comp. THE EDUCATION OF THE MINORITY CHILD: A COM-
PREHENSIVE BIBLIOGRAPHY OF 10,000 SELECTED ENTRIES. Chicago:
Integrated Education Associates, 1970. 530 p.

Covers all major minority groups between 1900 and 1970.

179 Willingham, Warren W., ed. SOURCE BOOK FOR HIGHER EDUCATION:
A CRITICAL GUIDE TO LITERATURE AND INFORMATION ON ACCESS
TO HIGHER EDUCATION. New York: Entrance Examination Board,
1973. 481 p.

An annotated bibliography on all phases of American higher
education.

180 Wilson, Louis N. "Bibliography of the Published Writings of President
G. Stanley Hall." AMERICAN JOURNAL OF PSYCHOLOGY 14 (1903):
417-30.

181 _____. BIBLIOGRAPHY OF CHILD STUDY FOR THE YEARS 1908-1909.
U.S. Bureau of Education Bulletin no. 11, 1911. Washington, D.C.:
Government Printing Office, 1911.

Later included some annual continuations.

182 _____. "Bibliography of the Published Writings of G. Stanley Hall:
1866-1924." NATIONAL ACADEMY OF SCIENCES OF THE UNITED
STATES OF AMERICA, BIOGRAPHICAL MEMOIR. Washington, D.C.:
National Academy of Sciences, 1929. 155-80.

183 Woodbury, Marda A. GUIDE TO SOURCES OF EDUCATIONAL INFOR-
MATION. Washington, D.C.: Information Resources Press, 1976. 371 p.

184 Wright, Edith A., and Phillips, Mary S. BULLETINS OF THE BUREAU OF
EDUCATION, 1906-1927. U.S. Bureau of Education Bulletin no. 17.
1928. Washington, D.C.: Government Printing Office, 1928. 65 p.

185 Wyer, James I., Jr., and Phelps, Martha L. BIBLIOGRAPHY OF EDU-
CATION FOR 1907. U.S. Bureau of Education Bulletin no. 3. 1908.
With subsequent annual volumes. Washington, D.C.: Government Print-
ing Office, 1908. 65 p.

> See Malcolm C. Hamilton, ed. EDUCATION LITERATURE,
> 1907-1932, 12 vols., New York: Garland Publishing Co.,
> 1978, which is a collected edition of the annual bibliographies
> with a cumulative proper name and subject index (Vol. 12).

Chapter 3

SOURCE COLLECTIONS

186 Archambault, Reginald D., ed. JOHN DEWEY ON EDUCATION: SE-LECTED WRITINGS. New York: Random House, 1964. 439 p.

187 Arrowood, Charles F., ed. THOMAS JEFFERSON AND EDUCATION IN A REPUBLIC. New York: McGraw-Hill, 1930. 183 p.

188 Babbidge, Homer D., Jr., ed. NOAH WEBSTER: ON BEING AMERI-CAN; SELECTED WRITINGS, 1783-1828. New York: Praeger, 1967. 270 p.

189 Best, John H., ed. BENJAMIN FRANKLIN ON EDUCATION. New York: Bureau of Publications, Teachers College, Columbia University, 1962. 174 p.

190 Best, John H., and Sidwell, Robert T., eds. THE AMERICAN LEGACY OF LEARNING: READINGS IN THE HISTORY OF EDUCATION. Phila-delphia: J.B. Lippincott, 1967. 467 p.

191 Bestor, Arthur E., Jr., ed. EDUCATION AND REFORM AT NEW HAR-MONY: CORRESPONDENCE OF WILLIAM MacLURE AND MARIE DU-CLOS FRETAGEOT, 1820-1833. Indianapolis: Indiana Historical Society, 1948. 281 p.

192 Borrowman, Merle L., ed. TEACHER EDUCATION IN AMERICA: A DOCUMENTARY HISTORY. New York: Teachers College Press, 1965. 251 p.

    Deals with teacher education in the United States: 1839-1946.

193 Bremner, Robert H., ed. CHILDREN AND YOUTH IN AMERICA: A DOCUMENTARY HISTORY. 3 vols. in 5. Cambridge, Mass.: Harvard University Press, 1970-74.

194 Brickman, William W., and Lehrer, Stanley, eds. A CENTURY OF HIGHER EDUCATION: CLASSICAL CITADEL TO COLLEGIATE COLOS- SUS. New York: Society for the Advancement of Education, 1962. 293 p.

195 Brubacher, John S. THE LAW AND HIGHER EDUCATION: A CASEBOOK. 2 vols. Rutherford, N.J.: Fairleigh Dickinson University Press, 1971.

196 _____, ed. HENRY BARNARD ON EDUCATION. New York: McGraw- Hill, 1931. 298 p.

197 Caldwell, Otis W., and Courtis, Stuart A. THEN AND NOW IN EDU- CATION, 1845-1923. Yonkers, N.Y.: World Book, 1923. 245 p.

198 Calhoun, Daniel, ed. THE EDUCATING OF AMERICANS: A DOCU- MENTARY HISTORY. Boston: Houghton Mifflin, 1969. 644 p.

199 Chadbourne, Ava H., comp. READINGS IN THE HISTORY OF EDUCA- TION IN MAINE. Bangor, Maine: Burr, 1932. 239 p.

200 Clews, Elsie W. EDUCATIONAL LEGISLATION AND ADMINISTRATION OF COLONIAL GOVERNMENTS. New York: Macmillan, 1899. 276 p.

201 Cohen, Sol. EDUCATION IN THE UNITED STATES: A DOCUMENTARY HISTORY. 5 vols. New York: Random House, 1974.

202 Coon, Charles L., ed. THE BEGINNINGS OF PUBLIC EDUCATION IN NORTH CAROLINA: A DOCUMENTARY HISTORY, 1790-1840. 2 vols. Raleigh, N.C.: Edwards and Broughton, 1908.

203 _____. NORTH CAROLINA SCHOOLS AND ACADEMIES, 1790-1840. Raleigh, N.C.: Edwards and Broughton, 1915. 846 p.

204 Cordasco, Francesco. "The Archives of American Educational History." THE REVIEW OF EDUCATION 2 (1976): 285-97.

205 Cowley, Elizabeth B. FREE LEARNING. Boston: Humphries, 1941. 194 p.

   Deals in sources on education in Massachusetts, Pennsylvania, Michigan, and California since colonial times.

206 Crane, Theodore R., ed. THE COLLEGES AND THE PUBLIC, 1787-1862. New York: Bureau of Publications, Teachers College, Columbia Univer- sity, 1963. 194 p.

207 _____. THE DIMENSIONS OF AMERICAN EDUCATION. Reading,
Mass.: Addison-Wesley, 1974. 265 p.

Covers the period from colonial times to the 1960s.

208 Cremin, Lawrence A., advisory ed. AMERICAN EDUCATION: ITS MEN,
IDEAS, AND INSTITUTIONS. 161 vols. in 2 series. New York: Arno
Press, New York Times, 1970-71.

A massive reprint of the basic materials in the history of
American education.

209 Cross, Barbara M., ed. THE EDUCATED WOMAN IN AMERICA: SE-
LECTED WRITINGS OF CATHARINE BEECHER, MARGARET FULLER, AND
M. CAREY THOMAS. New York: Teachers College Press, 1965. 175 p.

210 Cubberley, Ellwood Patterson, ed. READINGS IN PUBLIC EDUCATION
IN THE UNITED STATES: A COLLECTION OF SOURCES AND READ-
INGS TO ILLUSTRATE THE HISTORY OF EDUCATIONAL PRACTICE AND
PROGRESS IN THE UNITED STATES. Boston: Houghton Mifflin, 1934.
534 p.

211 Cubberley, Ellwood P[atterson]. and Elliot, Edward C., eds. STATE
AND COUNTY SCHOOL ADMINISTRATION: VOLUME II, SOURCE
BOOK. New York: Macmillan, 1915. 410 p.

212 Dabney, Charles W. UNIVERSAL EDUCATION IN THE SOUTH. 2 vols.
Chapel Hill: University of North Carolina Press, 1936.

213 Dworkin, Martin S., ed. DEWEY ON EDUCATION. New York: Bureau
of Publications, Teachers College, Columbia University, 1959.

214 Eby, Frederick, comp. EDUCATION IN TEXAS: SOURCE MATERIALS.
Austin: University of Texas, 1918. 963 p.

215 Elliot, Edward C., and Chambers, M.M., eds. CHARTERS AND BASIC
LAWS OF SELECTED AMERICAN UNIVERSITIES AND COLLEGES. New
York: Carnegie Foundation for the Advancement of Teaching, 1934.
483 p.

216 Evans, Henry R., and Wright, Edith A., comps. EXPRESSIONS IN EDU-
CATION BY BUILDERS OF AMERICAN DEMOCRACY. U.S. Office of
Education Bulletin no. 10. 1940. Washington, D.C.: Government
Printing Office, 1940. 90 p.

217 Fellman, David, ed. THE SUPREME COURT AND EDUCATION. New
York: Teachers College Press, 1969. 229 p.

Covers twenty-two major decisions between 1925 and 1968.

218 Finegan, Thomas E. FREE SCHOOLS. Albany: University of the State of New York, 1921. 682 p.

219 Fleming, Walter L. DOCUMENTARY HISTORY OF RECONSTRUCTION. Vol. 2. Cleveland: Clark, 1907. 410 p.

220 Fraser, Stewart E., ed. AMERICAN EDUCATION IN FOREIGN PERSPEC-TIVES: TWENTIETH CENTURY ESSAYS. New York: Wiley, 1969. 340 p.

  Covers writers from Great Britain, China, France, Germany, Sweden, and the USSR.

221 Garforth, F.W., ed. JOHN DEWEY: SELECTED EDUCATIONAL WRIT-INGS. London: Heinemann, 1966. 275 p.

222 Gartner, Lloyd P., ed. JEWISH EDUCATION IN THE UNITED STATES: A DOCUMENTARY HISTORY. New York: Teachers College Press, 1969. 224 p.

223 Goodsell, Willystine, ed. PIONEERS OF WOMEN'S EDUCATION IN THE UNITED STATES. New York: McGraw-Hill, 1931. 311 p.

224 Grattan, C. Hartley, ed. AMERICAN IDEAS ABOUT ADULT EDUCA-TION, 1710-1951. New York: Bureau of Publications, Teachers College, Columbia University, 1959. 140 p.

225 Greven, Philip J., Jr., ed. CHILD-REARING CONCEPTS, 1628-1861: HISTORICAL SOURCES. Itasca, Ill.: Peacock, 1973. 320 p.

226 Gross, Carl H., and Chandler, Charles C., eds. THE HISTORY OF AMERICAN EDUCATION THROUGH READINGS. Boston: D.C. Heath, 1964. 488 p.

227 Hillesheim, James W., and Merrill, George D., eds. THEORY AND PRACTICE IN THE HISTORY OF AMERICAN EDUCATION. Pacific Pali-sades, Calif.: Goodyear, 1971. 275 p.

228 Hillway, Tyrus, ed. AMERICAN EDUCATION: AN INTRODUCTION THROUGH READINGS. Boston: Houghton-Mifflin, 1964. 357 p.

  Covers from the colonial period to 1960s.

229 Hinsdale, B.A., comp. "Documents Illustrative of American Educational History." In REPORT OF THE COMMISSIONER OF EDUCATION FOR THE YEAR 1892-93, vol. 2, pp. 1225-414. Washington, D.C.: Govern-ment Printing Office, 1895.

230 Hofstadter, Richard, and Smith, Wilson, eds. AMERICAN HIGHER EDU-
CATION: A DOCUMENTARY HISTORY. 2 vols. Chicago: University
of Chicago Press, 1961.

Covers 1633 to mid-twentieth century.

231 Honeywell, Roy J. THE EDUCATIONAL WORK OF THOMAS JEFFER-
SON. Cambridge, Mass.: Harvard University Press, 1931. 287 p.

232 Joncich, Geraldine M., ed. PSYCHOLOGY AND THE SCIENCE OF
EDUCATION: SELECTED WRITINGS OF EDWARD L. THORNDIKE. New
York: Bureau of Publications, Teachers College, Columbia University,
1962. 245 p.

233 Jones, Howard M., ed. EMERSON ON EDUCATION. New York:
Teachers College Press, 1966. 227 p.

234 JOURNAL OF SOURCES IN EDUCATIONAL HISTORY. Oxford, Engl.:
Carfax Publishing, 1978-- .

Provides, in the form of microfiche, a selection of basic original source materials. An annual volume of three numbers
will comprise about twelve fiche and twelve hundred pages.

235 Katz, Michael B., ed. SCHOOL REFORM: PAST AND PRESENT. Boston: Little, Brown, 1971. 303 p.

Deals with the period 1826 through 1969.

236 _____. EDUCATION IN AMERICAN HISTORY: READINGS ON THE
SOCIAL ISSUES. New York: Praeger, 1973. 348 p.

237 Klain, Zora, ed. EDUCATIONAL ACTIVITIES OF NEW ENGLAND
QUAKERS: A SOURCE BOOK. Philadelphia: Westbrook, 1928. 185 p.

238 Kliebard, Herbert M., ed. RELIGION AND EDUCATION IN AMERICA:
A DOCUMENTARY HISTORY. Scranton, Pa.: International Textbook,
1969. 274 p.

239 Knight, Edgar W. WHAT COLLEGE PRESIDENTS SAY. Chapel Hill:
University of North Carolina Press, 1940. 340 p.

240 _____, ed. REPORTS ON EUROPEAN EDUCATION. New York:
McGraw-Hill, 1930. 319 p.

241 _____, ed. DOCUMENTARY HISTORY OF EDUCATION IN THE SOUTH
BEFORE 1860. 5 vols. Chapel Hill: University of North Carolina Press,
1949-53.

242 _____, ed. READINGS IN EDUCATIONAL ADMINISTRATION. New
York: Holt, 1953. 534 p.

243 Knight, Edgar W., and Hall, Clifton L., eds. READINGS IN AMERI-
CAN EDUCATIONAL HISTORY. New York: Appleton-Century-Crofts,
1951. 799 p.

244 Krug, Edward A., ed. CHARLES W. ELIOT AND POPULAR EDUCATION.
New York: Bureau of Publications, Teachers College, Columbia University, 1961. 166 p.

    Covers the period 1869 to 1905.

245 Lazerson, Marvin, and Grubb, W. Norton, eds. AMERICAN EDUCATION
AND VOCATIONALISM: A DOCUMENTARY HISTORY, 1870-1970. New
York: Teachers College Press, 1974. 176 p.

246 Lee, Gordon C., ed. CRUSADE AGAINST IGNORANCE: THOMAS
JEFFERSON ON EDUCATION. New York: Bureau of Publications,
Teachers College, Columbia University, 1961. 167 p.

247 Lewis, Elmer A., comp. LAWS RELATING TO VOCATIONAL EDUCA-
TION AND AGRICULTURAL EXTENSION. Washington, D.C.: Government Printing Office, 1941. 350 p.

    Covers laws enacted between 1914 and 1940.

248 McClusky, Neil G., S.J., ed. CATHOLIC EDUCATION IN AMERICA:
A DOCUMENTARY HISTORY. New York: Bureau of Education, Teachers
College, Columbia University, 1964. 205 p.

    Covers the period 1792 thru 1950.

249 Mann, Mary P. LIFE OF HORACE MANN. 1865. Reprint. Washington, D.C.: National Education Association, 1937. 602 p.

250 Martz, Velorus, and Ballinger, Stanley E. A GUIDE TO THE SOURCE
MATERIAL RELATING TO EDUCATION IN THE LAWS OF THE STATE OF
INDIANA, 1816-1851: PART ONE: 1816-1838. Bloomington: Bureau
of Research and Field Services, Indiana University, 1953. 145 p.

251 Martz, Velorus, and Smith, Henry L. SOURCE MATERIAL RELATING TO
THE DEVELOPMENT OF EDUCATION IN INDIANA. Bloomington: Bureau
of Cooperative Research and Field Services, 1945. 165 p.

252 Mayer, Frederick, ed. INTRODUCTORY READINGS IN EDUCATION.
Belmont, Calif.: Dickenson Publishing, 1966. 240 p.

253 Meriwether, Colyer. OUR COLONIAL CURRICULUM, 1606-1776. Washington, D.C.: Capital Publishing, 1907. 302 p.

254 Monroe, Paul, ed. READINGS IN THE FOUNDING OF THE AMERICAN PUBLIC SCHOOL SYSTEM. New York: Macmillan, 1940. 520 p.

> A microfilm of selected primary sources consulted for the preparation of the book is available from Xerox University Microfilms International, Ann Arbor, Michigan.

255 Noll, James W., and Kelly, Sam P., eds. FOUNDATIONS OF EDUCATION IN AMERICA: AN ANTHOLOGY OF MAJOR THOUGHTS AND SIGNIFICANT ACTIONS. New York: Harper and Row, 1970. 340 p.

> Covers from colonial times to the 1960s.

256 Norton, Arthur O., ed. THE FIRST STATE NORMAL SCHOOL IN AMERICA: THE JOURNALS OF CYRUS PEIRCE AND MARY SWIFT. Cambridge, Mass.: Harvard University Press, 1936. 186 p.

> On early teacher training in Massachusetts.

257 Peterson, Houston, ed. GREAT TEACHERS. New Brunswick, N.J.: Rutgers University Press, 1946. 351 p.

258 Pieper, George W. "The Educational Classics." HISTORY OF EDUCATION JOURNAL 4 (1952): 78-80.

259 Pratt, Daniel J. ANNALS OF PUBLIC EDUCATION IN THE STATE OF NEW YORK FROM 1626 TO 1746. Albany, N.Y.: Argus Co., 1872. 152 p.

260 Pyburn, Nita K., ed. DOCUMENTARY HISTORY OF EDUCATION IN FLORIDA, 1822-1860. Tallahassee: University of Florida Press, 1951. 240 p.

261 Raubinger, Frederick M., et al., eds. THE DEVELOPMENT OF SECONDARY EDUCATION. New York: Macmillan, 1969. 371 p.

262 Rippa, S. Alexander, ed. EDUCATIONAL IDEAS IN AMERICA: A DOCUMENTARY HISTORY. New York: David McKay, 1969. 609 p.

263 Rudolph, Frederick, ed. ESSAYS ON EDUCATION IN THE EARLY REPUBLIC. Cambridge, Mass.: Harvard University Press, 1965. 389 p.

264 Shalala, Donna E., et al. READINGS IN AMERICAN POLITICS AND EDUCATION. New York: MSS Information, 1973. 298 p.

265   Sizer, Theodore R., ed. THE AGE OF THE ACADEMIES. New York:
      Bureau of Publications, Teachers College, Columbia University, 1964.
      201 p.

      Deals with the academy movement between 1749 and 1885.

266   Skilbeck, Malcolm, ed. JOHN DEWEY. London: Collier-Macmillan,
      1970. 240 p.

267   Sloan, Douglas, ed. THE GREAT AWAKENING AND AMERICAN EDU-
      CATION: A DOCUMENTARY HISTORY. New York: Teachers College
      Press, 1973. 270 p.

268   Small, Walter H. EARLY NEW ENGLAND SCHOOLS. Boston: Ginn,
      1914. 401 p.

269   Smiley, Marjorie B., and Diekhoff, John S., eds. PROLOGUE TO
      TEACHING. New York: Oxford University Press, 1959. 189 p.

270   Smith, Wilson, ed. THEORIES OF EDUCATION IN EARLY AMERICA,
      1655-1819. Indianapolis: Bobbs-Merrill, 1973. 442 p.

271   Spurlock, Clark. EDUCATION AND THE SUPREME COURT. Urbana:
      University of Illinois Press, 1955. 202 p.

272   Strickland, Charles E., and Burgess, Charles, eds. HEALTH, GROWTH,
      AND HEREDITY: G. STANLEY HALL ON NATURAL EDUCATION. New
      York: Teachers College Press, 1965. 187 p.

273   Thomas, Maurice J., comp. PRESIDENTIAL STATEMENTS ON EDUCA-
      TION: EXCERPTS FROM INAUGURAL AND STATE OF THE UNION
      MESSAGES, 1789-1967. Pittsburgh: University of Pittsburgh Press, 1967.
      240 p.

274   Tyack, David B., ed. TURNING POINTS IN AMERICAN EDUCATION-
      AL HISTORY. Lexington, Mass.: Xerox College Publishing, 1976. 487 p.

      Originally published in 1967.

275   Ulich, Robert, ed. A SEQUENCE OF EDUCATIONAL INFLUENCES.
      Cambridge, Mass.: Harvard University Press, 1935. 190 p.

      Manuscript letters exchanged between European and American
      educators.

276   Vassar, Rena L., ed. SOCIAL HISTORY OF AMERICAN EDUCATION.
      2 vols. Chicago: Rand McNally, 1965.

Contents: vol. 1: COLONIAL TIMES TO 1860; vol. 2: TO PRESENT.

277   Weaver, David A., ed. BUILDERS OF AMERICAN UNIVERSITIES: IN-AUGURAL ADDRESSES, PRIVATELY CONTROLLED INSTITUTIONS. Alton, Ill.: Shurtleff College Press, 1950. 280 p.

278   Welter, Rush, ed. WRITINGS ON POPULAR EDUCATION: THE NINE-TEENTH CENTURY. Indianapolis: Bobbs-Merrill, 1971. 469 p.

279   Winn, Ralph B., ed. JOHN DEWEY: DICTIONARY OF EDUCATION. New York: Philosophical Library, 1959. 180 p.

280   Woody, Thomas. QUAKER EDUCATION IN THE COLONY AND STATE OF NEW JERSEY: A SOURCE BOOK. Philadelphia: University of Pennsylvania Press, 1923. 408 p.

281   _____, ed. EDUCATIONAL VIEWS OF BENJAMIN FRANKLIN. New York: McGraw-Hill, 1931. 315 p.

Chapter 4

HISTORIOGRAPHY OF AMERICAN EDUCATION

1. GENERAL HISTORIES

282 Anderson, Lewis F. HISTORY OF MANUAL AND INDUSTRIAL SCHOOL EDUCATION. New York: Appleton-Century-Crofts, 1976. 251 p.

283 Bailyn, Bernard. EDUCATION IN THE FORMING OF AMERICAN SOCIETY: NEEDS AND OPPORTUNITIES FOR STUDY. New York: Norton, 1972. 147 p.

> Originally issued by the Institute of Early American History and Culture at Williamsburg, Virginia.

284 Bayles, Ernest E., and Hood, Bruce L. GROWTH OF AMERICAN EDUCATIONAL THOUGHT AND PRACTICE. New York: Harper and Row, 1966. 305 p.

285 Berger, Michael L. THE PUBLIC EDUCATION SYSTEM. New York: Franklin Watts, 1977. 109 p.

286 Boone, Richard G. EDUCATION IN THE UNITED STATES, ITS HISTORY FROM THE EARLIEST SETTLEMENTS. New York: D. Appleton, 1889. 402 p.

287 Brickman, William W. EDUCATIONAL SYSTEMS IN THE UNITED STATES. New York: Center for Applied Research in Education, 1964. 118 p.

288 Brown, Elmer Ellsworth. THE MAKING OF OUR MIDDLE SCHOOLS: AN ACCOUNT OF THE DEVELOPMENT OF SECONDARY EDUCATION IN THE UNITED STATES. 1905. Reprint. Totowa, N.J.: Littlefield, Adams, 1970. 547 p.

> A reprint of a standard source work in the history of American education that first appeared in 1905.

289   Buetow, Harold A. OF SINGULAR BENEFIT: THE STORY OF CATHO-
      LIC EDUCATION IN THE UNITED STATES. New York: Macmillan,
      1970. 526 p.

      A comprehensive history that probably supersedes J.A. Burns,
      THE CATHOLIC SCHOOL SYSTEM IN THE UNITED STATES
      (1908), as well as his GROWTH AND DEVELOPMENT OF THE
      CATHOLIC SCHOOL SYSTEM IN THE UNITED STATES (1912),
      and B.J. Kohlbrenner's revision of these into, A HISTORY OF
      CATHOLIC EDUCATION IN THE UNITED STATES (1937), all
      out of print.

290   Bullock, Henry Allen. A HISTORY OF NEGRO EDUCATION IN THE
      SOUTH; FROM 1619 TO THE PRESENT. Cambridge, Mass.: Harvard
      University Press, 1967. 339 p.

291   Butts, R. Freeman. PUBLIC EDUCATION IN THE UNITED STATES: FROM
      REVOLUTION TO REFORM. New York: Holt, Rinehart and Winston,
      1978. 436 p.

292   Butts, R. Freeman, and Cremin, Lawrence A. A HISTORY OF EDUCA-
      TION IN AMERICAN CULTURE. New York: Holt, 1953. 628 p.

293   Church, Robert L., and Sedlak, Michael W. EDUCATION IN THE UNI-
      TED STATES: AN INTERPRETATIVE HISTORY. New York: Free Press,
      1976. 489 p.

294   Clifford, Geraldine J. THE SHAPE OF AMERICAN EDUCATION. Engle-
      wood Cliffs, N.J.: Prentice-Hall, 1975. 251 p.

      Attempts to "explain and to account for the predominant and
      determining characteristics of schools and colleges in this so-
      ciety."

295   Cordasco, Francesco. A BRIEF HISTORY OF EDUCATION. Rev. ed.
      Totowa, N.J.: Littlefield, Adams, 1976. 192 p.

      See: "Part 5: American Education," pp. 107-49.

296   Cremin, Lawrence A. THE AMERICAN COMMON SCHOOL: AN HIS-
      TORIC CONCEPTION. New York: Teachers College, Columbia Univer-
      sity, 1951. 248 p.

      Deals with the period 1815-50.

297   _____. A HISTORY OF AMERICAN EDUCATION. New York: Harper
      and Row, 1970-- .

      Intended as a three-volume comprehensive history of American
      Education. Vol. 1: AMERICAN EDUCATION: THE COLO-
      NIAL EXPERIENCE, 1607-1783. (1970).

298   _____. PUBLIC EDUCATION. New York: Basic Books, 1976. 100 p.

299   _____. TRADITIONS OF AMERICAN EDUCATION. New York: Basic Books, 1977. 172 p.

300 Cubberley, Ellwood Patterson. A BRIEF HISTORY OF EDUCATION; A HISTORY OF THE PRACTICE AND PROGRESS AND ORGANIZATION OF EDUCATION. Boston: Houghton Mifflin, 1922. 462 p.

An abridgement of Cubberley's earlier book, THE HISTORY OF EDUCATION (1920).

301   _____. PUBLIC EDUCATION IN THE UNITED STATES: A STUDY AND INTERPRETATION OF AMERICAN EDUCATIONAL HISTORY. Rev. ed. Boston: Houghton Mifflin, 1934. 782 p.

A revision of the 1919 edition, somewhat enlarged.

302   _____. THE HISTORY OF EDUCATION: EDUCATIONAL PRACTICE AND PROGRESS CONSIDERED AS A PHASE OF THE DEVELOPMENT AND SPREAD OF WESTERN CIVILIZATION. Boston and New York: Houghton Mifflin, 1948. 839 p.

303   _____. SYLLABUS OF LECTURES ON HISTORY OF EDUCATION. 1904. Reprint. 2d ed. Totowa, N.J.: Rowman and Littlefield, 1971. 360 p.

New introduction by Francesco Cordasco.

304 Curti, Merle. THE SOCIAL IDEAS OF AMERICAN EDUCATORS: WITH NEW CHAPTER ON THE LAST TWENTY-FIVE YEARS. Paterson, N.J.: Pageant Books, 1959. 613 p.

Challenges the classic concept of the role of the schools in our society.

305 Dexter, Edwin G. A HISTORY OF EDUCATION IN THE UNITED STATES. New York: Macmillan, 1904. 656 p.

306 Drake, William E. THE AMERICAN SCHOOL IN TRANSITION. New York: Prentice-Hall, 1955. 270 p.

307 Edwards, Newton, and Richey, Herman G. THE SCHOOL IN THE AMERICAN SOCIAL ORDER. 2d ed. Boston: Houghton Mifflin, 1963. 694 p.

308 Finney, Ross G. THE AMERICAN PUBLIC SCHOOL: A GENETIC STUDY OF PRINCIPLES, PRACTICES, AND PRESENT PROBLEMS. New York: Macmillan, 1921. 240 p.

309 French, William M. AMERICA'S EDUCATIONAL TRADITION: AN INTERPRETIVE HISTORY. Boston: D.C. Heath, 1964. 264 p.

310 Fuller, Edgar, and Pearson, J.B., eds. EDUCATION IN THE UNITED STATES: HISTORICAL DEVELOPMENT AND OUTLOOK. Washington, D.C.: National Education Association, 1969. 126 p.

311 Gabert, Glen. IN HOC SIGNO? A BRIEF HISTORY OF CATHOLIC PAROCHIAL EDUCATION IN AMERICA. Port Washington, N.Y.: Kennikat, 1973. 139 p.

A brief survey of Catholic parochial education from its beginnings to the present.

312 Gillett, Margaret. A HISTORY OF EDUCATION: THOUGHT AND PRACTICE. Toronto and New York: McGraw-Hill of Canada, 1966. 443 p.

313 Good, Harry G., and Teller, James D. A HISTORY OF AMERICAN EDUCATION. 3d ed. New York: Macmillan, 1973. 588 p.

314 Gross, Richard E. HERITAGE OF AMERICAN EDUCATION. Boston: Allyn and Bacon, 1962. 544 p.

315 Gutek, Gerald Lee. AN HISTORICAL INTRODUCTION TO AMERICAN EDUCATION. New York: Crowell, 1970. 246 p.

Sees formal education as a social process.

316 Henderson, John C. OUR NATIONAL SYSTEM OF EDUCATION. New York: Dodd, Mead, 1877. 285 p.

317 Karier, Clarence J. MAN, SOCIETY AND EDUCATION: A HISTORY OF AMERICAN EDUCATIONAL IDEAS. Chicago: Scott, Foresman, 1967. 334 p.

318 Knight, Edgar W. EDUCATION IN THE UNITED STATES. 3d rev. ed. Boston: Ginn, 1951. 753 p.

319 _____. FIFTY YEARS OF AMERICAN EDUCATION. New York: Ronald, 1952. 484 p.

320 Kraushaar, Otto F. AMERICAN NONPUBLIC SCHOOLS: PATTERNS OF DIVERSITY. Baltimore: Johns Hopkins Press, 1972. 387 p.

An extensive study of the private schools in the United States with extensive documentation.

321   Mayer, Frederick. AMERICAN IDEAS AND EDUCATION. Cleveland:
      Merrill, 1964. 638 p.

      A chronological examination; quotes from the primary sources.

322   Meyer, Adolph E. AN EDUCATIONAL HISTORY OF THE AMERICAN
      PEOPLE. 2d ed. New York: McGraw-Hill, 1967. 489 p.

323   _____. GRAND MASTERS OF EDUCATIONAL THOUGHT. New York:
      McGraw-Hill, 1975. 302 p.

      Includes chapters on Franklin, Jefferson, Noah Webster, Ben-
      jamin Rush, Samuel Knox, R.W. Emerson, Francis W. Parker,
      and John Dewey.

324   Monroe, Paul. FOUNDING OF THE AMERICAN PUBLIC SCHOOL SYS-
      TEM. 2 vols. New York: Macmillan, 1940.

      Volume 2 is a microfilm of documents in typeset comprising
      1,775 pages.

325   Mulhern, James A. A HISTORY OF EDUCATION: A SOCIAL INTER-
      PRETATION. New York: Ronald, 1959. 754 p.

326   Noble, Stuart G. A HISTORY OF AMERICAN EDUCATION. Rev. ed.
      New York: Rinehart, 1954. 552 p.

327   Parker, Samuel C. THE HISTORY OF MODERN ELEMENTARY EDUCA-
      TION. Boston: Ginn, 1912. 505 p. Reprint. Littlefield, Adams,
      1970.

      With an introduction by Francesco Cordasco. An historical
      overview from the Middle Ages to the present.

328   Perkinson, Henry J. TWO HUNDRED YEARS OF AMERICAN EDUCA-
      TIONAL THOUGHT. New York: David McKay, 1976. 376 p.

329   Potter, Robert E. THE STREAM OF AMERICAN EDUCATION. New
      York: American Book, 1967. 552 p.

330   Power, Edward J. MAIN CURRENTS IN THE HISTORY OF EDUCATION.
      2d ed. New York: McGraw-Hill, 1970. 628 p.

331   Pratte, Richard. THE PUBLIC SCHOOL MOVEMENT: A CRITICAL STUDY.
      New York: David McKay, 1973. 226 p.

      A concise history from colonial times to the present.

332   Pulliam, John D. HISTORY OF EDUCATION IN AMERICA. 2d ed.
      Columbus, Ohio: Charles E. Merrill, 1976. 185 p.

333   Reisner, Edward Hartman. THE EVOLUTION OF THE COMMON SCHOOL.
      New York: Macmillan, 1930. 590 p.

334   Rippa, S. Alexander. EDUCATION IN A FREE SOCIETY: AN AMERI-
      CAN HISTORY. 2d ed. New York: David McKay, 1976. 436 p.

335   Ryan, Patrick J. HISTORICAL FOUNDATIONS OF PUBLIC EDUCATION
      IN AMERICA. Dubuque, Iowa: William C. Brown, 1965. 335p.

      Deals in current public educational theory and practice.

336   Slosson, Edwin E. THE AMERICAN SPIRIT IN EDUCATION: A CHRON-
      ICLE OF GREAT TEACHERS. New Haven, Conn.: Yale University Press,
      1921. 309 p.

337   Smith, Frank. A HISTORY OF ENGLISH ELEMENTARY EDUCATION,
      1760-1902. London: University of London Press, 1931. 360 p. Re-
      print. New York: Augustus M. Kelley, 1970.

      Shows European influences on American educational practice.

338   Stone, Lawrence, ed. SCHOOLING AND SOCIETY: STUDIES IN THIS
      HISTORY OF EDUCATION. Baltimore and London: Johns Hopkins Uni-
      versity Press, 1976. 263 p.

      A compendium of studies from the sixteenth century to the
      present.

339   Swett, John. AMERICAN PUBLIC SCHOOLS. New York: American
      Book, 1900. 240 p.

340   Thayer, Vivian T. FORMATIVE IDEAS IN AMERICAN EDUCATION:
      FROM THE COLONIAL PERIOD TO THE PRESENT. New York: Dodd,
      Mead, 1965. 394 p.

341   Thwing, Charles F. A HISTORY OF EDUCATION IN THE UNITED
      STATES SINCE THE CIVIL WAR. Boston: Houghton Mifflin, 1910. 347 p.

342   Warren, Donald R. HISTORY, EDUCATION AND PUBLIC POLICY.
      Berkeley, Calif.: McCutcheon, 1978. 186 p.

343   Welter, Rush. POPULAR EDUCATION AND DEMOCRATIC THOUGHT
      IN AMERICA. New York: Columbia University Press, 1962. 473 p.
      Traces the role of colonial and republican precedents in the be-
      lief in public education and their extension in the Jacksonian era.

344   Wiggin, Gladys A. EDUCATION AND NATIONALISM: AN HISTORI-
       CAL INTERPRETATION OF AMERICAN EDUCATION. New York:
       McGraw-Hill, 1962. 518 p.

345   Winship, Albert E. GREAT AMERICAN EDUCATORS. New York: Ameri-
       can Book, 1900. 220 p.

346   Woody, Thomas. A HISTORY OF WOMEN'S EDUCATION IN THE UNI-
       TED STATES. 2 vols. 1929. Reprint. New York: Octagon Books,
       1966.

       Volume 2 contains bibliographical materials (pp. 481-589).

2. SPECIALIZED STUDIES

347   Altbach, Philip G., and Kelly, Gail P. EDUCATION AND COLO-
       NIALISM. New York: Longman, 1978. 372 p.

       Includes chapters on the education of American Indians, on
       blacks, and women in the nineteenth century, and "educa-
       tional colonialism and the American Working Class."

348   Andersson, Theodore. "Bilingual Education: The American Experience."
       MODERN LANGUAGE JOURNAL 55 (1971): 427-40.

349   Andersson, Theodore, and Boyer, Mildred, eds. BILINGUAL SCHOOL-
       ING IN THE UNITED STATES. 2 vols. Detroit: Blaine Ethridge, 1976.

       With a new introduction and supplemental bibliographies by
       Francesco Cordasco.

350   Appel, John J. "American Negro and Immigrant Experiences: Similari-
       ties and Differences." AMERICAN QUARTERLY 18 (1966): 95-103.

351   Atzmon, Ezri. "The Educational Programs for Immigrants in the United
       States." HISTORY OF EDUCATIONAL JOURNAL 9 (1958): 75-80.

352   Bailyn, Bernard. "Education as a Discipline: Some Historical Notes."
       In THE DISCIPLINE OF EDUCATION, edited by John Walton and James
       L. Kuethe, pp. 125-39. Madison: University of Wisconsin Press, 1963.

       Also, see: "Comments," by Wilson Smith, Ibid., pp. 139-44.

353   Barzun, Jacques. "History: The Muse and Her Doctors." AMERICAN
       HISTORICAL REVIEW 77 (1972): 36-64.

354   Baum, Willa Klug. "Oral History: A Revived Tradition at the Bancroft
       Library." PACIFIC NORTHWESTERN QUARTERLY 58 (1967): 57-64.

355   Baylor, Ruth M. ELIZABETH PALMER PEABODY: KINDERGARTEN PIO-
       NEER. Philadelphia: University of Pennsylvania Press, 1965. 228 p.

356   Beach, Mark. "History of Education." REVIEW OF EDUCATIONAL
       RESEARCH 39 (1969): 561-76.

           An overview and general review of the literature that is keyed
           to a bibliography.

357   Benjamin, H.H. "An Approach to the Study of Causation in Educational
       History." HISTORY OF EDUCATION JOURNAL 6 (1954): 137-52.

358   Berkhofer, Robert F. "Clio and the Culture Concept: Some Impressions
       of a Changing Relationship in American Historiography." SOCIAL SCI-
       ENCE QUARTERLY 53 (1972): 297-320.

359   Bernier, Normand R., and Williams, Jack E. BEYOND BELIEFS: IDEO-
       LOGICAL FOUNDATIONS OF AMERICAN EDUCATION. Englewood
       Cliffs, N.J.: Prentice-Hall, 1973. 422 p.

360   Berrol, Selma C. "Education and the Italian and Jewish Community Ex-
       perience." In THE INTERACTION BETWEEN ITALIANS AND JEWS IN
       AMERICA, edited by Jean Scarpaci, pp. 31-41. Staten Island, N.Y.:
       American Italian Historical Association, 1975.

361   Bledstein, Burton J. THE CULTURE OF PROFESSIONALISM: THE MID-
       DLE CLASS AND THE DEVELOPMENT OF HIGHER EDUCATION IN
       AMERICA. New York: Norton, 1976. 240 p.

362   Blow, Susan E. "The History of the Kindergarten in the United States."
       OUTLOOK 55 (1897): 932-38.

363   Bodnar, John. "Materialism and Morality: Slavic American Immigrants
       and Education, 1890-1940." JOURNAL OF ETHNIC STUDIES 3 (1976):
       1-19.

364   Boone, Richard Gause. A HISTORY OF EDUCATION IN INDIANA.
       New York: D. Appleton, 1892. 454 p.

365   Borrowman, Merle L. "Studies in the History of American Education."
       REVIEW OF EDUCATION 1 (1975): 56-66.

366   Bourne, Randolph S. THE GARY SCHOOLS. New ed. Cambridge:
       M.I.T. Press, 1970. 323 p.

           Includes a sociohistorical study of the Gary system by Adeline
           Levine and Murray Levine, and an abridged version of the sum-

mary report on the Gary schools written by Abraham Flexner in 1918.

367   Bowles, Samuel, and Gintis, Herbert. SCHOOLING IN CAPITALIST AMERICA: EDUCATIONAL REFORM AND THE CONTRADICTIONS OF ECONOMIC LIFE. New York: Basic Books, 1976. 340 p.

See education as a tool of social policy. See review: Allan Horlick. REVIEW OF EDUCATION 3 (1977): 168-81.

368   Brickman, William W. "Educational Literature Review: Educational History of the United States." SCHOOL AND SOCIETY 72 (1950): 436-44.

369   _____. "An Historical Survey of Foreign Writings on American Educational History." PAEDAGOGICA HISTORICA 2 (1962): 5-21.

370   _____. "Conant, Koerner, and the History of Education." SCHOOL AND SOCIETY 92 (1964): 135-39.

371   _____. "Revisionism and the Study of the History of Education." HISTORY OF EDUCATION QUARTERLY 4 (1964): 209-23.

Critical of revisionist historiography and especially of Bernard Bailyn.

372   Burgess, Charles. "History of Education." REVIEW OF EDUCATIONAL RESEARCH 37 (1967): 12-20.

373   Burnham, William H., and Suzzallo, Henry. THE HISTORY OF EDUCATION AS A PROFESSIONAL SUBJECT. New York: Columbia University Press, 1908. 110 p.

374   Butts, R. Freeman. "Civilization Building and the Modernization Process: A Framework for the Reinterpretation of the History of Education." HISTORY OF EDUCATION QUARTERLY 7 (1967): 147-74.

Uses terms "revisionism," "reinterpretation," and "reconstruction" essentially synonymously to arrive at a schematic. Also see: "Response to Professor Butts," by George F. Kneller, Ibid., pp. 175-81.

375   _____. "The Public School: Assaults on a Great Idea." THE NATION 216 (1973): 553-60.

Also, see R. Freeman Butts, "The Public Purpose of the Public School." TEACHERS COLLEGE RECORD 75 (1973): 207-21, and "Public Education and the Public Faith." EDUCATIONAL QUEST 18, Memphis State University (1974).

376 _____. "Public Education and Political Community." HISTORY OF EDUCATION QUARTERLY 14 (1974): 165-83.

An overview which seeks to look ahead as to the probable shape of the historiography of education in the ensuing fifteen years.

377 Calam, John. PARSONS AND PEDAGOGUES: THE S.P.G. ADVENTURE IN AMERICAN EDUCATION. New York: Columbia University Press, 1971. 249 p.

Deals with activities of the Society for the Propagation of the Gospel in Foreign Parts (1702-1883).

378 Callahan, Raymond E. EDUCATION AND THE CULT OF EFFICIENCY. Chicago: University of Chicago Press, 1962. 273 p.

379 Carnay, Martin. EDUCATION AS CULTURAL IMPERIALISM. New York: David McKay, 1974. 378 p.

A revisionist interpretation.

380 Carnoy, Martin, and Levin, Henry M. THE LIMITS OF EDUCATIONAL REFORM. New York: David McKay, 1976. 290 p.

381 Cartwright, William H., and Watson, Richard L., eds. THE REINTERPRETATION OF AMERICAN HISTORY AND CULTURE. Washington, D.C.: National Council for the Social Studies, 1973. 554 p.

Seeks to assess the revisionist historiography of the 1960s. For a similar assessment of the 1950s, also see John Higham, THE RECONSTRUCTION OF AMERICAN HISTORY, and Irwin Unger, "The New Left and American History," AMERICAN HISTORICAL REVIEW 72 (1967): 1237-63.

382 Chaper, Jesse H. "Establishment Clause and Aid to Parochial Schools." CALIFORNIA LAW REVIEW 56 (1958): 260-341.

383 Childs, John L., et al. "A Review Symposium: Lawrence A. Cremin's THE GENIUS OF AMERICAN EDUCATION." HISTORY OF EDUCATION QUARTERLY 7 (1967): 102-33.

384 Church, Robert L. "Economists as Experts: The Rise of an Academic Profession in America, 1870-1917." In THE UNIVERSITY IN SOCIETY, vol. 2, edited by Lawrence Stone, pp. 571-609. Princeton: Princeton University Press, 1974.

In the same volume, also see: James McLachlan, "The Choice of Hercules: American Student Societies in the Early 19th Century," pp. 449-94, and James M. McPherson, "The New

Puritanism: Values and Goals of Freedmen's Education in America," pp. 611-39.

385 _____. "History of Education as a Field of Study." In ENCYCLOPE-DIA OF EDUCATION, vol. 4, edited by Lee C. Deighton, pp. 415-24. New York: Macmillan, 1971.

386 Clegg, Ambrose A., Jr. "Church Groups and Federal Aid to Education." HISTORY OF EDUCATION QUARTERLY 4 (1964): 137-54.

387 Clement, Rufus E. "The Church School as a Factor in Negro Life." JOURNAL OF NEGRO HISTORY 12 (1927): 5-12.

388 Clifford, Geraldine J. "'Psyching' Psycho-History." HISTORY OF EDU-CATION QUARTERLY 11 (1970): 413-25.

> Based upon Sudhir Kakar, FREDERICK TAYLOR: A STUDY IN PERSONALITY AND INNOVATION, 1970, using Freudian and Eriksonian terms.

389 _____. "Home and School in 19th Century America: Some Personal-History Reports from the United States." HISTORY OF EDUCATION QUARTERLY 18 (1978): 3-34.

390 Cohen, David K. "Immigrants and the Schools." REVIEW OF EDUCA-TIONAL RESEARCH 4 (1970): 13-17.

> Really an overview of immigrant children and IQ retardation and measures of cognitive progress.

391 Cohen, David K., and Lazerson, Marvin. "Education and the Corporate Order." SOCIALIST REVOLUTION 2 (1972): 47-72.

> Essentially about vocational education and educational change.

392 Cohen, Sol. PROGRESSIVES AND URBAN SCHOOL REFORM: THE PUBLIC EDUCATION ASSOCIATION OF NEW YORK CITY, 1895-1954. New York: Bureau of Publications, Teachers College, Columbia University, 1964. 273 p.

393 _____. "Sir Michael E. Sadler and the Sociopolitical Analysis of Edu-cation." HISTORY OF EDUCATION QUARTERLY 7 (1967): 281-94.

> Sir Michael Sadler was a member of the Bryce Commission, and a professor of education at the University of Manchester, England.

394 _____. "English Writers on the American Common Schools, 1884-1904." SCHOOL REVIEW 76 (1968): 127-46.

395   _____. "The Industrial Education Movement, 1907-17." AMERICAN QUARTERLY 20 (1968): 95-110.

396   _____. "New Perspectives in the History of American Education, 1960-1970." HISTORY OF EDUCATION [England] 2 (1973): 79-96.

397   _____. "The History of the History of American Education, 1900-1976: The Uses of the Past." HARVARD EDUCATIONAL REVIEW 46 (1976): 298-330.

398   Conway, J. "Perspectives on the History of Women's Education in the United States." HISTORY OF EDUCATION QUARTERLY 14 (1974): 1-12.

399   Cordasco, Francesco. "The Promethean Ethic: Higher Education and Social Imperatives." PEABODY JOURNAL OF EDUCATION 44 (1967): 195-209.

400   _____. "The Challenge of the Non-English Speaking Child in the American School." SCHOOL AND SOCIETY 96 (1968): 198-201.

       On the Title VII amendments to the Elementary and Secondary Education Act.

401   _____. "Leonard Covello and the Community School." SCHOOL AND SOCIETY 98 (1970): 298-99.

402   _____. "The Catholic Urban School: The Patterns of Survival." NOTRE DAME UNIVERSITY JOURNAL OF EDUCATION 2 (1971): 61-67.

403   _____. "Henry Barnard's American Journal of Education." HISTORY OF EDUCATION QUARTERLY 11 (1971): 328-32.

404   _____. "America and the Quest for Equal Educational Opportunity: A Prolegomenon and Overview." BRITISH JOURNAL OF EDUCATIONAL STUDIES 21 (1973): 50-63.

405   _____. "The Children of Immigrants in Schools: Historical Analogues of Educational Deprivation." JOURNAL OF NEGRO EDUCATION 42 (1973): 44-53.

       Limited to New York City: 1890-1915.

406   _____. "Reforming Teacher Education in the 1970's." SCHOOL AND SOCIETY 101 (1973): 381-84.

407   _____. "The Teachers College Contributions to Education." HISTORY OF EDUCATION QUARTERLY 14 (1974): 149-53.

408   _____. "Spanish-Speaking Children in American Schools." INTERNA-
TIONAL MIGRATION REVIEW 9 (1975): 379-82.

> Also appears in modified form in: INTELLECT 101 (1975):
> 242-43.

409   Covello, Leonard. THE SOCIAL BACKGROUND OF THE ITALO-AMERI-
CAN SCHOOL CHILD: A STUDY OF THE SOUTHERN ITALIAN FAMILY
MORES AND THEIR EFFECT ON THE SCHOOL SITUATION IN ITALY
AND AMERICA. Edited and with an introduction by Francesco Cordasco.
Leiden, The Netherlands: E.J. Brill, 1967; Totowa, N.J.: Rowman and
Littlefield, 1972. 488 p.

410   Cremin, Lawrence A. THE TRANSFORMATION OF THE SCHOOL: PRO-
GRESSIVISM IN AMERICAN EDUCATION, 1876-1957. New York: Random House, 1964. 387 p.

411   _____. THE GENIUS OF AMERICAN EDUCATION. Pittsburgh: University of Pittsburgh Press, 1965. 122 p.

> Also see: "A Review Symposium." HISTORY OF EDUCATION
> QUARTERLY 7 (1967): 102-33.

412   _____. THE WONDERFUL WORLD OF ELWOOD PATTERSON CUBBER-
LEY: AN ESSAY ON THE HISTORIOGRAPHY OF AMERICAN EDUCA-
TION. New York: Bureau of Publications, Teachers College, Columbia
University, 1965. 81 p.

413   _____. "Curriculum-Making in the United States." TEACHERS COL-
LEGE RECORD 73 (1971): 207-22.

414   _____. "Notes Toward a Theory of Education." In NOTES ON EDU-
CATION (Institute of Philosophy and Politics of Education, Teachers College, Columbia University 1 (1973). 43 p.

> Also see: Lawrence A. Cremin, AMERICAN EDUCATION:
> SOME NOTES TOWARD A NEW HISTORY. Bloomington:
> University of Indiana Press, 1972.

415   _____. "The Family as Educator: Some Comments on the Recent Historiography." TEACHERS COLLEGE RECORD 76 (1974): 250-65.

416   _____, et al. "The Role of the History of Education in the Professional
Preparation of Teachers." HISTORY OF EDUCATION JOURNAL 7 (1955-
56): 38-62.

417   Cross, Robert D. "Recent Histories of U.S. Catholic Education." HIS-
TORY OF EDUCATION QUARTERLY 14 (1974): 125-30.

418 Cutler, William W. "Oral History: Its Nature and Uses for Educational
     History." HISTORY OF EDUCATION QUARTERLY 11 (1971): 184-94.

419 "Early History of the Kindergarten in St. Louis, Mo." In UNITED STATES
     BUREAU OF EDUCATION, REPORT OF THE COMMISSIONER, 1896-1897,
     vol. 1, pp. 899-922. Washington, D.C.: 1898.

420 Eisle, J. Christopher. "John Dewey and the Immigrants." HISTORY OF
     EDUCATION QUARTERLY 15 (1975): 67-85.

         Also see: Clarence J. Karier, "John Dewey and the New
         Liberalism: Some Reflections and Responses." HISTORY OF
         EDUCATION QUARTERLY 15 (1975): 417-43.

421 Endes, Raymond J. "Elementary School Functions in the United States:
     An Historical Analysis." PAEDAGOGICA HISTORICA 7 (1967): 378-416.

422 Evans, John W. "Catholics and the Blair Education Bill." CATHOLIC
     HISTORICAL REVIEW 46 (1960): 273-98.

423 Findley, James. "Education and the Church Controversy. The Later
     Career of Dwight L. Moody." NEW ENGLAND QUARTERLY 39 (1966):
     210-32.

424 Finkelstein, Barbara. "Pedagogy as Intrusion: Teaching Values in Popu-
     lar Primary Schools in 19th Century America." HISTORY OF CHILDHOOD
     QUARTERLY: THE JOURNAL OF PSYCHOHISTORY 2 (1975): 368-69.

425 Fisher, Berenice M. "History, Social Science, and Education: Some
     Kinks in the Academic Procession." HISTORY OF EDUCATION QUAR-
     TERLY 11 (1971): 426-34.

         Also see: George W. Stocking, "On the Limits of 'Presentism'
         and 'Historicism' in the Historiography of the Behavioral Sci-
         ences." JOURNAL OF THE HISTORY OF THE BEHAVIORAL
         SCIENCES 1 (1965): 211-17, and Robert A. Skotheim, AMERI-
         CAN INTELLECTUAL HISTORIES AND HISTORIANS, 1966.

426 Freund, Paul A. "Public Aid to Parochial Schools." HARVARD LAW RE-
     VIEW 82 (1969): 1680-692.

427 Friedman, Norman L. "New Orders and Old: Historians, Educationists,
     and the Dynamics of Academic Imperialism." AMERICAN BEHAVIORAL
     SCIENTIST 9 (1965): 24-29.

428 [Fund for the Advancement of Education.] Committee on the Role of
     Education in American History. EDUCATION AND AMERICAN HISTORY.
     New York: 1965. 45 p.

A revision and an expansion of its 1957 statement on the subject.

429 Gilbert, Felix, and Graubard, Stephen R., eds. HISTORICAL STUDIES TODAY. New York: Norton, 1972. 469 p.

Essays by twenty-two historians on all aspects of historical enquiry. See particularly: John E. Talbott, "Education in Intellectual and Social History," pp. 193-210.

430 Gobbel, Luther L. CHURCH-STATE RELATIONSHIPS IN EDUCATION IN NORTH CAROLINA SINCE 1776. Durham, N.C.: Duke University Press, 1938. 251 p.

431 Good, Harry G. "The Approach to the History of Education." SCHOOL AND SOCIETY 20 (1924): 231-37.

432 Greeley, Andrew M., and McCready, William C. CATHOLIC SCHOOLS IN A DECLINING CHURCH. Mission, Kans.: Sheed and Ward, 1976. 483 p.

433 Greene, Maxine. "The Professional Significance of History of Education." HISTORY OF EDUCATION QUARTERLY 7 (1967): 182-90.

434 _____. "Identities and Contours: An Approach to Educational History." EDUCATIONAL RESEARCHER 2 (1973): 5-17.

435 Greer, Colin. "Immigrants, Negroes and the Public Schools." THE URBAN REVIEW 3 (1969): 9-12.

436 _____. THE GREAT SCHOOL LEGEND: A REVISIONIST INTERPRETATION OF AMERICAN PUBLIC EDUCATION. New York: Basic Books, 1972. 206 p.

437 Hansen, Allen O. "Integrative Anthropological Method in History of Culture and Education." EDUCATIONAL FORUM 1 (1937): 361-78.

438 Hendrick, Irving G. "History of Education and Teacher Preparation: A Cautious Analysis." JOURNAL OF TEACHER EDUCATION 17 (1966): 71-76.

439 Herbst, Jurgen. THE GERMAN HISTORICAL SCHOOL IN AMERICAN SCHOLARSHIP: A STUDY IN THE TRANSFER OF CULTURE. Ithaca, N.Y.: Cornell University Press, 1965. 262 p.

Deals with its impact--especially on the social sciences.

440 _____. "American College History: Re-Examination Underway." HIS-
TORY OF EDUCATION QUARTERLY 14 (1974): 259-65.

    Suggests historians are more interested in demographic social
    analysis.

441 Herzog, John D. "Deliberate Instruction and Household Structure: A
Cross-Cultural Study." HARVARD EDUCATIONAL REVIEW 32 (1962):
301-42.

442 Hiner, N. Ray. "Professions in Process: Changing Relations Between
Historians and Educators, 1896-1911." HISTORY OF EDUCATION QUAR-
TERLY 12 (1972): 34-56.

    Also see: David D. Van Tassel, RECORDING AMERICA'S
    PAST: AN INTERPRETATION OF THE DEVELOPMENT OF
    HISTORICAL STUDIES IN AMERICA. Chicago: University
    of Chicago Press, 1960.

443 [History of Education]. "Doing History of Education." HISTORY OF
EDUCATION QUARTERLY 9 (1969): 324-29, 343-59, 360-71, 372-75.

    Also see: Paul Nash, ed. HISTORY AND EDUCATION:
    THE EDUCATIONAL USES OF THE PAST, 1970.

444 Holsinger, M. Paul. "The Oregon School Bill Controversy, 1922-1925."
PACIFIC HISTORICAL REVIEW 37 (1968): 327-41.

445 Hood, Bruce L. "The Historian of Education: Some Notes on His Role."
HISTORY OF EDUCATION QUARTERLY 9 (1969): 372-75.

446 Horlick, Allan S. "Good History and Historical Questions." HISTORY
OF EDUCATION QUARTERLY 13 (1973): 173-83.

    See also: the author's, "The Rewriting of American Education-
    al History." NEW YORK UNIVERSITY EDUCATION QUAR-
    TERLY (1974): 3-7.

447 Itzkoff, Seymour W. A NEW PUBLIC EDUCATION. New York: David
McKay, 1976. 372 p.

448 Jenkins, Elizabeth. "How the Kindergarten Found Its Way to America."
WISCONSIN MAGAZINE OF HISTORY 14 (1930-31): 48-62.

449 Judd, Charles H. "Changing Conceptions of Secondary and Higher Education in America." SCHOOL REVIEW 45 (1937): 93-104.

450 Kaestle, Carl F. "Social Reform and the Urban School." HISTORY OF
EDUCATION QUARTERLY 12 (1972): 211-28.

451 _____. THE EVOLUTION OF AN URBAN SCHOOL SYSTEM: NEW YORK CITY, 1750-1850. Cambridge, Mass.: Harvard University Press, 1973. 205 p.

452 _____. "Conflict and Concensus Revised: Notes Toward a Reinterpretation of American Educational History." HARVARD EDUCATIONAL REVIEW 46 (1976): 390-96.

453 Kahn, Akbert S. "Relevance: Some Historical Perspectives, Past, Present, and Future." JOURNAL OF EDUCATION 154 (1971): 49-57.

454 Kalisch, Philip, and Hutton, Harry. "Davidson's Influence on Educational Historiography." HISTORY OF EDUCATION QUARTERLY 6 (1966): 79-87.

   Also see: Thomas Davidson, HISTORY OF EDUCATION, 1900.

455 Karier, Clarence; Violas, Paul; and Spring, Joel. ROOTS OF CRISIS: AMERICAN EDUCATION IN THE TWENTIETH CENTURY. Chicago: Rand McNally, 1973. 383 p.

456 Katz, Michael B. "The Emergence of Bureaucracy in Urban Education: The Boston Case, 1850-1884." HISTORY OF EDUCATION QUARTERLY 8 (1968): 155-88, 319-57.

457 _____. THE IRONY OF EARLY SCHOOL REFORM: EDUCATIONAL INNOVATION IN MID-NINETEENTH CENTURY MASSACHUSETTS. Cambridge, Mass.: Harvard University Press, 1968. 325 p.

458 _____. "From Voluntarism to Bureaucracy in American Education." SOCIOLOGY OF EDUCATION 44 (1971): 297-332.

459 _____. "The Present Moment in Educational Reform." HARVARD EDUCATIONAL REVIEW 41 (1971): 342-59.

460 _____. CLASS, BUREAUCRACY AND SCHOOLS. New York: Praeger, 1975. 208 p.

461 Kloss, Heinz. THE AMERICAN BILINGUAL TRADITION. Rowley, Mass.: Newbury House, 1977. 347 p.

462 Krug, Edward A. THE SHAPING OF THE AMERICAN HIGH SCHOOL. New York: Harper, 1964. 486 p.

Also see, Krug, Edward A., THE SHAPING OF THE AMERI-
CAN HIGH SCHOOL. Univ. of Wisconsin, 1972, which
continues the story to 1941.

463 _____. SALIENT DATES IN AMERICAN EDUCATION: 1635-1964.
New York: Harper and Row, 1966. 159 p.

464 Lannie, Vincent P. PUBLIC MONEY AND PAROCHIAL EDUCATION:
BISHOP HUGHES, GOVERNOR SEWARD, AND THE NEW YORK SCHOOL
CONTROVERSY. Cleveland: Press of Case Western Reserve University,
1968. 282 p.

465 LaNoue, George R. "Religious Schools and 'Secular' Subjects." HAR-
VARD EDUCATIONAL REVIEW 32 (1962): 255-91.

466 Lazerson, Marvin. ORIGINS OF THE URBAN SCHOOL: PUBLIC EDU-
CATION IN MASSACHUSETTS, 1870-1915. Cambridge, Mass.: Harvard
University Press, 1971. 278 p.

467 _____. "Revisionism and American Educational History." HARVARD
EDUCATIONAL REVIEW 43 (1973): 269-83.

468 _____. "Understanding American Catholic Educational History." HIS-
TORY OF EDUCATION QUARTERLY 17 (1977): 297-317.

An interpretive framework for understanding the history of
Catholic education in the United States.

469 Leslie, W. Bruce. "Localism, Denominationalism, and Institutional Strategies in Urbanizing America: Three Pennsylvania Colleges, 1870-1915."
HISTORY OF EDUCATION QUARTERLY 17 (1977): 235-56.

An examination of Bucknell University, Franklin and Marshall
College, and Swarthmore College.

470 Lewis, H. Graham. "Bailyn and Cremin on Cubberley and History of
Education." EDUCATIONAL THEORY 17 (1967): 56-69.

471 Lilge, Frederic. "The Functionalist Fallacy and the History of Education."
SCHOOL AND SOCIETY 65 (1947): 241-43.

472 Lord, Daniel C. "The Historian as Villain: The Historian's Role in the
Training of Teachers." THE HISTORIAN 34 (1972): 407-20.

473 Lutz, Alma. EMMA WILLARD: PIONEER EDUCATOR OF AMERICAN
WOMEN. Boston: Beacon, 1964. 143 p.

474 McAvoy, Thomas T. "Public Schools vs. Catholic Schools and James McMaster." REVIEW OF POLITICS 28 (1966): 19-46.

475 McBride, Paul. "The Co-op Industrial Education Experiment, 1900-1917." HISTORY OF EDUCATION QUARTERLY 14 (1974): 209-21.

476 McLachlan, James. AMERICAN BOARDING SCHOOLS: A HISTORICAL STUDY. New York: Charles Scribner Sons, 1970. 381 p.

> First comprehensive history of the American private boarding school from earliest times to the present.

477 Mattingly, Paul H. "Useful History and Black Identity." HISTORY OF EDUCATION QUARTERLY 10 (1970): 338-50.

478 _____. THE CLASSLESS PROFESSION: AMERICAN SCHOOLMEN IN THE NINETEENTH CENTURY. New York: New York University Press, 1975. 235 p.

> Attempts to "explain the historical dynamics behind the professionalization of the American teacher."

479 Mays, Arthur B. "Fifty Years of Progress in Vocational and Practical Arts Education." AMERICAN VOCATIONAL JOURNAL 31 (1956): 29-38.

480 Mehl, Bernard. "New Writings and the Status of the History of Education." HISTORY OF EDUCATION JOURNAL 8 (1957): 108-16.

481 Mitchell, Fredric, and Skelton, James W. "The Church-State Conflict in Early Indian Education." HISTORY OF EDUCATION QUARTERLY 6 (1966): 41-51.

482 Nash, Paul. "History of Education." REVIEW OF EDUCATIONAL RESEARCH 34 (1964): 37-54.

483 Nevin, David, and Bills, Robert E. THE SCHOOLS THAT FEAR BUILT: SEGREGATIONIST ACADEMIES IN THE SOUTH. Washington, D.C.: Acropolis Books, 1976. 186 p.

484 Patterson, Orlando. "Rethinking Black History." HARVARD EDUCATIONAL REVIEW 41 (1971): 297-315.

> Also see: Eugene D. Genovese, ROLL JORDAN, ROLL: THE WORLD THAT SLAVES MADE. New York: Pantheon, 1974.

485   Peabody, Elizabeth P.   "Kindergarten Culture."   In UNITED STATES
      BUREAU OF EDUCATION, REPORT OF THE COMMISSIONER, 1870,
      pp. 354-59. Washington, D.C.: Government Printing Office, 1870.

486   _____.   "The Objects of the Kindergarten."   In UNITED STATES BUREAU
      OF EDUCATION, REPORT OF THE COMMISSIONER, 1871, pp. 529-34.
      Washington, D.C.: Government Printing Office, 1872.

487   Perkinson, Henry J.   "The Role of Religion in American Education: An
      Historical Interpretation."   PAEDAGOGICA HISTORICA 5 (1965): 109-21.

488   _____.   THE IMPERFECT PANACEA: AMERICAN FAITH IN EDUCATION,
      1865-1965. New York: Random House, 1968. 234 p.

      Especially see the bibliographical notes, pp. 223-39, and also
      his: THE POSSIBILITIES OF ERROR, 1971.

489   Platt, Anthony M.   THE CHILD SAVERS: THE INVENTION OF DELIN-
      QUENCY. Chicago: University of Chicago Press, 1977. 240 p.

490   Pratte, Richard.   THE PUBLIC SCHOOL MOVEMENT: A CRITICAL
      STUDY. New York: David McKay, 1973. 226 p.

491   Quinan, Richard J.   "Growth and Development of Catholic Education in
      the Archdiocese of Boston."   CATHOLIC HISTORICAL REVIEW 22 (1936):
      27-41.

492   Rainsford, George N.   CONGRESS AND HIGHER EDUCATION IN THE
      NINETEENTH CENTURY. Nashville: University of Tennessee Press, 1972.
      156 p.

493   Ravitch, Diane.   "On the History of Minority Group Education in the
      United States."   TEACHERS COLLEGE RECORD 78 (1976): 213-28.

494   _____.   "The Revisionists Revisited."   NATIONAL ACADEMY OF EDU-
      CATION PROCEEDINGS 4 (1977): 35-42.

495   _____.   THE REVISIONISTS REVISITED: A CRITIQUE OF THE RADICAL
      ATTACK ON THE SCHOOLS. New York: Basic Books, 1978. 194 p.

      A review of the works of the radical historians of education.
      Notices of the revisionism of Michael B. Katz, Colin Greer,
      Clarence Karier, Paul Violas, Joel Spring, Walter Feinberg,
      Samuel Bowles, and Herbert Gintis.

496   Rehberg, Richard S., and Rosenthal, Evelyn.   CLASS AND MERIT IN
      THE AMERICAN HIGH SCHOOL: AN ASSESSMENT OF THE REVISION-

IST AND MERITOCRATIC ARGUMENTS. New York: Longman, 1978. 337 p.

Social and economic inequality in American schools in the 1960s and 1970s.

497   Rempson, Joe L. "Urban Minorities: Education of Immigrants." In THE ENCYCLOPEDIA OF EDUCATION, vol. 9, edited by Lee C. Deighton, pp. 319-99. New York: Macmillan, 1971.

498   Riley, Glenda. "Origins of the Argument for Improved Female Education." HISTORY OF EDUCATION QUARTERLY 9 (1969): 455-70.

499   Rist, Ray C. THE URBAN SCHOOL: A FACTORY FOR FAILURE. Cambridge: M.I.T. Press, 1973. 265 p.

500   Rooke, Patricia T. "From Pollyana to Jeremiah: Recent Interpretations of American Educational History." JOURNAL OF EDUCATIONAL THOUGHT 9 (1975): 15-28.

501   Rothman, David J. THE DISCOVERY OF THE ASYLUM: SOCIAL ORDER AND DISORDER IN THE NEW REPUBLIC. Boston: Little, Brown, 1971. 376 p.

On the shift from noninstitutional to institutional solutions.

502   Roucek, Joseph. "The Foreign Roots of American Educational History." EDUCATIONAL FORUM 27 (1962): 47-57.

503   Rudolph, Frederick. CURRICULUM: A HISTORY OF THE AMERICAN UNDERGRADUATE COURSE OF STUDY SINCE 1636. San Francisco: Jossey-Bass, 1977. 362 p.

Places the curriculum in a broad setting of time and place and sees it as an instrument of many purposes and persons (including the students) rather than essentially as only a reflection of college catalogs, curriculum committees, and faculty debates on the subject.

504   Sacks, Seymour, et al. CITY SCHOOLS/SUBURBAN SCHOOLS: A HISTORY OF FISCAL CONFLICT. Syracuse, N.Y.: Syracuse University Press, 1972. 201 p.

505   Sanders, James W. "Catholic Elementary-School Enrollment: Chicago, 1925-65." ELEMENTARY SCHOOL JOURNAL 68 (1967): 88-96.

506   _____. THE EDUCATION OF AN URBAN MINORITY: CATHOLICS IN CHICAGO, 1833-1965. New York: Oxford University Press, 1977. 277 p.

507 Schlossman, Steven L. "Before Home Start: Notes Toward a History of
Parent Education in America, 1897-1929." HARVARD EDUCATIONAL
REVIEW 46 (1976): 436-67.

508 Schultz, Stanley K. THE CULTURE FACTORY: BOSTON PUBLIC
SCHOOLS, 1789-1860. New York: Oxford University Press, 1973.
394 p.

509 Scott, Ronald M. "The Social History of Education: Three Alternatives."
HISTORY OF EDUCATION QUARTERLY 10 (1970): 242-54.

> Examines the works of Berenice M. Fisher and Michael B.
> Katz, among others.

510 Selevan, Ida C. "The Education of Jewish Immigrants in Pittsburgh,
1862-1932." YIVO [Yiddish Scientific Institute, New York] 15 (1974):
124-43.

511 Sheedy, Morgan M. "The Catholic Parochial Schools of the United
States." In UNITED STATES BUREAU OF EDUCATION, REPORT OF THE
COMMISSIONER, 1903, vol. 1, pp. 1079-1101. Washington, D.C.:
Government Printing Office, 1905.

512 Sherman, Robert R., and Kirschner, Joseph. UNDERSTANDING HISTORY
OF EDUCATION. Cambridge, Mass.: Schenckman Publishing, 1976.
226 p.

513 Sievers, Harry J. "The Catholic Indian School Issue and the Presidential
Election of 1892." CATHOLIC HISTORICAL REVIEW 38 (1952): 129-55.

514 Sloan, Douglas. THE SCOTTISH ENLIGHTENMENT AND THE AMERICAN
COLLEGE IDEAL. New York: Teachers College Press, Columbia University, 1971. 298 p.

> Reviews eighteenth-century Scottish academies and Presbyterian
> academies in the American colonies.

515 _____. "Historiography and the History of Education." In REVIEW OF
RESEARCH IN EDUCATION, edited by Fred N. Kerlinger, pp. 239-69.
Itasca, Ill.: F.E. Peacock, 1973.

516 Smith, Timothy L. "Immigrant Social Aspirations and American Education,
1880-1930." AMERICAN QUARTERLY 21 (1969): 523-43.

517 _____. "Native Blacks and Foreign Whites: Varying Responses to Educational Opportunity in America, 1880-1950." PERSPECTIVES IN AMERI-
CAN HISTORY 6 (1972): 309-37.

518 Smith, Wilson. "The New Historian of American Education: Some Notes for a Portrait." HARVARD EDUCATIONAL REVIEW 31 (1961): 136-43.

519 Spring, Joel H. EDUCATION AND THE RISE OF THE CORPORATE STATE. Boston: Beacon, 1972. 206 p.

520 _____. THE SORTING MACHINE: NATIONAL EDUCATIONAL POLICY SINCE 1945. New York: David McKay, 1976. 309 p.

521 _____. AMERICAN EDUCATION: AN INTRODUCTION TO SOCIAL AND POLITICAL ASPECTS. New York: Longman, 1978. 234 p.

    Educational policy in the 1960s and 1970s with an analysis of the structure of power in American education.

522 Stock, Phyllis. BETTER THAN RUBIES: A HISTORY OF WOMEN'S EDU-CATION. New York: G.P. Putnam's Sons, 1978. 252 p.

    A history of women's education in the western world from classical times to the present with special emphasis on the United States.

523 Stocking, George W. "On the Limits of 'Presentism' and 'Historicism' in the Historiography of the Behavioral Sciences." JOURNAL OF THE HISTORY OF THE BEHAVIORAL SCIENCES 1 (1965): 211-17.

524 Storr, Richard J. "The Education of History: Some Impressions." HARVARD EDUCATIONAL REVIEW 31 (1961): 124-35.

525 _____. "The Role of Education in American History: A Memorandum for the Committee Advising the Fund for the Advancement of Education in Regard to the Subject." HARVARD EDUCATIONAL REVIEW 46 (1976): 331-54.

526 Stoutemeyer, J.H. "The Teaching of the History of Education in Normal Schools." SCHOOL AND SOCIETY 7 (1918): 517-80.

527 Swift, Fletcher H. A HISTORY OF PUBLIC PERMANENT COMMON SCHOOL FUNDS IN THE UNITED STATES, 1795-1905. New York: Holt, 1907. 493 p.

528 _____. "The Specific Objectives of a Professional Course in the History of Education." TEACHERS COLLEGE RECORD 23 (1922): 12-18.

529 Talbott, John E. "The History of Education." DAEDALUS 41 (1971): 133-50.

The entire issue deals with history and methodology and related issues.

530 Thomas, Alan M. "American Education and the Immigrant." TEACHERS
COLLEGE RECORD 55 (1953-54): 253-67.

531 Tyack, David B. "The History of Education and the Preparation of Teachers: A Reappraisal." JOURNAL OF TEACHER EDUCATION 19 (1965):
427-31.

532 _____. "Bureaucracy and the Common School: The Example of Portland, Oregon, 1851-1913." AMERICAN QUARTERLY 19 (1967): 475-98.

533 _____. "The Perils of Pluralism." AMERICAN HISTORICAL REVIEW
74 (1968): 74-98.

534 _____. "New Perspectives on the History of American Education." In
THE STATE OF AMERICAN HISTORY, edited by Herbert J. Bass, pp. 22-
42. Chicago: Quadrangle, 1970.

535 _____. THE ONE BEST SYSTEM: A HISTORY OF AMERICAN URBAN
EDUCATION. Cambridge, Mass.: Harvard University Press, 1974. 353 p.

536 _____. "Ways of Selling: An Essay on the History of Compulsory
Schooling." HARVARD EDUCATIONAL REVIEW 46 (1976): 355-89.

537 Urban, Wayne J. "A Philosophical Critique of Michael Katz's Educational History." In PROCEEDINGS OF THE PHILOSOPHY OF EDUCATION
SOCIETY, edited by Brian Crittenden, pp. 94-103. 1973.

538 _____. "Some Historiographical Problems in Revisionist Educational History." AMERICAN EDUCATIONAL RESEARCH JOURNAL 12 (1975): 45-
63.

539 "[Urban Education]: Needs and Opportunities for Historical Research."
HISTORY OF EDUCATION QUARTERLY 9 (1969): 281-325.

540 Veysey, Laurence. "Toward a New Direction in Educational History:
Prospect and Retrospect." HISTORY OF EDUCATION QUARTERLY 9
(1969): 343-58.

541 Warren, Donald R. TO ENFORCE EDUCATION: A HISTORY OF THE
FOUNDING YEARS OF THE UNITED STATES OFFICE OF EDUCATION.
Detroit: Wayne State University Press, 1974. 239 p.

542 Weeks, Edward. THE LOWELLS AND THEIR INSTITUTE. Boston: Little, Brown, 1966. 202 p.

543 Weinberg, Meyer. A CHANCE TO LEARN: THE HISTORY OF RACE AND EDUCATION IN THE UNITED STATES. New York: Cambridge University Press, 1977. 471 p.

544 Welter, Rush. "Reason, Rhetoric, and Reality in American Educational History." REVIEW OF EDUCATION 2 (1976): 91-99.

545 Wendt, Erhard F. "Brief History of Industrial Arts and Vocational Education." INDUSTRIAL ARTS AND VOCATIONAL EDUCATION 35 (1946): 151-54.

546 Wesley, Edgar B. "Lo, the Poor History of Education." HISTORY OF EDUCATION QUARTERLY 9 (1969): 329-42.

547 Whitehead, John S. THE SEPARATION OF COLLEGE AND STATE: COLUMBIA, DARTMOUTH, HARVARD, AND YALE, 1776-1876. New Haven, Conn.: Yale University Press, 1973. 262 p.

548 Williamson, E.G. "Historical Perspectives of the Vocational Guidance Movement." PERSONAL AND GUIDANCE JOURNAL 42 (1964): 854-59.

549 Winter, Nathan H. JEWISH EDUCATION IN A PLURALIST SOCIETY: SAMSON BENDERLY AND JEWISH EDUCATION IN THE UNITED STATES. New York: New York University Press, 1966. 262 p.

550 Wirth, Arthur G. "Philosophical Issues in the Vocational-Liberal Studies Controversy, 1900-1917: John Dewey Versus the Social Efficiency Philosophers." STUDIES IN PHILOSOPHY AND EDUCATION 7 (1974): 169-82.

551 Wise, Arthur E. RICH SCHOOLS, POOR SCHOOLS: THE PROMISE OF EQUAL EDUCATIONAL OPPORTUNITY. Chicago: University of Chicago Press, 1969. 228 p.

552 Wollenberg, Charles M. ALL DELIBERATE SPEED: SEGREGATION AND EXCLUSION IN CALIFORNIA SCHOOLS, 1855-1975. Berkeley: University of California Press, 1977. 201 p.

553 Wood, James E., Jr. "Religion and Public Education in Historical Perspective." JOURNAL OF CHURCH AND STATE 14 (1972): 397-414.

Chapter 5

THE AMERICAN COLLEGE AND UNIVERSITY

1. GENERAL HISTORIES AND STUDIES

554 Adams, Herbert B. "American Pioneers of University Extension." EDU-
CATIONAL REVIEW 2 (1891): 220-30.

555 _____. "Educational Extension in the United States." In UNITED
STATES BUREAU OF EDUCATION, REPORT OF THE COMMISSIONER,
1899-1900, vol. 1, pp. 175-379. Washington, D.C.: Government Printing Office, 1901.

556 Ahern, Patrick H. "The First Faculty of the Catholic University of
America." CATHOLIC HISTORICAL REVIEW 38 (1947): 129-57.

557 Altbach, Philip G. STUDENT POLITICS IN AMERICA: A HISTORICAL
ANALYSIS. New York: McGraw-Hill, 1974. 185 p.

558 Altman, Robert A. THE UPPER DIVISION COLLEGE. San Francisco:
Jossey-Bass, 1970. 201 p.

559 Angell, James B. "University Education in the United States." PRO-
CEEDINGS, AMERICAN PHILOSOPHICAL SOCIETY 66 (1927): 645-54.

560 Aptheker, Herbert. "The Negro College Student in the 1920s -- Years
of Preparation and Protest: An Introduction." SCIENCE AND SOCIETY
33 (1969): 150-67.

561 Atwood, Rufus B. "The Origin and Development of the Negro Public
College, with Especial Reference to the Land-Grant College." JOURNAL
OF NEGRO EDUCATION 31 (1962): 240-50.

562 Avorn, Jerry L., et al. UP AGAINST THE IVY WALL: A HISTORY OF
THE COLUMBIA CRISIS. New York: Atheneum, 1969. 307 p.

Deals with the revolt at Columbia University in the 1960s.

563 Badger, Henry G. "Negro Colleges and Universities: 1900-1950."
JOURNAL OF NEGRO EDUCATION 21 (1952): 89-93.

564 Barnes, Sherman B. "Learning and Piety in Ohio Colleges, 1865-1900."
OHIO HISTORICAL QUARTERLY 79 (1960): 327-52.

565 _____. "The Entry of Science and History in the College Curriculum,
1865-1914." HISTORY OF EDUCATION QUARTERLY 4 (1964): 44-58.

566 Barzun, Jacques. THE AMERICAN UNIVERSITY: HOW IT RUNS, WHERE
IT IS GOING. New York: Harper and Row, 1968. 319 p.

567 Bay, Christian. "Political and Apolitical Students: Facts in Search of
Theory." JOURNAL OF SOCIAL ISSUES 23 (1967): 76-91.

568 Beard, Charles A. "The Quest for Academic Power." JOURNAL OF
HIGHER EDUCATION 3 (1932): 464-69.

569 Becker, Carl. "The Cornell Tradition: Freedom and Responsibility."
BULLETIN, AMERICAN ASSOCIATION OF UNIVERSITY PROFESSORS 26
(1940): 509-22.

570 Beecher, Henry K., and Altschule, Mark. MEDICINE AT HARVARD:
THE FIRST 300 YEARS. Hanover, N.H.: University Press of New England, 1977. 587 p.

571 Ben-David, Joseph. AMERICAN HIGHER EDUCATION: DIRECTIONS
OLD AND NEW. New York: McGraw-Hill, 1972. 184 p.

572 Ben-David, Joseph, and Zlocower, Abraham. "Universities and Academic
Systems in Modern Societies." EUROPEAN JOURNAL OF SOCIOLOGY
3 (1962): 45-84.

573 Berelson, Bernard. GRADUATE EDUCATION IN THE UNITED STATES.
New York: McGraw-Hill, 1960. 346 p.

    Considered a major study of the history and nature of graduate
    study and of graduate institutions.

574 Berube, Maurice R. THE URBAN UNIVERSITY IN AMERICA. Westport,
Conn.: Greenwood Press, 1978. 149 p.

    A history of the city university in America with recommenda-
    tions for creation of federally supported "urban grant" institu-
    tions of higher education.

575 Bestor, Arthur. "The American University: A Historical Interpretation of Current Issues." COLLEGE AND UNIVERSITY 32 (1957): 175-88.

576 Bittner, W.S. THE UNIVERSITY EXTENSION MOVEMENT. U.S. Bureau of Education Bulletin No. 84, 1919. Washington, D.C.: Government Printing Office, 1920. 124 p.

577 Blackburn, Robert, et al. CHANGING PRACTICES IN UNDERGRADUATE EDUCATION. Berkeley, Calif.: Carnegie Council on Policy Studies in Higher Education, 1976. 186 p.

578 Blackmar, Frank W. THE HISTORY OF FEDERAL AND STATE AID TO HIGHER EDUCATION IN THE UNITED STATES. U.S. Bureau of Education Information Circular No. 1, 1890. Washington, D.C.: Government Printing Office, 1890. 343 p.

579 _____. HIGHER EDUCATION IN KANSAS. U.S. Bureau of Education Information Circular No. 2, 1900. Washington, D.C.: Government Printing Office, 1900. 166 p.

580 Bledstein, Barton. THE CULTURE OF PROFESSIONALISM: THE MIDDLE CLASS AND THE DEVELOPMENT OF HIGHER EDUCATION IN AMERICA. New York: Norton, 1976. 354 p.

     The middle class support of the university as an "institutional matrix" promoting "social faith in merit, competence, discipline, and control" as its essential theme.

581 Blocker, Clyde E.; Plummer, Robert H.; and Richardson, Richard C., Jr. THE TWO-YEAR COLLEGE: A SOCIAL SYNTHESIS. Englewood Cliffs, N.J.: Prentice-Hall, 1965. 298 p.

582 Bloomfield, Maxwell. AMERICAN LAWYERS IN A CHANGING SOCIETY, 1776-1876. Cambridge, Mass.: Harvard University Press, 1976. 397 p.

583 Bond, Horace M. "Evolution and Present Status of Negro Higher Education in the United States." JOURNAL OF NEGRO EDUCATION 17 (1948): 224-35.

584 _____. "The Origin and Development of the Negro Church-Related College." JOURNAL OF NEGRO EDUCATION 29 (1960): 217-26.

585 Bowles, Frank, and DaCosta, Frank A. BETWEEN TWO WORLDS: A PROFILE OF NEGRO HIGHER EDUCATION. New York: McGraw-Hill, 1971. 240 p.

586   Brewer, Joseph, and Heiges, Donald. "The Search for Unity in Higher
       Education." HARVARD EDUCATIONAL REVIEW 16 (1946): 21-43.

587   Broome, Edwin C. "A Historical and Critical Discussion of College Ad-
       mission Requirements." COLUMBIA UNIVERSITY CONTRIBUTIONS TO
       PHILOSOPHY 11 (1903).

           Reprinted by the College Entrance Examination Board, Prince-
           ton, 1963, 1968.

588   Brubacher, John S. "The Autonomy of the University." JOURNAL OF
       HIGHER EDUCATION 38 (1967): 237-49.

589   Brubacher, John S., and Willis, Rudy. HIGHER EDUCATION IN TRANSI-
       TION: A HISTORY OF AMERICAN COLLEGES AND UNIVERSITIES,
       1636-1976. New York: Harper and Row, 1976. 536 p.

           A chronological and topical history from colonial times to the
           present. Also includes: "A Bibliography of American College
           and University Histories," pp. 515-27.

590   Brunner, Henry S. LAND-GRANT COLLEGES AND UNIVERSITIES, 1862-
       1962. U.S. Office of Education Bulletin No. 13, 1962. Washington,
       D.C.: Government Printing Office, 1962. 180 p.

591   Bush, George G. HISTORY OF HIGHER EDUCATION IN MASSACHU-
       SETTS. U.S. Bureau of Education Information Circular No. 6. Washing-
       ton, D.C.: Government Printing Office, 1891. 445 p.

592   Byse, Clark. "The University of Due Process: A Somewhat Different
       View." BULLETIN, AMERICAN ASSOCIATION OF UNIVERSITY PRO-
       FESSORS 54 (1968): 143-48.

593   Caldwell, E.W. "An Introduction to the History of Higher Education in
       Nebraska." NEBRASKA HISTORY MAGAZINE 3 (1892): 210-29.

594   Caliver, Ambrose. "The Role of the Federal Government in the Higher
       Education of Negroes, 1865-1949." PHYLON 10 (1949): 370-80.

595   Carmichael, Oliver C. "The Roots of Higher Education in Minnesota."
       MINNESOTA HISTORY 34 (1954): 90-95.

596   Carnegie Commission on Higher Education. THE OPEN DOOR COL-
       LEGES: POLICIES FOR COMMUNITY COLLEGES. New York: McGraw-
       Hill, 1970. 280 p.

597 _____. LESS TIME, MORE OPTIONS: EDUCATION BEYOND THE HIGH SCHOOL. New York: McGraw-Hill, 1971. 240 p.

598 _____. REFORM ON CAMPUS: CHANGING STUDENTS, CHANGING ACADEMIC PROGRAMS. New York: McGraw-Hill, 1972. 190 p.

599 _____. COLLEGE GRADUATES AND JOBS: ADJUSTING TO A NEW LABOR MARKET SITUATION. New York: McGraw-Hill, 1973. 220 p.

600 _____. THE PURPOSE AND PERFORMANCE OF HIGHER EDUCATION IN THE UNITED STATES. New York: McGraw-Hill, 1973. 250 p.

601 Carrell, William D. "American College Professors; 1750-1800." HISTORY OF EDUCATION QUARTERLY 8 (1968): 289-305.

602 _____. "Biographical List of American College Professors to 1800." HISTORY OF EDUCATION QUARTERLY 8 (1968): 358-74.

603 Chambers, Merritt M. "A Decade of Progress in Higher Education Law." EDUCATIONAL FORUM 29 (1964): 79-84.

604 Churchill, Alfred V. "Oberlin Students, Students, Sinners, and Adolescents in the 1870s and 1880s." NORTHWEST OHIO QUARTERLY 25 (1952-53): 41-71.

605 Clapp, Gordon R. "The College Charter." JOURNAL OF HIGHER EDUCATION 5 (1943): 79-87.

606 Clark, Felton G. "The Development and Present Status of Publicly-Supported Higher Education for Negroes." JOURNAL OF NEGRO EDUCATION 27 (1958): 221-32.

607 Clement, Rufus E. "The Historical Development of Higher Education for American Negroes." JOURNAL OF NEGRO EDUCATION 35 (1966): 299-305.

608 Cohen, Michael, and March, James G. LEADERSHIP AND AMBIGUITY: THE AMERICAN COLLEGE PRESIDENT. New York: McGraw-Hill, 1974. 270 p.

609 Compayre, Gabriel. "Higher and Secondary Education in the United States." In UNITED STATES BUREAU OF EDUCATION, REPORT OF THE COMMISSIONER, 1895-1896, vol. 2, pp. 1153-74. Washington, D.C.: Government Printing Office, 1896.

610 Conant, James B. THE CITADEL OF LEARNING. New Haven, Conn.: Yale University Press, 1956. 79 p.

611 Cope, Jackson I. "William James's Correspondence with Daniel Coit Gilman, 1877-1881." JOURNAL OF THE HISTORY OF IDEAS 12 (1951): 609-27.

612 Corner, George W. "Apprenticed to Aesculapius: The American Medical Student, 1765-1965." PROCEEDINGS, AMERICAN PHILOSOPHICAL SOCIETY 109 (1965): 249-58.

613 Coser, Lewis. "Some Reflections on Academic Freedom Today." DISSENT 11 (1964): 76-79.

614 Cowley, W.H. "College and University Teaching, 1858-1958." EDUCATIONAL RECORD 39 (1958): 311-26.

615 _____. "Three Curricular Conflicts." LIBERAL EDUCATION 46 (1960): 467-83.

616 _____. "Some Myths About Professors, Presidents, and Trustees." TEACHERS COLLEGE RECORD 64 (1962): 159-71.

617 Curti, Merle. "The American Scholar in Three Wars." JOURNAL OF THE HISTORY OF IDEAS 3 (1942): 241-64.

618 Curti, Merle, and Nash, Roderick. PHILANTHROPY IN THE SHAPING OF AMERICAN HIGHER EDUCATION. New Brunswick, N.J.: Rutgers University Press, 1965. 340 p.

619 Daniel, W. Harrison. "Southern Baptists and Education, 1865-1900: A Case Study." MARYLAND HISTORY MAGAZINE 64 (1969): 218-47.

620 Darlington, C.D. "Freedom and Responsibility in Academic Life." BULLETIN OF THE ATOMIC SCIENTISTS 13 (1957): 131-34.

621 Dennis, Lawrence E., and Kaufman, Joseph F., eds. THE COLLEGE AND THE STUDENT. Washington, D.C.: American Council on Education, 1966. 390 p.

622 DeVane, William C. THE AMERICAN UNIVERSITY IN THE TWENTIETH CENTURY. Baton Rouge: Louisiana State University Press, 1957. 72 p.

623 _____. HIGHER EDUCATION IN TWENTIETH-CENTURY AMERICA. Cambridge, Mass.: Harvard University Press, 1965. 150 p.

624 Donnan, Elizabeth. "A Nineteenth Century Cause Celebre." BULLETIN, AMERICAN ASSOCIATION OF UNIVERSITY PROFESSORS 38 (1952): 368-89.

625 Dunbar, Willis F. "Public Versus Private Control of Higher Education in Michigan." MISSISSIPPI VALLEY HISTORICAL REVIEW 22 (1935-36): 385-407.

626 Eckelberry, R.H. THE HISTORY OF THE MUNICIPAL UNIVERSITY IN THE UNITED STATES. U.S. Office of Education Bulletin No. 2, 1932. Washington, D.C.: Government Printing Office, 1932. 213 p.

627 Eddy, Edward D., Jr. COLLEGES FOR OUR LAND AND TIME: THE LAND GRANT IDEA IN AMERICAN EDUCATION. New York: Harper and Bros., 1956. 328 p.

628 Edwards, Marcia. "College Enrollment During Times of Depression." JOURNAL OF HIGHER EDUCATION 3 (1932): 11-16.

629 _____. STUDIES IN AMERICAN GRADUATE EDUCATION. New York: Carnegie Foundation for the Advancement of Teaching, 1944. 71 p.

630 Eells, Walter C. "The Center of Population of Negro Higher Education." JOURNAL OF NEGRO EDUCATION 5 (1936): 595-98.

631 _____. "Higher Education of Negroes in the United States." JOURNAL OF NEGRO EDUCATION 24 (1955): 426-34.

632 _____. "Honorary Ph.Ds in the 20th Century." SCHOOL AND SOCIETY 85 (1957): 74-75.

633 _____. "The Early History of Sabbatical Leave." BULLETIN, AMERICAN ASSOCIATION OF UNIVERSITY PROFESSORS 48 (1962): 253-56.

634 Eells, Walter C., and Hollis, Ernest V. "The Origin and Development of the Public College in the United States." JOURNAL OF NEGRO EDUCATION 31 (1962): 221-29.

635 Engel, Mary. "The Case of Alexander Winchell: A Chapter in the History of Academic Freedom." HISTORY OF EDUCATION JOURNAL 10 (1959): 73-80.

   Also see: HISTORY OF EDUCATION JOURNAL 7 (1956): 37-43, for a similar case at Vanderbilt University in 1878, by way of comparison.

636 Fellman, David. "Academic Freedom in American Public Law." TEACH-
ERS COLLEGE RECORD 62 (1961): 368-86.

637 Ferrari, Michael R. PROFILES OF AMERICAN COLLEGE PRESIDENTS.
East Lansing: Michigan State University Press, 1970. 175 p.

638 Flexner, Abraham. MEDICAL EDUCATION IN THE UNITED STATES AND
CANADA. New York: Carnegie Foundation, 1910. 346 p.

See also Flexner's article, "Medical Education in the United States,"
ATLANTIC 105 (1910): 797-804.

639 _____. "Medical Education, 1900-1924." EDUCATIONAL RECORD 5
(1924): 75-91.

640 _____. UNIVERSITIES: AMERICAN, ENGLISH, GERMAN. New York:
Oxford University Press, 1930. 381 p.

641 Ford, Charles E. "Botany Texts: A Survey of Their Development in
American Higher Education, 1643-1906." HISTORY OF EDUCATIONAL
QUARTERLY 4 (1964): 59-71.

642 Frankel, Charles, ed. ISSUES IN UNIVERSITY EDUCATION: ESSAYS
BY TEN AMERICAN SCHOLARS. New York: Harper and Bros., 1959.
175 p.

643 Franklin, John H. "Jim Crow Goes to College: The Genesis of Legal
Segregation in Southern Schools." SOUTH ATLANTIC QUARTERLY 58
(1959): 225-35.

644 Frazier, E. Franklin. "Graduate Education in Negro Colleges and Universities." JOURNAL OF NEGRO EDUCATION 2 (1933): 329-41.

645 Gerhard, Dietrich. "The Emergence of the Credit System in American
Education Considered as a Problem of Social and Intellectual History."
BULLETIN, AMERICAN ASSOCIATION OF UNIVERSITY PROFESSORS,
1955, pp. 647-68.

646 Gideonese, Harry D. "Changing Issues in Academic Freedom in the United States Today." PROCEEDINGS, AMERICAN PHILOSOPHICAL SOCIETY
94 (1950): 91-104.

647 Glass, Bentley. "The Academic Scientist, 1940-1960." BULLETIN,
AMERICAN ASSOCIATION OF UNIVERSITY PROFESSORS 46 (1960):
149-54.

648 Glazer, Penina. "The New Left, a Style of Protest." JOURNAL OF HIGHER EDUCATION 38 (1967): 119-30.

649 Gleazer, Edmund J. PROJECT FOCUS: A FORECAST STUDY OF COMMUNITY COLLEGES. New York: McGraw-Hill, 1973. 239 p.

650 Graubard, Stephen R., ed. AMERICAN HIGHER EDUCATION: TOWARD AN UNCERTAIN FUTURE. 2 vols. Boston: American Academy of Arts and Sciences, 1974-75.

    Issued as entire issues of DAEDALUS 103 (1974); 104 (1975). Includes essays on all facets of contemporary American higher education.

651 Greeley, Andrew M. FROM BACKWATER TO MAINSTREAM: A PROFILE OF CATHOLIC HIGHER EDUCATION. New York: McGraw-Hill, 1969. 210 p.

652 Gruber, Carol S. MARS AND MINERVA: WORLD WAR I AND THE USES OF THE HIGHER LEARNING IN AMERICA. Baton Rouge: Louisiana State University Press, 1976. 310 p.

653 Gustad, John W. "They March to a Different Drummer: Another Look at College Teachers." EDUCATIONAL RECORD 40 (1959): 204-12.

654 Hall, E.W. HISTORY OF HIGHER EDUCATION IN MAINE. U.S. Bureau of Education Information Circular No. 3, 1903. Washington, D.C.: Government Printing Office, 1903. 241 p.

655 Hall, G. Stanley. "On the History of American College Textbooks and Teaching in Logic, Ethics, Psychology, and Allied Subjects." PROCEEDINGS, AMERICAN ANTIQUARIAN SOCIETY 9 (1893-94): 137-74.

656 Handlin, Oscar, and Handlin, Mary. THE AMERICAN COLLEGE AND AMERICAN CULTURE: SOCIALIZATION AS A FUNCTION OF HIGHER EDUCATION. New York: McGraw-Hill, 1970. 260 p.

657 Harris, Seymour, ed. HIGHER EDUCATION IN THE UNITED STATES: THE ECONOMIC PROBLEMS. Cambridge, Mass.: Harvard University Press, 1960. 252 p.

658 Hassenger, Robert, ed. THE SHAPE OF CATHOLIC HIGHER EDUCATION. Chicago: University of Chicago Press, 1967. 378 p.

659 Hawkins, Hugh. "Three University Presidents Testify." AMERICAN QUARTERLY 11 (1959): 99-119.

660 _____. "Charles W. Eliot, Daniel C. Gilman, and the Nurture of American Scholarship." NEW ENGLAND QUARTERLY 39 (1966): 291-308.

661 Heath, G. Louis. VANDALS IN THE BOMB FACTORY: THE HISTORY AND LITERATURE OF THE STUDENTS FOR A DEMOCRATIC SOCIETY. Metuchen, N.J.: Scarecrow Press, 1976. 485 p.

662 Hefferlin, J.B. Lon. DYNAMICS OF ACADEMIC REFORM. San Francisco: Jossey-Bass, 1969. 240 p.

663 Henry, David D. CHALLENGES PAST, CHALLENGES PRESENT: AN ANALYSIS OF AMERICAN HIGHER EDUCATION SINCE 1930. San Francisco: Jossey-Bass, 1975. 320 p.

664 Hepburn, William M. "Academic Freedom and Tenure." BULLETIN, AMERICAN ASSOCIATION OF UNIVERSITY PROFESSORS 23 (1937): 642-53.

665 Herbst, Jurgen. "From Moral Philosophy to Sociology: Albion W. Small." HARVARD EDUCATIONAL REVIEW 29 (1959): 227-44.

666 _____. "Liberal Education and the Graduate Schools: An Historical View of College Reform." HISTORY OF EDUCATIONAL QUARTERLY 2 (1962): 244-58.

667 _____. "From Religion to Politics: Debates and Confrontations over American College Governance in the Mid-Eighteenth Century." HARVARD EDUCATIONAL REVIEW 46 (1976): 397-424.

668 Hills, E.C. "The Degree of Doctor of Philosophy." BULLETIN, AMERICAN ASSOCIATION OF UNIVERSITY PROFESSORS 13 (1927): 163-85.

669 "The History of the Preceptorial or Tutorial System." BULLETIN, AMERICAN ASSOCIATION OF UNIVERSITY PROFESSORS 19 (1920): 534-62.

670 Hofstadter, Richard, and Metzger, Walter P. THE DEVELOPMENT OF ACADEMIC FREEDOM IN THE UNITED STATES. New York: Columbia University Press, 1955. 527 p.

671 Holley, Howard L. "Medical Education in Alabama." ALABAMA REVIEW 7 (1954): 245-63.

672 Hollis, Ernest V. "Forces That Have Shaped Doctoral Work in the United States." BULLETIN, AMERICAN ASSOCIATION OF UNIVERSITY PROFESSORS 31 (1945): 357-82.

673   Hughes, Robert M., and Turner, Joseph A. "Notes on Higher Education of Women in Virginia." WILLIAM AND MARY COLLEGE QUARTERLY HISTORICAL MAGAZINE 9 (1929): 325-34.

674   Jencks, Christopher, and Riesman, David. "The American Negro College." HARVARD EDUCATIONAL REVIEW 37 (1967): 3-60.

      Also see: Ibid, "Four Responses and a Reply," pp. 451-68.

675   _____. "The War Between the Generations." TEACHERS COLLEGE RECORD 69 (1967): 1-22.

676   John, Walton C. GRADUATE STUDY IN UNIVERSITIES AND COLLEGES IN THE UNITED STATES. U.S. Office of Education Bulletin No. 20, 1934. Washington, D.C.: Government Printing Office, 1935. 234 p.

677   Johnson, B. Lamar. ISLANDS ON INNOVATION EXPANDING: CHANGES IN THE COMMUNITY COLLEGE. Beverly Hills, Calif.: Glencoe Press, 1969. 240 p.

678   Johnson, Michael T. "Constitutional Rights of College Students." TEXAS LAW REVIEW 42 (1964): 344-63.

679   Joncich, Geraldine. "Scientists and the Schools of the Nineteenth Century: The Case of American Physicists." AMERICAN QUARTERLY 18 (1966): 667-85.

680   Jones, Howard M. "The American Concept of Academic Freedom." BULLETIN, AMERICAN ASSOCIATION OF UNIVERSITY PROFESSORS 46 (1960): 66-72.

681   Jones, Howard M., et al. "On the Conflict Between the Liberal Arts and the Schools of Education." AMERICAN COUNCIL OF LEARNED SOCIETIES NEWSLETTER 5 (1954): 17-38.

682   Kaysen, Carl, ed. CONTENT AND CONTEXT: ESSAYS ON COLLEGE EDUCATION. New York: McGraw-Hill, 1973. 320 p.

683   Keeton, Morris T. MODELS AND MAVERICKS: A PROFILE OF PRIVATE LIBERAL ARTS COLLEGES. New York: McGraw-Hill, 1971. 180 p.

684   Kelly, Robert L. "The Colleges and the National Recovery Act." BULLETIN, AMERICAN ASSOCIATION OF UNIVERSITY PROFESSORS 19 (1933): 478-82.

685   Keniston, Kenneth. "The Sources of Student Dissent." JOURNAL OF SOCIAL ISSUES 23 (1967): 108-37.

686   Kennedy, Sister M. St. Mel. "The Changing Academic Characteristics of the Nineteenth Century American College Teacher." PAEDAGOGICA HISTORICA 5 (1965): 351-401.

687   Kerr, Clark. THE USES OF THE UNIVERSITY. Cambridge, Mass.: Harvard University Press, 1963. 140 p.

688   Kinney, Stanley N. "The Speaker Ban Extended at the University of Michigan, 1920-1935." HISTORY OF EDUCATION JOURNAL 8 (1956): 1-17.

689   Knight, Edgar W. "Some Early Discussions of the College Curriculum." SOUTH ATLANTIC QUARTERLY 34 (1935): 60-78.

690   Knight, George W., and Commons, John R. THE HISTORY OF HIGHER EDUCATION IN OHIO. U.S. Bureau of Education Information Circular No. 5, 1891. Washington, D.C.: Government Printing Office, 1891. 258 p.

691   Kohlbrenner, Bernard J. "Religion and Higher Education: An Historical Perspective." HISTORY OF EDUCATION QUARTERLY 1 (1961): 45-56.

692   Kouwenhoven, John A. "The New York Undergraduate, 1830-1850." COLUMBIA UNIVERSITY QUARTERLY 31 (1939): 75-103.

693   Kraus, Charles A. "The Evolution of the American Graduate School." BULLETIN, AMERICAN ASSOCIATION OF UNIVERSITY PROFESSORS 38 (1951): 497-506.

694   Lansing, Marion F. "Seventy-Five Years of Higher Education for Women." OUTLOOK 52 (1912): 360-65.

       Written in commemoration of the seventy-fifth anniversary of the founding of Mt. Holyoke College (for women).

695   Larson, Vernon C. "The Development of Short Courses at the Land Grant Institutions." AGRICULTURAL HISTORY 31 (1957): 31-35.

696   Lawler, Justus G. THE CATHOLIC DIMENSION IN HIGHER EDUCATION. Westminster, Md.: Newman Press, 1959. 302 p.

697   Leflar, Robert A. "Legal Education in Arkansas: A Brief History of the Law School." ARKANSAS HISTORICAL QUARTERLY 21 (1962): 99-131.

698   Levine, Arthur, and Weingart, John. REFORM OF UNDERGRADUATE EDUCATION. San Francisco: Jossey-Bass, 1973. 160 p.

699 Lewis, Alvin F. HISTORY OF HIGHER EDUCATION IN KENTUCKY.
U.S. Bureau of Education Information Circular No. 3, 1899. Washington, D.C.: Government Printing Office, 1899. 350 p.

700 Lewis, Guy. "The Beginning of Organized Collegiate Sport." AMERICAN QUARTERLY 22 (1970): 222-29.

701 Lipset, Seymour M. "Students and Politics in Comparative Perspective." DAEDALUS 97 (1968): 1-28.

702 Logan, Frenise A. "The Movement in North Carolina to Establish a State Supported College for Negroes." NORTH CAROLINA HISTORICAL REVIEW 35 (1958): 167-80.

703 Logan, Rayford W. "The Evolution of Private Colleges for Negroes." JOURNAL OF NEGRO EDUCATION 37 (1958): 213-20.

704 Ludlum, Robert P. "Academic Freedom and Tenure: A History." ANTIOCH REVIEW 10 (1950): 3-34.

705 McClelland, Clarence P. "The Education of Females in Early Illinois." JOURNAL OF THE ILLINOIS STATE HISTORICAL SOCIETY 36 (1943): 378-407.

706 McDowell, F.M. THE JUNIOR COLLEGE. U.S. Bureau of Education Bulletin No. 35, 1919. Washington, D.C.: Government Printing Office, 1919. 139 p.

707 McGiffert, Michael. THE HIGHER LEARNING IN COLORADO: AN HISTORICAL STUDY, 1860-1940. Denver: Swallow, 1964. 110 p.

708 McGrath, Earl J. "The Control of Higher Education in America." EDUCATIONAL RECORD 17 (1936): 259-79.

709 _____. THE GRADUATE SCHOOL AND THE DECLINE OF LIBERAL EDUCATION. New York: Institute of Higher Education, Teachers College, Columbia University, 1959. 65 p.

710 _____. THE PREDOMINATELY NEGRO COLLEGES AND UNIVERSITIES IN TRANSITION. New York: Teachers College, Columbia University, 1965. 204 p.

711 McLean, Malcolm S. "Impact of World War II Upon Institutions for the Higher Education of the Negro." JOURNAL OF NEGRO EDUCATION 11 (1942): 338-45.

712 Martin, William H. "Desegregation in Higher Education." TEACHERS COLLEGE RECORD 62 (1960): 36-47.

713 Mayhew, Lewis B. THE CARNEGIE COMMISSION ON HIGHER EDUCA-TION: A CRITICAL ANALYSIS OF THE REPORTS AND RECOMMENDA-TIONS. San Francisco: Jossey-Bass, 1973. 441 p.

714 _____. LEGACY OF THE SEVENTIES: EXPERIMENT, ECONOMY, EQUALITY, AND EXPEDIENCY IN AMERICAN HIGHER EDUCATION. San Francisco: Jossey-Bass, 1978. 366 p.

 A description of the "educational revolution" of the late 1960s and the 1970s in American higher education.

715 Medsker, Leland J. THE JUNIOR COLLEGE: PROGRESS AND PROS-PECT. New York: McGraw-Hill, 1960. 367 p.

716 Medsker, Leland L., and Tillery, Dale. BREAKING THE ACCESS BAR-RIERS: A PROFILE OF THE TWO-YEAR COLLEGES. New York: McGraw-Hill, 1971. 190 p.

717 Meriwether, Colyer. HISTORY OF HIGHER EDUCATION IN SOUTH CAROLINA: WITH A SKETCH OF THE FREE SCHOOL SYSTEM. U.S. Bureau of Education Information Circular No. 3, 1888. Washington, D.C.: Government Printing Office, 1889. 247 p.

718 Merriam, Lucius S. HIGHER EDUCATION IN TENNESSEE. U.S. Bureau of Education Information Circular No. 5, 1893. Washington, D.C.: Government Printing Office, 1893. 287 p.

719 Metzger, Walter P. "The German Contribution to the American Theory of Academic Freedom." BULLETIN, AMERICAN ASSOCIATION OF UNI-VERSITY PROFESSORS 41 (1955): 214-30.

720 Meyer, Richard J. "Academic Freedom in the United States." BRITISH JOURNAL OF EDUCATIONAL STUDIES 15 (1967): 28-39.

721 Miller, Douglas T. "The Transformation of Higher Education in America, 1865-1875, As Reflected in THE NATION." EDUCATIONAL THEORY 11 (1961): 187-92.

722 Morrison, Jack. THE RISE OF THE ARTS ON THE AMERICAN CAMPUS. New York: McGraw-Hill, 1973. 180 p.

723 Nevins, Allan. THE STATE UNIVERSITIES AND DEMOCRACY. Urbana: University of Illinois Press, 1962. 160 p.

724   Newcomer, Mabel. A CENTURY OF HIGHER EDUCATION FOR AMERI-
       CAN WOMEN. New York: Harper and Bros., 1959. 266 p.

725   Neyland, Leedell W. "State Supported Higher Education Among Negroes
       in the State of Florida." FLORIDA HISTORICAL QUARTERLY 43 (1964):
       105-22.

726   Nichols, Egbert Ray. "A Historical Sketch of Intercollegiate Debating."
       QUARTERLY JOURNAL OF SPEECH 203 (1937): 259-78.

727   Novak, Steven J. THE RIGHTS OF YOUTH: AMERICAN COLLEGES
       AND STUDENT REVOLT, 1798-1815. Cambridge, Mass.: Harvard Uni-
       versity Press, 1977. 280 p.

728   Paine, N. Emmons. "Instruction in Psychiatry in American Medical Col-
       leges." AMERICAN JOURNAL OF PSYCHIATRY 50 (1894): 372-80.

729   Payton, Phillip W. "Origins of the Terms 'Major and Minor' in Ameri-
       can Higher Education." HISTORY OF EDUCATION QUARTERLY 1 (1961):
       57-63.

730   Peterson, George E. THE NEW ENGLAND COLLEGE IN THE AGE OF
       THE UNIVERSITY. Amherst, Mass.: Amherst College Press, 1964. 260 p.

731   "Philanthropy in the History of American Higher Education." BULLETIN,
       AMERICAN ASSOCIATION OF UNIVERSITY PROFESSORS 9 (1923): 356-
       68.

732   Piedmont, Eugene B. "Changing Racial Attitudes at a Southern University:
       1947-1964." JOURNAL OF NEGRO EDUCATION 36 (1967): 32-41.

733   "The Place of University Extension in American Education." U.S. BU-
       REAU OF EDUCATION, REPORT OF THE COMMISSIONER, 1891-1892.
       Vol. 2, pp. 743-52. Washington, D.C.: U.S. Government Printing
       Office, 1894.

734   Poret, George. "The Establishment of the First Permanent Chair of Edu-
       cation in an American University." PEABODY JOURNAL OF EDUCATION
       13 (1936): 20-28.

735   Powell, J.P. "Some Nineteenth Century Views on the University Curri-
       culum." HISTORY OF EDUCATION QUARTERLY 5 (1965): 97-109.

736   Power, Edward J. HISTORY OF CATHOLIC HIGHER EDUCATION IN
       THE UNITED STATES. Milwaukee: Bruce Publishing, 1958. 383 p.

737 Price, Richard Rees. THE FINANCIAL SUPPORT OF STATE UNIVERSITIES. Cambridge, Mass.: Harvard University Press, 1924. 205 p.

738 Radin, Max. "The Loyalty Oath at the University of California." BULLETIN, AMERICAN ASSOCIATION OF UNIVERSITY PROFESSORS 36 (1950): 237-48.

739 Raphael, Theophile, and Gordon, Mary A. "Psychoses Among College Students." AMERICAN JOURNAL OF PSYCHIATRY 95 (1938): 659-75.

740 Reber, Louis E. UNIVERSITY EXTENSION IN THE UNITED STATES. U.S. Bureau of Education Bulletin No. 19, 1914. Washington, D.C.: Government Printing Office, 1914. 63 p.

741 Richardson, Eudora R. "The Case of the Women's Colleges in the South." SOUTH ATLANTIC QUARTERLY 29 (1930): 126-39.

742 Robinson, Mabel L. THE CURRICULUM OF THE WOMAN'S COLLEGE. U.S. Bureau of Education Bulletin No. 6, 1918. Washington, D.C.: Government Printing Office, 1918. 140 p.

743 Rockwell, Leo L. "Academic Freedom--German Origin and American Development." BULLETIN, AMERICAN ASSOCIATION OF UNIVERSITY PROFESSORS 36 (1950): 225-36.

744 Ross, Earle D. "Religious Influences in the Development of State Colleges and Universities." INDIANA MAGAZINE OF HISTORY 46 (1950): 343-62.

745 Ross, Hugh. "University Influence in the Genesis and Growth of Junior Colleges in California." HISTORY OF EDUCATION QUARTERLY 3 (1963): 145-52.

746 Rudolph, Frederick. THE AMERICAN COLLEGE AND UNIVERSITY: A HISTORY. New York: Knopf, 1962. 516 p.

747 Rudy, S. Willis. "The Revolution in American Higher Education: 1865-1900." HARVARD EDUCATIONAL REVIEW 21 (1951): 155-74.

748 _____. "Eliot and Gilman: The History of an Academic Friendship." TEACHERS COLLEGE RECORD 54 (1953): 307-18.

749 _____. THE EVOLVING LIBERAL ARTS CURRICULUM: A HISTORICAL REVIEW OF BASIC THEMES. New York: Teachers College, Columbia University, 1960. 180 p.

750 Ryan, W. Carson, Jr. THE LITERATURE OF AMERICAN SCHOOL AND COLLEGE ATHLETICS. Bulletin No. 24. New York: Carnegie Foundation for the Advancement of Teaching, 1929. 180 p.

751 _____. STUDIES IN EARLY GRADUATE EDUCATION. Bulletin No. 30. New York: Carnegie Foundation for the Advancement of Teaching, 1939. 167 p.

752 Sack, Saul. "The Higher Education of Women in Pennsylvania." PENNSYLVANIA MAGAZINE OF HISTORY AND BIOGRAPHY 83 (1959): 29-73.

753 _____. "Student Life in the Nineteenth Century." PENNSYLVANIA MAGAZINE OF HISTORY AND BIOGRAPHY 85 (1961): 255-88.

754 Sammartino, Peter. A HISTORY OF HIGHER EDUCATION IN NEW JERSEY. South Brunswick, N.J.: A.S. Barnes, 1978. 196 p.

755 Sampson, Edward E. "Student Activism and the Decade of Protest." JOURNAL OF SOCIAL ISSUES 23 (1967): 1-33.

756 Sanford, Nevitt, ed. THE AMERICAN COLLEGE: A PSYCHOLOGICAL AND SOCIAL INTERPRETATION OF THE HIGHER LEARNING. New York: Wiley, 1962. 1,084 p.

757 Savio, Mario. "The Uncertain Future of the Multiversity: A Partisan Scrutiny of Berkeley's Muscatine Report." HARPER'S, October 1966, pp. 88-94.

758 Schmidt, George P. THE OLD TIME COLLEGE PRESIDENT. New York: Columbia University Press, 1930. 251 p.

759 _____. THE LIBERAL ARTS COLLEGE: A CHAPTER IN AMERICAN CULTURAL HISTORY. New Brunswick, N.J.: Rutgers University Press, 1957. 310 p.

760 Sears, Jesse B. PHILANTHROPY IN THE HISTORY OF AMERICAN HIGHER EDUCATION. U.S. Bureau of Education Bulletin No. 26, 1922. Washington, D.C.: Government Printing Office, 1922. 112 p.

761 Seavey, Warren A. "Dismissal of Students: Due Process." HARVARD LAW REVIEW 70 (1956-57): 1406-410.

762 Sekora, John. "The Emergence of Negro Higher Education in America: A Review." RACE 10 (1968): 79-87.

763 Selden, William K. ACCREDITATION: A STRUGGLE OVER STANDARDS IN HIGHER EDUCATION. New York: Harper and Row, 1960. 138 p.

764 _____. "The Governance of Higher Education." EDUCATIONAL RECORD 45 (1964): 317-24.

765 _____. "Some Observations on the Governance of the American University." TEACHERS COLLEGE RECORD 68 (1967): 277-88.

766 "The Selection, Retention, and Promotion of Undergraduates in American Universities." BULLETIN, AMERICAN ASSOCIATION OF UNIVERSITY PROFESSORS 12 (1926): 373-481.

767 Sherzer, Jane. "The Higher Education of Women in the Ohio Valley Previous to 1840." OHIO HISTORICAL QUARTERLY 25 (1916): 1-26.

768 Shryock, Richard H. "The Academic Profession in the United States." BULLETIN, AMERICAN ASSOCIATION OF UNIVERSITY PROFESSORS 38 (1952): 32-70.

769 Sims, David H. "Religious Education in Negro Colleges and Universities." JOURNAL OF NEGRO HISTORY 5 (1920): 166-207.

770 Slosson, Edwin E. GREAT AMERICAN UNIVERSITIES. New York: Macmillan, 1910. 528 p.

771 Small, Albion. "Fifty Years of Sociology in the United States (1865-1915)." AMERICAN JOURNAL OF SOCIOLOGY 21 (1916): 721-864.

772 Smith, Anna T. "Coeducation in the Schools and Colleges of the United States." In U.S. BUREAU OF EDUCATION, REPORT OF THE COMMISSIONER, 1903. Vol. 1, pp. 1047-78. Washington, D.C.: Government Printing Office, 1905.

773 Snow, M.S. HIGHER EDUCATION IN MISSOURI. U.S. Bureau of Education Information Circular No. 2, 1898. Washington, D.C.: Government Printing Office, 1898. 164 p.

774 Snyder, Henry N. "The Denominational College in Southern Education." SOUTH ATLANTIC QUARTERLY 5 (1906): 8-20.

775 Starr, Joseph R. "The Hatch Act and Academic Freedom." BULLETIN, AMERICAN ASSOCIATION OF UNIVERSITY PROFESSORS 27 (1941): 61-69.

776 Stephan, A. Stephen. "Backgrounds and Beginnings of University Exten-
     sion in America." HARVARD EDUCATIONAL REVIEW 18 (1948): 99-108.

777 Stone, James Champion and DeNevi, Donald P., comps. PORTRAITS
     OF THE AMERICAN UNIVERSITY, 1890-1910. San Francisco: Jossey-
     Bass, 1971. 380 p.

778 Storr, Richard J. "Academic Culture and the History of American Higher
     Education." JOURNAL OF GENERAL EDUCATION 5 (1950): 6-16.

779 _____. THE BEGINNING OF THE FUTURE: AN HISTORICAL AP-
     PROACH TO GRADUATE EDUCATION IN THE ARTS AND SCIENCES.
     New York: McGraw-Hill, 1973. 99 p.

780 "A Study of the Medical Course: Its History and Future." BULLETIN,
     AMERICAN ASSOCIATION OF UNIVERSITY PROFESSORS 11 (1925):
     354-64.

781 Sykes, Frederick H. "The Social Basis of the New Education for Women."
     TEACHERS COLLEGE RECORD 18 (1917): 226-42.

782 Taylor, Harold. STUDENTS WITHOUT TEACHERS: THE CRISIS IN THE
     UNIVERSITY. New York: McGraw-Hill, 1969. 333 p.

783 Tewkesbury, Donald G. THE FOUNDING OF AMERICAN COLLEGES
     AND UNIVERSITIES BEFORE THE CIVIL WAR: WITH PARTICULAR REFER-
     ENCE TO THE RELIGIOUS INFLUENCES BEARING UPON THE COLLEGE
     MOVEMENT. New York: Archon Press, 1965. 254 p.

     First published by Teachers College, Columbia University, in
     1932.

784 Thelin, John R. THE CULTIVATION OF IVY: A SAGA OF THE COL-
     LEGE IN AMERICA. Cambridge, Mass.: Schenckman Publishing, 1976.
     90 p.

785 Thwing, Charles F. THE AMERICAN AND THE GERMAN UNIVERSITY:
     ONE HUNDRED YEARS OF HISTORY. New York: Macmillan, 1928.
     238 p.

786 Tolman, W.H. HISTORY OF HIGHER EDUCATION IN RHODE ISLAND.
     U.S. Bureau of Education Information Circular No. 1. 1894. Washing-
     ton, D.C.: Government Printing Office, 1894. 210 p.

787 "Toryism in American College Government." BULLETIN, AMERICAN
     ASSOCIATION OF UNIVERSITY PROFESSORS 9 (1923): 349-56.

788 Trow, Martin. PROBLEMS IN THE TRANSITION FROM ELITE TO MASS HIGHER EDUCATION. Berkeley, Calif.: Carnegie Commission on Higher Education, 1973. 240 p.

789 _____, ed. TEACHERS AND STUDENTS: ASPECTS OF AMERICAN HIGHER EDUCATION. New York: McGraw-Hill, 1975. 170 p.

790 Tucker, William J. "Administrative Problems of the Historic College." EDUCATIONAL REVIEW 43 (1912): 433-48.

791 "The University of California Loyalty Oath Situation." BULLETIN, AMERICAN ASSOCIATION OF UNIVERSITY PROFESSORS 37 (1951): 92-101.

792 Vesey, Laurence R. THE EMERGENCE OF THE AMERICAN UNIVERSITY. Chicago: University of Chicago Press, 1965. 505 p.

793 Visher, Stephan S. "J. McKeen Cattell and American Science." SCHOOL AND SOCIETY 66 (1947): 449-52.

794 Webb, Walter P. "The Historical Seminar: Its Outer Shell and Its Inner Spirit." MISSISSIPPI VALLEY HISTORICAL REVIEW 42 (1955): 3-23.

795 Wechsler, Harold S. THE QUALIFIED STUDENT: A HISTORY OF SELEC-TIVE COLLEGE ADMISSION IN AMERICA. New York: John Wiley and Sons, 1977. 341 p.

796 Whitehead, John. THE SEPARATION OF COLLEGE AND STATE: CO-LUMBIA, DARTMOUTH, HARVARD AND YALE, 1776-1876. New Haven, Conn.: Yale University Press, 1973. 262 p.

797 Whitehead, Matthew J. "Origin and Establishment of the Negro College Deanship." JOURNAL OF NEGRO EDUCATION 14 (1945): 166-73.

798 Wilson, Ruth D. "Negro Colleges of Liberal Arts." AMERICAN SCHOL-AR 19 (1950): 461-70.

799 Woodburn, James A. HIGHER EDUCATION IN INDIANA. U.S. Bureau of Education Information Circular No. 1. 1891. Washington, D.C.: Government Printing Office, 1891. 200 p.

800 Wriston, Henry M. ACADEMIC PROCESSION: REFLECTIONS OF A COLLEGE PRESIDENT. New York: Columbia University Press, 1959. 222 p.

2. INSTITUTIONAL HISTORIES AND STUDIES

801 Adams, Herbert B. THE COLLEGE OF WILLIAM AND MARY. U.S.
Bureau of Education Information Circular No. 1, 1887. Washington,
D.C.: Government Printing Office, 1887. 89 p.

802 Ambrose, Stephen E. DUTY, HONOR, COUNTRY: A HISTORY OF
WEST POINT. Baltimore, Md.: Johns Hopkins University Press, 1966.
375 p.

803 "Amherst Plan for Reading and Study." BULLETIN, AMERICAN ASSOCIA-
TION OF UNIVERSITY PROFESSORS 9 (1923): 238-48.

804 Barnard, John. FROM EVANGELICANISM TO PROGRESSIVISM AT
OBERLIN COLLEGE, 1866-1917. Columbus: Ohio State University,
1969. 171 p.

805 Battle, W.J. "A Concise History of the University of Texas, 1883-1950."
SOUTHWESTERN HISTORICAL QUARTERLY 54 (1951): 391-411.

806 Bell, Daniel. THE REFORMING OF GENERAL EDUCATION: THE
COLUMBIA COLLEGE EXPERIENCE IN ITS NATIONAL SETTING. New
York: Columbia University Press, 1966. 320 p.

807 Bergendoff, Conrad. AUGUSTANA. A PROFESSION OF FAITH: A
HISTORY OF AUGUSTANA COLLEGE, 1860-1935. Rock Island, Ill.:
Augustana Library, 1969. 220 p.

808 Bigglestone, W.E. "Oberlin College and the Negro Student, 1865-1940."
JOURNAL OF NEGRO EDUCATION 56 (1971): 198-219.

809 Bishop, Morris. A HISTORY OF CORNELL. Ithaca, N.Y.: Cornell
University Press, 1962. 651 p.

810 Blanshard, Frances. FRANK AYDELOTTE OF SWARTHMORE. Middletown, Conn.: Wesleyan University Press, 1970. 429 p.

811 Blegen, Theodore C. "The Minnesota Historical Society and the University of Minnesota." MINNESOTA HISTORY 23 (1942): 1-9.

812 Bond, Horace Mann. EDUCATION FOR FREEDOM: A HISTORY OF
LINCOLN UNIVERSITY, PENNSYLVANIA. Lincoln, Pa.: Lincoln University Press, 1976. 616 p.

813 Bordin, Ruth. THE UNIVERSITY OF MICHIGAN: A PICTORIAL HISTORY.
Ann Arbor: University of Michigan Press, 1967. 212 p.

814   Brawley, Benjamin. A HISTORY OF MOREHOUSE COLLEGE. College Park, Md.: McGrath, 1970. 218 p.

815   Bronson, Walter C. THE HISTORY OF BROWN UNIVERSITY, 1764-1914. Providence: Brown University Press, 1914. 547 p.

816   Brooks, Robert P. THE UNIVERSITY OF GEORGIA UNDER SIXTEEN ADMINISTRATIONS, 1785-1955. Athens: University of Georgia Press, 1956. 260 p.

817   Bruce, Philip A. HISTORY OF THE UNIVERSITY OF VIRGINIA, 1819-1919: THE LENGTHENED SHADOW OF ONE MAN [THOMAS JEFFERSON]. 5 vols. New York: Macmillan, 1920.

818   Buck, Paul, ed. SOCIAL SCIENCES AT HARVARD, 1860-1920: FROM INCULCATION TO THE OPEN MIND. Cambridge, Mass.: Harvard University Press, 1965. 320 p.

819   Carey, James C. KANSAS STATE UNIVERSITY: THE QUEST FOR IDENTITY. Lawrence, Kans.: Regents Press of Kansas, 1977. 333 p.

820   Carron, Malcolm. THE CONTRACT COLLEGES OF CORNELL UNIVERSITY: A COOPERATIVE EDUCATIONAL ENTERPRISE. Ithaca, N.Y.: Cornell University Press, 1958. 186 p.

821   Carstensen, Vernon. "The University as Head of the Iowa Public School System." IOWA JOURNAL OF HISTORY 53 (1955): 213-46.

822   Cary, Harold W. THE UNIVERSITY OF MASSACHUSETTS: A HISTORY OF ONE HUNDRED YEARS. Amherst: University of Massachusetts Press, 1962. 340 p.

823   Cheyney, Edward P. HISTORY OF THE UNIVERSITY OF PENNSYLVANIA, 1740-1940. Philadelphia: University of Pennsylvania Press, 1940. 461 p.

824   Clark, Burton R. THE DISTINCTIVE COLLEGE: ANTIOCH, REED AND SWARTHMORE. Chicago: Aldine, 1970. 160 p.

825   Columbia University. Faculty of Philosophy. A HISTORY OF THE FACULTY OF PHILOSOPHY, COLUMBIA UNIVERSITY. New York: Columbia University Press, 1957. 308 p.

826   Cordasco, Francesco. THE SHAPING OF AMERICAN GRADUATE EDUCATION: DANIEL COIT GILMAN AND THE PROTEAN PH.D. Totowa, N.J.: Rowman and Littlefield, 1973. 163 p.

Originally appeared in 1959. Places Gilman (1831–1908), first president of Johns Hopkins University, in the historical framework of the development of graduate education in the United States.

827 Correll, Charles M. "The First Century of Kansas State University." KANSAS HISTORICAL QUARTERLY 38 (1962): 409–44.

828 Covert, James T. A POINT OF PRIDE: THE UNIVERSITY OF PORT-LAND STORY. Portland, Oreg.: University of Portland Press, 1976. 328 p.

829 Cremin, Lawrence A., et al. HISTORY OF TEACHERS COLLEGE, COLUMBIA UNIVERSITY. New York: Columbia University Press, 1954. 289 p.

830 Cross, Arthur L. "The University of Michigan and the Training of the Students for the War." MICHIGAN HISTORY 4 (1928): 112–40.

831 Cumberland, William Henry. THE HISTORY OF BUENA VISTA COL-LEGE. Ames: Iowa State University Press, 1966. 233 p.

832 Cunningham, John T. UNIVERSITY IN THE FOREST: THE STORY OF DREW UNIVERSITY. Florham Park, N.J.: Afton Publishing Co., 1972. 288 p.

833 Curti, Merle E. THE UNIVERSITY OF WISCONSIN: A HISTORY, 1848–1925. 2 vols. Madison: University of Wisconsin Press, 1949.

834 Dexter, Franklin B. BIOGRAPHICAL SKETCHES OF THE GRADUATES OF YALE COLLEGE WITH ANNALS OF THE COLLEGE HISTORY. 6 vols. New York: Holt, 1885–1912.

835 _____. SKETCH OF THE HISTORY OF YALE UNIVERSITY. New York: Holt, 1887. 108 p.

836 _____, ed. DOCUMENTARY HISTORY OF YALE UNIVERSITY. New Haven, Conn.: Yale University Press, 1916. 382 p.

837 Dickey, John J. THE DARTMOUTH EXPERIENCE. Hanover, N.H.: University Press of New England, 1978. 308 p.

838 Duberman, Martin. BLACK MOUNTAIN: AN EXPLORATION IN COM-MUNITY. New York: Dutton, 1972. 236 p.

839 Dunbar, Willis F. THE MICHIGAN RECORD IN HIGHER EDUCATION.

Detroit: Wayne State University Press, 1963. 410 p.

840 Dyer, John P. TULANE: THE BIOGRAPHY OF A UNIVERSITY, 1834-1965. New York: Harper and Row, 1966. 370 p.

841 Ellsworth, Frank L. LAW ON THE MIDWAY: THE FOUNDING OF THE UNIVERSITY OF CHICAGO LAW SCHOOL. Chicago: University of Chicago Press, 1977. 191 p.

842 English, Thomas H. EMORY UNIVERSITY, 1915-1965: A SEMICENTENNIAL HISTORY. Atlanta: Emory University Press, 1966. 120 p.

843 Eschenbacher, Herman F. THE UNIVERSITY OF RHODE ISLAND: A HISTORY OF LAND-GRANT EDUCATION IN RHODE ISLAND. New York: Appleton-Century-Crofts, 1967. 548 p.

844 Evjen, Harry. "Illinois State University, 1852-1868." JOURNAL OF THE ILLINOIS STATE HISTORICAL SOCIETY 31 (1938): 54-71.

845 Fairchild, James H. OBERLIN, THE COLONY AND THE COLLEGE. Oberlin, Ohio: E.J. Goodrich, 1883. 377 p.

846 Faulkner, William H. "The Academic Schools of the University of Virginia." UNIVERSITY OF VIRGINIA ALUMNI BULLETIN. 3 ser. 14. (1921): 73-85.

847 First, Wesley, ed. UNIVERSITY ON THE HEIGHTS. New York: Doubleday, 1969. 199 p.

About Columbia University, New York City.

848 Fleming, Thomas J. WESTPOINT: THE MEN AND TIMES OF THE UNITED STATES MILITARY ACADEMY. New York: Morrow, 1969. 402 p.

849 Forman, Sidney. "Scandal Among Cadets: An Historical Verdict." TEACHERS COLLEGE RECORD 66 (1965): 485-91.

850 Furniss, Edgar S. THE GRADUATE SCHOOL OF YALE: A BRIEF HISTORY. New Haven, Conn.: Yale University Press, 1965. 140 p.

851 Garrison, George P. "The First Twenty-Five Years of the University of Texas." SOUTHWESTERN HISTORICAL QUARTERLY 60 (1956): 106-17.

852 Gates, Charles M. THE FIRST CENTURY AT THE UNIVERSITY OF WASHINGTON, 1861-1961. Seattle: University of Washington Press, 1961. 252 p.

853 Geiger, Louis G. UNIVERSITY OF THE NORTHERN PLAINS: A HIS-
TORY OF THE UNIVERSITY OF NORTH DAKOTA, 1883-1958. Grand
Forks: University of North Dakota Press, 1958. 491 p.

854 Gettelman, Marvin E. "College President on the Prairie: John H. Finley and Knox College in the 1890s." HISTORY OF EDUCATION QUAR-
TERLY 9 (1969): 129-53.

855 Goodspeed, Thomas W. A HISTORY OF THE UNIVERSITY OF CHICAGO.
Chicago: University of Chicago Press, 1916. 522 p.

856 Gray, James. OPEN WIDE THE DOOR: THE STORY OF THE UNIVER-
SITY OF MINNESOTA. New York: G.P. Putnam's Sons, 1958. 256 p.

857 Greenbaum, Leonard. A SPECIAL INTEREST: THE ATOMIC ENERGY
COMMISSION: ARGONNE NATIONAL LABORATORY AND THE MID-
WESTERN UNIVERSITIES. Ann Arbor: University of Michigan Press,
1971. 222 p.

858 Hanawalt, Leslie I. A PLACE OF LIGHT: THE HISTORY OF WAYNE
STATE UNIVERSITY. Detroit: Wayne State University Press, 1968. 512 p.

859 Hartshorne, E.Y. "Growth and Metabolism in the Harvard Faculty of
Arts and Sciences, 1920-1940." HARVARD EDUCATIONAL REVIEW 12
(1942): 143-64.

860 Havighurst, Walter. THE MIAMI YEARS: 1809-1959. New York: G.P.
Putnam's Sons, 1958. 254 p.

861 Hawkins, Hugh D. "Sevge William Brown and His Influence on the Johns
Hopkins University." MARYLAND HISTORICAL MAGAZINE 52 (1957):
173-86.

862 _____. PIONEER: A HISTORY OF THE JOHNS HOPKINS UNIVER-
SITY, 1874-1889. Ithaca, N.Y.: Cornell University Press, 1960. 368 p.

863 Headley, Leal A., and Jarchow, Merrill E. CARLETON: THE FIRST
CENTURY. Northfield, Minn.: Carleton College, 1966. 489 p.

864 Herbst, Jurgen. "Francis Greenwood Peabody: Harvard's Theologian of
the Social Gospel." HARVARD THEOLOGICAL REVIEW 54 (1961): 45-
69.

865 Hickerson, Frank R. "The Founding of the Toledo University of Arts and
Trades." NORTHWEST OHIO QUARTERLY 20 (1948): 68-86, 97-119.

866 _____. "The University of Toledo Comes of Age." NORTHWEST OHIO QUARTERLY 21 (1949): 38-68.

867 Hogan, Peter E. "Americanism and the Catholic University of America." CATHOLIC HISTORICAL REVIEW 33 (1947): 158-90.

868 Holden, Reuben A. YALE: A PICTORIAL HISTORY. New Haven, Conn.: Yale University Press, 1967. 296 p.

869 Holmes, Dwight O.W. "Fifty Years of Howard University." JOURNAL OF NEGRO HISTORY 3 (1918): 128-38, 368-80.

870 Holsten, George H., Jr. BICENTENNIAL YEAR: THE STORY OF A RUTGERS CELEBRATION. New Brunswick, N.J.: Rutgers University Press, 1968. 294 p.

871 Hoxie, R. Gordon, et al. A HISTORY OF THE FACULTY OF POLITICAL SCIENCE, COLUMBIA UNIVERSITY. New York: Columbia University Press, 1955. 326 p.

872 Humphrey, David C. FROM KING'S COLLEGE TO COLUMBIA, 1746-1800. New York: Columbia University Press, 1976. 378 p.

873 Hutchins, Robert M. "The University of Chicago and the Bachelor's Degree." EDUCATIONAL RECORD 23 (1942): 567-73.

874 _____. "The University of Chicago: Its Past Record and Its Future Mission." SCHOOL AND SOCIETY 62 (1945): 65-69.

875 Jackson, L.P. "The Origin of Hampton Institute." JOURNAL OF NEGRO HISTORY 10 (1925): 131-49.

876 Johnson, Henry C., Jr., and Johanningmeier, Erwin. TEACHERS FOR THE PRAIRIE: THE UNIVERSITY OF ILLINOIS AND THE SCHOOLS, 1868-1945. Urbana: University of Illinois Press, 1972. 508 p.

877 Jones, Thomas F. A PAIR OF LAWN SLEEVES: A BIOGRAPHY OF WILLIAM SMITH (1727-1803). New York: Chilton, 1972. 210 p.

878 Kahn, E.J., Jr. HARVARD: THROUGH CHANGE AND THROUGH STORM. New York: Norton, 1969. 388 p.

879 Kelley, Brooks M. YALE: A HISTORY. New Haven, Conn.: Yale University Press, 1974. 245 p.

880 Kendall, Elaine. "PECULIAR INSTITUTIONS": AN INFORMAL HISTORY OF THE SEVEN SISTERS COLLEGES. New York: G.P. Putnam's Sons, 1975. 360 p.

881 Kersey, Harry A., Jr. JOHN MILTON GREGORY AND THE UNIVERSITY OF ILLINOIS. Urbana: University of Illinois Press, 1968. 252 p.

882 Klapperman, Gilbert. THE STORY OF YESHIVA UNIVERSITY: THE FIRST JEWISH UNIVERSITY IN AMERICA. New York: Macmillan, 1969. 310 p.

883 Knepper, George W. NEW LAMPS FOR OLD. A CENTENNIAL PUBLICATION: ONE HUNDRED YEARS OF URBAN EDUCATION AT THE UNIVERSITY OF AKRON. Akron, Ohio: Akron University Press, 1970. 407 p.

884 Kropp, Simon F. THAT ALL MAY LEARN: NEW MEXICO STATE UNIVERSITY, 1888-1964. Las Cruces: New Mexico State University Press, 1972. 401 p.

885 Kuhn, Madison. MICHIGAN STATE: THE FIRST HUNDRED YEARS, 1855-1955. East Lansing: Michigan State University Press, 1955. 501 p.

886 Lazerson, Marvin. "F.A.P. Barnard and Columbia College: Prologue to a University." HISTORY OF EDUCATION QUARTERLY 6 (1966): 49-64.

887 Lipset, Seymour Martin, and Riesman, David. EDUCATION AND POLITICS AT HARVARD. New York: McGraw-Hill, 1975. 270 p.

888 Lockmiller, David A. "The Establishment of the North Carolina College of Agriculture and Mechanic Arts." NORTH CAROLINA HISTORICAL REVIEW 16 (1939): 273-95.

889 Logan, Rayford W. HOWARD UNIVERSITY, THE FIRST HUNDRED YEARS, 1867-1967. New York: New York University Press, 1969. 658 p.

890 McCormick, Richard P. RUTGERS: A BICENTENNIAL HISTORY. New Brunswick, N.J.: Rutgers University Press, 1966. 336 p.

891 Madsen, David. "Daniel Coit Gilman at the Carnegie Institute of Washington." HISTORY OF EDUCATION QUARTERLY 9 (1969): 154-86.

892 Manley, Robert N. CENTENNIAL HISTORY OF THE UNIVERSITY OF NEBRASKA. Vol. 1: FRONTIER UNIVERSITY (1869-1919). Lincoln: University of Nebraska Press, 1969. 331 p.

893 Meigs, Cornelia L. WHAT MAKES A COLLEGE? A HISTORY OF BRYN
MAWR. New York: Macmillan, 1956. 277 p.

894 Merryman, John Edward. THE INDIANA STORY, 1875-1975: PENNSYL-
VANIA'S FIRST UNIVERSITY. Indiana, Pa.: Indiana Publishing, 1976.
458 p.

895 Miller, Russell E. LIGHT ON THE HILL: A HISTORY OF TUFTS COL-
LEGE, 1852-1952. Boston: Beacon, 1966. 734 p.

896 Mitchell, J. Pearce. STANFORD UNIVERSITY, 1916-1941. Stanford,
Calif.: Stanford University Press, 1958. 167 p.

897 Morgan, Joy E. HORACE MANN AT ANTIOCH. Washington, D.C.:
National Education Association, 1938. 150 p.

898 Morison, Samuel Eliot. THE FOUNDING OF HARVARD COLLEGE.
Cambridge, Mass.: Harvard University Press, 1935. 472 p.

899 _____. HARVARD COLLEGE IN THE SEVENTEENTH CENTURY. 2
vols. Cambridge, Mass.: Harvard University Press, 1936.

900 _____. THREE CENTURIES OF HARVARD, 1636-1936. Cambridge,
Mass.: Harvard University Press, 1936. 512 p.

901 _____. "The Harvard Presidency." NEW ENGLAND QUARTERLY 31
(1958): 435-46.

902 Morison, Samuel Eliot, ed. THE DEVELOPMENT OF HARVARD UNIVER-
SITY SINCE THE INAUGURATION OF PRESIDENT ELIOT, 1869-1929.
Cambridge, Mass.: Harvard University Press, 1930. 660 p.

903 Murphy, William Michael, and Bruckner, D.J.R. THE IDEA OF THE
UNIVERSITY OF CHICAGO. Chicago: University of Chicago Press,
1976. 533 p.

904 Myers, Burton D. "A Study of Faculty Appointments at Indiana University, 1824-1937." INDIANA MAGAZINE OF HISTORY 60 (1944): 129-
55.

905 Nissenbaum, Stephen, ed. THE GREAT AWAKENING AT YALE COLLEGE.
Belmont, Calif.: Wadsworth Publishing, 1972. 180 p.

   Refers to the religious revivalism of 1740-45.

906 Parker, Franklin. "A Golden Age in American Education: Chicago in the 1890s." SCHOOL AND SOCIETY 89 (1961): 146-52.

907 Patrick, George T.W. "Founding the Psychological Laboratory of the State University of Iowa." IOWA JOURNAL OF HISTORY 30 (1932): 404-16.

908 Peckham, Howard H. THE MAKING OF THE UNIVERSITY OF MICHI-GAN, 1817-1967. Ann Arbor: University of Michigan Press, 1967. 276 p.

909 Pennypacker, Samuel W. "The University of Pennsylvania in Its Relations to the State of Pennsylvania." PENNSYLVANIA MAGAZINE OF HISTORY AND BIOGRAPHY 15 (1891): 88-100.

910 Phelps, Reginald H. "150 Years of Phi Beta Kappa at Harvard." AMERI-CAN SCHOLAR 1 (1932): 58-63.

911 Pickard, J.L. "Historical Sketch of the State University of Iowa." AN-NALS OF IOWA 4 (1899): 1-66.

912 Pierson, George W. YALE: COLLEGE AND UNIVERSITY, 1871-1937. YALE: THE UNIVERSITY COLLEGE, 1921-1937. New Haven, Conn.: Yale University Press, 1955. 740 p.

913 Pilkington, Walter. HAMILTON COLLEGE, 1812-1964. Clinton, N.Y.: Hamilton College Press, 1962. 406 p.

914 Plochmann, George K. THE ORDEAL OF SOUTHERN ILLINOIS UNIVER-SITY. Carbondale: Southern Illinois Press, 1959. 662 p.

915 Porter, Earl W. TRINITY AND DUKE, 1892-1924: FOUNDATIONS OF DUKE UNIVERSITY. Durham, N.C.: Duke University Press, 1964. 350 p.

916 Pusey, William W. III. THE INTERRUPTED DREAM: THE EDUCATIONAL PROGRAM AT WASHINGTON COLLEGE (WASHINGTON AND LEE UNI-VERSITY), 1850-1880. Lexington, Va.: Liberty Hall Press of Washington and Lee University, 1976. 62 p.

917 Rainey, Homer P. THE TOWER AND THE DOME: A FREE UNIVERSITY VERSUS POLITICAL CONTROL. Austin: Pruett, 1971. 151 p.

About the battles this president (Rainey) had with the University of Texas Regents which cost him his job in the 1940s.

918   Rand, Benjamin. "Philosophical Instruction in Harvard University from 1636 to 1906." HARVARD GRADUATES MAGAZINE 37 (1928-29): 29-47, 188-200, 296-311.

919   Richardson, Leon Burr. A STUDY OF THE LIBERAL COLLEGE. Hanover, N.H.: Dartmouth College Publications, 1924. 282 p.

920   _____. HISTORY OF DARTMOUTH COLLEGE. 2 vols. Hanover, N.H.: Dartmouth College Publications, 1932.

921   Riesman, David, and Jencks, Christopher. "A Case Study in Vignette: San Francisco State College." TEACHERS COLLEGE RECORD 63 (1962): 233-66.

922   Roach, Helen. "The Early Speaking Societies at Columbia College." BULLETIN, AMERICAN ASSOCIATION OF UNIVERSITY PROFESSORS 41 (1955): 639-44.

923   Roberts, O.M. "A History of the Establishment of the University of the State of Texas." SOUTHWESTERN HISTORICAL QUARTERLY 1 (1898): 233-65.

924   Ross, Earle D. THE LAND-GRANT IDEA AT IOWA STATE COLLEGE: A CENTENNIAL TRIAL BALANCE, 1858-1958. Ames: Iowa State College Press, 1958. 310 p.

925   Sack, Saul. A HISTORY OF HIGHER EDUCATION IN PENNSYLVANIA. Harrisburg: PENNSYLVANIA HISTORICAL SOCIETY, 1960. 1,197 p.

926   Schmidt, George P. DOUGLAS COLLEGE: A HISTORY. New Brunswick, N.J.: Rutgers University Press, 1968. 282 p.

927   Schwab, John C. "The Yale College Curriculum, 1701-1901." EDUCATIONAL REVIEW 22 (1901): 1-17.

928   Sellers, Charles Coleman. DICKINSON COLLEGE: A HISTORY. Middletown, Conn.: Wesleyan University Press, 1973.

929   Servin, Manuel P., and Wilson, Iris Higbie. SOUTHERN CALIFORNIA AND ITS UNIVERSITY: A HISTORY OF USC, 1880-1964. Los Angeles: Ward Ritchie, 1969. 319 p.

930   Sherwood, Sidney. THE UNIVERSITY OF THE STATE OF NEW YORK: HISTORY OF HIGHER EDUCATION IN THE STATE OF NEW YORK. U.S. Bureau of Education Information Circular No. 3. Washington, D.C.: Government Printing Office, 1900. 538 p.

931   Simons, William E. LIBERAL EDUCATION IN THE SERVICE ACADEMIES.
       New York: Teachers College Press, 1965. 250 p.

932   Solberg, Winton U. "The Conflict Between Religion and Secularism at
       the University of Illinois, 1867-1894." AMERICAN QUARTERLY 18
       (1966): 183-99.

933   _____. "The University of Illinois and the Reform of Discipline in the
       Modern University, 1868-1891." BULLETIN, AMERICAN ASSOCIATION
       OF UNIVERSITY PROFESSORS 52 (1966): 305-14.

934   _____. THE UNIVERSITY OF ILLINOIS, 1867-1894: AN INTELLECTU-
       AL AND CULTURAL HISTORY. Urbana: University of Illinois Press,
       1968. 494 p.

935   Stadtman, Verne A. THE UNIVERSITY OF CALIFORNIA, 1868-1968.
       New York: McGraw-Hill, 1970. 594 p.

936   Stephens, Frank F. A HISTORY OF THE UNIVERSITY OF MISSOURI.
       Columbia: University of Missouri Press, 1962. 460 p.

937   Stephenson, Wendell H. "Herbert B. Adams and Southern Historical
       Scholarship at the Johns Hopkins University." MARYLAND HISTORICAL
       MAGAZINE 42 (1947): 1-20.

938   Stone, Irving, ed. THERE WAS A LIGHT: AUTOBIOGRAPHY OF A
       UNIVERSITY, BERKELEY: 1868-1968. New York: Doubleday, 1970.
       454 p.

939   Storr, Richard J. HARPER'S UNIVERSITY: THE BEGINNINGS, A HIS-
       TORY OF THE UNIVERSITY OF CHICAGO. Chicago: University of
       Chicago Press, 1966. 411 p.

940   Thornton, Harrison J. "Coeducation at the State University of Iowa."
       IOWA JOURNAL OF HISTORY 44 (1947): 380-412.

           Deals with the period: 1840-60.

941   Thwing, Charles F. NOTES ON THE HISTORY OF THE COLLEGE FOR
       WOMEN AT WESTERN RESERVE UNIVERSITY FOR ITS TWENTY-FIVE
       YEARS, 1888-1913. Cleveland: Press Case Western Reserve University,
       1913. 60 p.

942   Wagner, Geoffrey. THE END OF EDUCATION: THE EXPERIENCE OF
       THE CITY UNIVERSITY OF NEW YORK WITH OPEN ENROLLMENT AND
       THE THREAT TO HIGHER EDUCATION IN AMERICA. Cranbury, N.J.:
       A.S. Barnes and Co., 1976. 252 p.

943   Wallace, Francis. NOTRE DAME: ITS PEOPLE AND ITS LEGENDS.
New York: David McKay, 1969. 273 p.

944   Warch, Richard. SCHOOL OF THE PROPHETS: YALE COLLEGE, 1701-
1740. New Haven, Conn.: Yale University Press, 1973. 240 p.

945   Wertenbaker, Thomas J. PRINCETON, 1746-1896. Princeton, N.J.:
Princeton University Press, 1946. 424 p.

946   Westerberg, Virginia. "A History of the University Elementary School,
State University of Iowa, 1915-1958." PAEDAGOGICA HISTORICA 4
(1964): 457-96.

947   Whetzel, H.H. "The History of Industrial Fellowships at the Department
of Plant Pathology at Cornell University." AGRICULTURAL HISTORY 19
(1945): 99-103.

948   Whittemore, Richard. "Nicholas Murray Butler and the Teaching Profession." HISTORY OF EDUCATION QUARTERLY 1 (1961): 22-37.

949   _____. "Sovereignty in the University: Teachers College and Columbia." TEACHERS COLLEGE RECORD 46 (1965): 509-8.

950   Widmayer, Charles E. HOPKINS AT DARTMOUTH. Hanover, N.H.:
University Press of New England, 1977. 312 p.

951   Williamson, Harold F., and Wild, Payson S. NORTHWESTERN UNIVER-
SITY: A HISTORY, 1850-1975. Evanston, Ill.: Northwestern University
Press, 1976. 407 p.

952   Wilson, Louis R. THE UNIVERSITY OF NORTH CAROLINA, 1900-1930:
THE MAKING OF A MODERN UNIVERSITY. Chapel Hill: University
of North Carolina Press, 1957. 633 p.

Chapter 6

THE COLONIAL PERIOD: 1607-1783

953   "Accounts of the College." WILLIAM AND MARY COLLEGE QUARTERLY HISTORICAL MAGAZINE 8 (1900): 166-71.

954   American Antiquarian Society. "The Colonial Scene--1602-1800." AMERICAN ANTIQUARIAN SOCIETY 80: 53-160.

955   Anderson, Dice R. "The Teacher of Jefferson and Marshall." SOUTH ATLANTIC QUARTERLY 15 (1916): 327-43.

Refers to Chancellor Thomas Wythe (1726-1806).

956   Baldwin, Simeon E. "The Ecclesiastical Constitution of Yale College." PAPERS, NEW HAVEN COLONY HISTORICAL SOCIETY 3 (1882): 406-42.

957   Bell, Whitfield, J., Jr. "Philadelphia Medical Students in Europe, 1750-1800." PENNSYLVANIA MAGAZINE OF HISTORY AND BIOGRAPHY 67 (1943): 1-29.

958   _____. "Benjamin Franklin and the German Charity Schools." PRO-CEEDINGS, AMERICAN PHILOSOPHICAL SOCIETY 99 (1955): 381-87.

959   _____. EARLY AMERICAN SCIENCE NEEDS AND OPPORTUNITIES FOR STUDY. Williamsburg, Va.: Institute for Early American History and Culture, 1955. vii, 85 p.

960   Belok, Michael V. "The Courtesy Tradition and Early Schoolbooks." HISTORY OF EDUCATION QUARTERLY 8 (1968): 306-18.

961   Boorstin, Daniel J. THE LOST WORLD OF THOMAS JEFFERSON. New York: Holt, 1948. 306 p.

962   _____. THE AMERICANS: THE COLONIAL EXPERIENCE. New York: Random House, 1958. 434 p.

963 Brasch, Frederick E. "The Newtonian Epoch in the American Colonies."
PROCEEDINGS, AMERICAN ANTIQUARIAN SOCIETY 49 (1939): 314-32.

964 Bridenbaugh, Carl. "The New England Town: A Way of Life in American Antiquarian Society." PROCEEDINGS, AMERICAN ANTIQUARIAN
SOCIETY 56 (1947): 19-48.

965 _____. SEAT OF EMPIRE: THE POLITICAL ROLE OF EIGHTEENTH
CENTURY WILLIAMSBURG. New ed. Williamsburg, Va.: Colonial Williamsburg, 1958. 85 p.

    Series 1. Distributed by H. Holt, New York.

966 _____. THE SPIRIT OF '76. New York: Oxford University Press, 1976.
162 p.

967 Bridenbaugh, Carl, and Bridenbaugh, Jessica. REBELS AND GENTLE-
MEN: PHILADELPHIA IN THE AGE OF FRANKLIN. New York: Rey-
nal and Hitchcock, 1942. 393 p.

968 Bridenbaugh, Carl. MYTHS AND REALITIES: SOCIETIES OF THE CO-
LONIAL SOUTH. Baton Rouge: Louisiana State University Press, 1952.
208 p.

969 Brinton, Howard H. "Quaker Contributions to Higher Education in Colonial America." PENNSYLVANIA HISTORY 25 (1958): 234-50.

970 Broderick, Francis L. "Pulpit, Physics, and Politics: The Curriculum of
the College of New Jersey, 1746-1794." WILLIAM AND MARY QUAR-
TERLY 6 (1949): 42-67.

971 Buranelli, Vincent. "Colonial Philosophy." WILLIAM AND MARY
QUARTERLY 16 (1949): 343-62.

972 Bush, George G. "The First Common Schools of New England." U.S.
BUREAU OF EDUCATION, REPORT OF THE COMMISSIONER, 1896-97.
Vol. 2, pp. 1165-86. Washington, D.C.: Government Printing Office,
1898.

973 Butterfield L[ymon].H., ed. "A Sketch of the Revolution and Improvement in Science, Arts, and Literature in America." WILLIAM AND
MARY QUARTERLY 10 (1953): 597-627.

    A reprint from Samuel Miller: "A Brief Retrospect of the
    Eighteenth Century" (1803).

974   _____, ed. JOHN WITHERSPOON COMES TO AMERICA. Princeton,
       N.J.: Princeton University Library, 1953. 160 p.

       Collected correspondence: 1766-70.

975   Cadbury, Henry J. "John Harvard's Library." PUBLICATIONS, COLO-
       NIAL SOCIETY OF MASSACHUSETTS 34 (1940): 353-88.

976   Campbell, H.G. "The Syms and Eaton Schools and Their Successors."
       WILLIAM AND MARY QUARTERLY 20 (1940): 1-61.

977   Carrell, William D. "American College Professors: 1750-1800." HIS-
       TORY OF EDUCATION QUARTERLY 8 (1968): 289-305.

978   Castaneda, Carlos E. "The Beginnings of University Life in America."
       CATHOLIC HISTORICAL REVIEW 24 (1938): 153-74.

979   Castel, Albert. "The Founding Fathers and the Vision of a National Uni-
       versity." HISTORY OF EDUCATION QUARTERLY 4 (1964): 280-302.

980   Chase, Wayland J. "The Great Awakening and Its Educational Conse-
       quences." SCHOOL AND SOCIETY 35 (1932): 443-49.

981   Cohen, I. Bernard. SOME EARLY TOOLS OF AMERICAN SCIENCE:
       AN ACCOUNT OF THE EARLY SCIENTIFIC INSTRUMENTS AND MINERO-
       LOGICAL AND BIOLOGICAL COLLECTIONS IN HARVARD UNIVERSITY.
       Cambridge, Mass.: Harvard University Press, 1950. 201 p.

982   Cohen, Sheldon S. "Benjamin Trumbull, The Years at Yale, 1755-1759."
       HISTORY OF EDUCATION QUARTERLY 6 (1966): 33-48.

983   _____. "Tradition and Change in the Ivy League: Benjamin Trumbull,
       the Years at Yale, 1755-1759." HISTORY OF EDUCATION QUARTERLY
       6 (1966): 33-48.

984   _____. "The Yale College Journal of Benjamin Trumbull." HISTORY
       OF EDUCATION QUARTERLY 8 (1968): 375-85.

985   _____. A HISTORY OF COLONIAL EDUCATION, 1607-1776. New
       York: Wiley, 1974. 228 p.

986   Cole, N.M. "The Licensing of Schoolmasters in Colonial Massachusetts."
       HISTORY OF EDUCATION JOURNAL 8 (1956): 68-74.

987   Come, D.R. "The Influence of Princeton on Higher Education in the
       South Before 1825." WILLIAM AND MARY QUARTERLY 2 (1945): 352-96.

988 Connor, R.D.W. "The Genesis of Higher Education in North Carolina."
NORTH CAROLINA HISTORICAL REVIEW 28 (1951): 1-14.

Covers: 1763-89.

989 Conroy, Graham P. "Berkeley and Education in America." JOURNAL
OF THE HISTORY OF IDEAS 21 (1960): 211-20.

990 Coolidge, Calvin. "George Washington and Education." NATIONAL
EDUCATION ASSOCIATION JOURNAL 15 (1926): 94-102.

991 "Correspondence of Ezra Stiles, President of Yale College, and James
Madison, President of William and Mary." WILLIAM AND MARY COL-
LEGE QUARTERLY HISTORICAL MAGAZINE 7 (1927): 292-96.

992 Corry, John P. "Education in Colonial Georgia." GEORGIA HISTORI-
CAL QUARTERLY 16 (1932): 136-45.

993 Cremin, Lawrence A. AMERICAN EDUCATION: THE COLONIAL EX-
PERIENCE, 1607-1783. New York: Harper and Row, 1970. 688 p.

994 Culleton, Leo. "William and Mary College vs Frewen, Chancery Suit,
1702." VIRGINIA MAGAZINE OF HISTORY AND BIOGRAPHY 24
(1916): 374-78.

995 Curti, Merle. THE GROWTH OF AMERICAN THOUGHT. 3d ed. New
York: Harper and Row, 1964. 939 p.

996 Cutts, A.B. "Educational Influence of Aberdeen in Seventeenth Century
Virginia." WILLIAM AND MARY COLLEGE QUARTERLY HISTORICAL
MAGAZINE 15 (1935): 229-49.

997 Davis, Andrew M. "The First Scholarship at Harvard." PROCEEDINGS,
AMERICAN ANTIQUARIAN SOCIETY 5 (1884): 129-40.

998 _____. "John Harvard's Life in America, 1637-1638." PUBLICATIONS,
COLONIAL SOCIETY OF MASSACHUSETTS 12 (1908): 4-44.

999 Dexter, Franklin B. THE FOUNDING OF YALE COLLEGE. New Haven,
Conn.: New Haven Colonial Historical Society, 1882. 31 p.

Published as volume 3 of the papers of the society.

1000 _____. "On Some Social Distinctions at Harvard and Yale Before the
Revolution." PROCEEDINGS, AMERICAN ANTIQUARIAN SOCIETY 9
(1893): 34-59.

1001 _____. "Thomas Clap and His Writings." PAPERS, NEW HAVEN CO-LONY HISTORICAL SOCIETY 5 (1894): 247-74.

1002 _____. "An Historical Sketch of the Powers and Duties of the Presidency in Yale College." PROCEEDINGS, AMERICAN ANTIQUARIAN SOCIETY 12 (1896): 27-42.

1003 _____. EARLY PRIVATE LIBRARIES IN NEW ENGLAND. Worcester, Mass.: Davis Press, 1907. 15 p.

1004 _____. "Student Life at Yale in the Early Days of Connecticut Hall." PAPERS, NEW HAVEN COLONY HISTORICAL SOCIETY 7 (1908): 288-97.

1005 _____. "Yale College in Saybrook." PAPERS, NEW HAVEN COLONY HISTORICAL SOCIETY 7 (1908): 129-40.

1006 _____. "The Removal of Yale College to New Haven in October 1716." PAPERS, NEW HAVEN HISTORICAL SOCIETY 9 (1918): 70-89.

1007 "Documents of William and Mary College: Recently Discovered." WILLIAM AND MARY COLLEGE QUARTERLY HISTORICAL MAGAZINE 10 (1930): 239-53.

1008 Dudley, Thomas. "The Harvard College Charter of 1650." PUBLICATIONS, COLONIAL SOCIETY OF MASSACHUSETTS 31 (1935): 1-16.

1009 Durim, R. "The Role of the Presidents in the American College of the Colonial Period." HISTORY OF EDUCATION QUARTERLY 1 (1961): 23-31.

1010 Easterby, J.H. "The South Carolina Education Bill of 1770." SOUTH CAROLINA HISTORICAL MAGAZINE 48 (1947): 95-111.

1011 Eaves, Robert W. "A History of the Educational Developments of Alexandria, Virginia, Prior to 1800." WILLIAM AND MARY COLLEGE QUARTERLY HISTORICAL MAGAZINE 16 (1936): 111-61.

1012 Edes, Henry H. "A Letter of President Dunster of Harvard to a Committee of the General Court in 1653, Concerning the Affairs of Harvard College." PUBLICATIONS, COLONIAL SOCIETY OF MASSACHUSETTS 3 (1897): 415-25.

1013 _____. "A College Commencement: Some Harvard Theses of 1663, and a Note on Their Significance." PUBLICATIONS, COLONIAL SOCIETY OF MASSACHUSETTS 5 (1898): 322-40.

1014 Eells, Walter C. "The First Directory of American Colleges." HISTORY OF EDUCATION QUARTERLY 9 (1962): 225-33.

1015 Ellis, Joseph J. THE NEW ENGLAND MIND IN TRANSITION; SAMUEL JOHNSON OF CONNECTICUT, 1696-1772. New Haven, Conn.: Yale University Press, 1973. 292 p.

1016 Ferris, Florence L. "Indian Schools in Colonial Days." JOURNAL OF AMERICAN HISTORY 6 (1912): 141-58.

1017 Fiering, Norman S. "President Samuel Johnson and the Circle of Knowledge." WILLIAM AND MARY QUARTERLY 28, Ser. 3 (1971): 199-236.

1018 "Finances of the College in 1775-1795." WILLIAM AND MARY QUARTERLY HISTORICAL MAGAZINE 11 (1903): 149-53.

1019 Finegan, Thomas E. "Colonial Schools and Colleges in New York." NEW YORK STATE HISTORICAL ASSOCIATION, PROCEEDINGS 14 (1917): 165-82.

1020 "The First Chair in Law and Police at William and Mary College." WILLIAM AND MARY COLLEGE QUARTERLY HISTORICAL MAGAZINE 4 (1896): 264-65.

1021 Fish, Carl R. "The English Parish and Education at the Beginning of American Colonization." SCHOOL REVIEW 23 (1915): 433-49.

1022 Ford, Paul L. THE NEW ENGLAND PRIMER. New York: Teachers College Press, 1962. 78 p.

1023 Foster, Francis A. "The Burning of Harvard Hall in 1764, and Its Consequences." PUBLICATIONS, COLONIAL SOCIETY OF MASSACHUSETTS 14 (1911): 2-43.

1024 Foster, Margery S. OUT OF SMALL BEGINNINGS. . . . : AN ECONOMIC HISTORY OF HARVARD COLLEGE IN THE PURITAN PERIOD (1636-1712). Cambridge, Mass.: Harvard University Press, 1962. 280 p.

1025 Fox, Bertha S. "Provost Smith and the Quest for Funds." PENNSYLVANIA HISTORY 2 (1935): 225-38.

1026 Frost, S.E., Jr. "Higher Education Among the American Indians During the Colonial Period." HISTORY OF EDUCATION JOURNAL 9 (1958): 59-66.

1027 Fuller, Henry M. "Bishop Berkeley as a Benefactor of Yale." YALE UNIVERSITY LIBRARY GAZETTE 33 (1953): 1-18.

1028 Ganter, Herbert L. "Documents Relating to the Early History of the College of William and Mary and to the History of the Church in Virginia." WILLIAM AND MARY COLLEGE QUARTERLY HISTORICAL MAGAZINE 19-20 (1939-40): 348-75, 446-70, 114-37, 212-36, 391-96, 524-44.

1029 Goodwin, Mary F. "Christianizing and Educating the Negro in Colonial Virginia." HISTORICAL MAGAZINE OF THE PROTESTANT EPISCOPAL CHURCH 10 (1932): 143-52.

1030 Grabo, Norman S. "The Veiled Vision: The Role of Aesthetics in Early American Intellectual History." WILLIAM AND MARY QUARTERLY 19 (1962): 493-510.

1031 Greene, Evarts B. "The Anglican Outlook on the American Colonies in the Early Eighteenth Century." AMERICAN HISTORICAL REVIEW 20 (1914): 64-85.

1032 Gummere, R.M. "The Classical Element in Early New England Almanacs." HARVARD LIBRARY REVIEW 9 (1955): 181-96.

1033 Halber, Mabel. "Moravian Influence on Higher Education in Colonial America." PENNSYLVANIA HISTORY 25 (1958): 205-22.

1034 Hansen, Allen O. LIBERALISM AND AMERICAN EDUCATION IN THE EIGHTEENTH CENTURY. New York: Macmillan, 1926. 317 p.

1035 Haskett, Richard C. "Princeton Before the Revolution." WILLIAM AND MARY QUARTERLY 5 (1949): 90-93.

1036 Hendrick, I.G. "A Reappraisal of Colonial New Hampshire's Effort in Public Education." HISTORY OF EDUCATION QUARTERLY 6 (1966): 43-60.

1037 Herbst, Jurgen. "The First Three American Colleges: Schools of the Reformation." PERSPECTIVES IN AMERICAN HISTORY 8 (1974): 5-54.

1038 Hindle, Brooke. "The Quaker Background and Science in Colonial Philadelphia." ISIS 46 (1955): 243-50.

1039 _____. THE PURSUIT OF SCIENCE IN REVOLUTIONARY AMERICA, 1735-1789. Chapel Hill: University of North Carolina Press, 1956. 410 p.

1040 ____. TECHNOLOGY IN EARLY AMERICA. Chapel Hill: University of North Carolina Press, 1966. 145 p.

1041 Hooker, Richard J., ed. THE CAROLINA BACKCOUNTRY ON THE EVE OF REVOLUTION. Chapel Hill: University of North Carolina Press, 1953. 305 p.

1042 Hornberger, Theodore. "A Note on the Probable Source of Provost Smith's Famous Curriculum for the College of Philadelphia." PENNSYLVANIA MAGAZINE OF HISTORY AND BIOGRAPHY 68 (1934): 370-77.

1043 ____. "Samuel Johnson of Yale and King's College: A Note on the Relation of Science and Religion in Provincial America." NEW ENGLAND QUARTERLY 8 (1935): 378-97.

1044 ____. SCIENTIFIC THOUGHT IN THE AMERICAN COLLEGES: 1638-1800. Austin: University of Texas Press, 1945. 108 p.

1045 Hudson, Winthrop S. "The Morison Myth Concerning the Founding of Harvard College." CHURCH HISTORY 8 (1939): 148-59.

1046 Hughes, Robert M. "William and Mary, The First American Law School." WILLIAM AND MARY COLLEGE QUARTERLY HISTORICAL MAGAZINE 2 (1922): 40-48.

1047 Humphrey, David C. "Colonial Colleges and English Dissenting Academies: A Study in Transatlantic Culture." HISTORY OF EDUCATION QUARTERLY 12 (1972): 184-97.

1048 ____. "British Influences on Eighteenth Century American Education." HISTORY OF EDUCATION QUARTERLY 13 (1973): 63-72.

1049 Ingraham, George H. "The Story of the Log College." JOURNAL OF THE PRESBYTERIAN HISTORICAL SOCIETY 12 (1927): 487-511.

1050 Jackson, George L. THE DEVELOPMENT OF SCHOOL SUPPORT IN COLONIAL MASSACHUSETTS. New York: Teachers College, Columbia University Press, 1909. 95 p.

1051 Jackson, Joseph. "A Philadelphia Schoolmaster of the Eighteenth Century." PENNSYLVANIA MAGAZINE OF HISTORY AND BIOGRAPHY 25 (1911): 315-32.

1052 Jernegan, Marcus W. "Factors Influencing the Development of American Education Before the Revolution." PROCEEDINGS, MISSISSIPPI VALLEY HISTORICAL ASSOCIATION 5 (1911-12): 190-206.

1053 _____. "The Beginnings of Public Education in New England." SCHOOL REVIEW 23 (1915): 319-30, 361-80.

1054 _____. "The Educational Development of the Southern Colonies." THE SCHOOL REVIEW: A JOURNAL OF SECONDARY EDUCATION 27 (1919): 360-76, 405-25.

1055 Jones, E. Alfred. "Two Professors of William and Mary College." WILLIAM AND MARY COLLEGE QUARTERLY HISTORICAL MAGAZINE 26 (1918): 221-31.

> Refers to Rev. Thomas Gwatkin and Dr. Samuel Henley.

1056 Jorgenson, Lloyd P. "The American Faith in Education." HISTORY OF EDUCATION JOURNAL 4 (1952): 11-17.

> Deals with the doctrine of man's perfectability as a basic American tenet in education.

1057 "Journal of the Meetings of the President and Masters of William and Mary College." WILLIAM AND MARY COLLEGE QUARTERLY HISTORICAL MAGAZINE 1 (1893): 130-37, 214-20; 2 (1893): 50-57, 122-27; 2 (1894): 208-10, 256-58; 3 (1894): 60-64, 128-32; 3 (1895): 195-97, 262-65; 4 (1895): 43-46, 130-32; 4 (1896): 187-92; 5 (1896): 15-17, 83-89; 5 (1897): 187-89, 224-29; 13 (1904): 15-22, 133-37; 13 (1905): 148-56, 230-35; 14 (1906): 242-46; 15 (1906): 1-14, 134-42; 15 (1907): 164-74, 264-69.

1058 Kaestle, Carl F. "Common Schools Before the Common School Revival: New York Schooling in the 1790s." HISTORY OF EDUCATION QUARTERLY 12 (1972): 465-500.

1059 Kemp, William W. THE SUPPORT OF SCHOOLS IN COLONIAL NEW YORK BY THE SOCIETY FOR THE PROPAGATION OF THE GOSPEL IN FOREIGN PARTS. New York: Teachers College, Columbia University, 1913. 279 p.

1060 Kiefer, Sister Monica. "Early American Childhood in the Middle Atlantic Area." PENNSYLVANIA MAGAZINE OF HISTORY AND BIOGRAPHY 68 (1944): 3-37.

1061 Kilpatrick, William H. THE DUTCH SCHOOLS OF NEW NETHERLAND AND COLONIAL NEW YORK. U.S. Bureau of Education Bulletin No. 12. Washington, D.C.: Government Printing Office, 1912. 239 p.

1062 Kimmel, Herbert. "The Status of Mathematics and Mathematical Instruction During the Colonial Period." SCHOOL AND SOCIETY 9 (1919): 195-202.

1063 Kingsley, William L. "History of Yale." AMERICAN JOURNAL OF EDUCATION 5 (1858): 541-66.

1064 Kirkpatrick, J[ohn].E. "The British College in the American Colonies." SCHOOL AND SOCIETY 17 (1923): 449-53.

Refers to Harvard, William and Mary, Yale, Brown, and Dartmouth colleges.

1065 _____. "Constitutional Development of the College of William and Mary." WILLIAM AND MARY COLLEGE QUARTERLY HISTORICAL MAGAZINE 6 (1926): 95-108.

Deals with the period: 1693-1779.

1066 Klassen, Frank. "Persistence and Change in Eighteenth Century Colonial Education." HISTORY OF EDUCATION QUARTERLY 2 (1962): 83-99.

1067 Klein, Milton M. "Church, State and Education: Testing the Issue in Colonial New York." NEW YORK HISTORY 45 (1964): 291-303.

1068 Knight, Edgar W. "Early Opposition to the Teaching of American Children Abroad." EDUCATIONAL FORUM 11 (1947): 193-204.

1069 _____. "An Improved Plan of Education, 1775: An Eighteenth Century Activity Curriculum." SCHOOL AND SOCIETY 69 (1949): 409-11.

1070 Knight, J.W. "The Development of a Curriculum in the Early American Colleges." HISTORY OF EDUCATION QUARTERLY 1 (1961): 64-75.

Refers to use of a Cambridge model from the seventeenth century well into the eighteenth century.

1071 Koch, Adrienne. "Pragmatic Wisdom and the American Enlightenment." WILLIAM AND MARY QUARTERLY 18 (1961): 313-29.

1072 Kohlbrenner, Bernard. "Religion and Higher Education: An Historical Perspective." HISTORY OF EDUCATION QUARTERLY 1 (1961): 45-56.

Notes that with the exception of the College of Pennsylvania, the other eight major early American colleges were strongly denominational.

1073 Kraus, Joe W. "The Development of a Curriculum in the Early American Colleges." HISTORY OF EDUCATION QUARTERLY 1 (1961): 64-76.

Notes the heavy reliance on British curricular models.

1074 _____. "Private Libraries in Colonial America." JOURNAL OF LIBRARY HISTORY 9 (1974): 31-53.

1075 Lamerton, E.V. "Colonial Libraries of Pennsylvania." PENNSYLVANIA MAGAZINE OF HISTORY AND BIOGRAPHY 42 (1918): 193-234.

1076 Land, Robert H. "Henrico and Its College." WILLIAM AND MARY QUARTERLY HISTORICAL MAGAZINE 18 (1938): 453-98.

1077 Landrum, Grace W. "The First Colonial Grammar in English." WILLIAM AND MARY COLLEGE QUARTERLY HISTORICAL MAGAZINE 19 (1939): 272-85.

1078 Lane, William C. "Benjamin Franklin's Relations with Harvard College." PUBLICATIONS, COLONIAL SOCIETY OF MASSACHUSETTS 10 (1906): 229-39.

1079 Larned, Ellen D. "Yale Boys of the Last Century: The Journal of Elijah Backus, Jr., at Yale College from January 1 to December 31, 1977." CONNECTICUT QUARTERLY 1 (1895): 355-61.

1080 Law, William C. "Early Harvard Broadsides." PROCEEDINGS, AMERICAN ANTIQUARIAN SOCIETY 24 (1914): 264-304.

1081 Lawrence, James B. "Religious Education of the Negro in the Colony of Georgia." GEORGIA HISTORICAL QUARTERLY 14 (1930): 41-57.

1082 Littlefield, George E. "Elijah Corlet and the 'Faire Grammar Schoole' at Cambridge." PUBLICATIONS, COLONIAL SOCIETY OF MASSACHU-SETTS 17 (1913): 131-42.

1083 Lively, Bruce R. "William Smith, the College and Academy of Philadel-phia and Pennsylvania Politics, 1753-1758." HISTORICAL MAGAZINE OF THE PROTESTANT EPISCOPAL CHURCH 38 (1969): 237-58.

1084 Lockridge, Kenneth A. LITERACY IN COLONIAL NEW ENGLAND: AN ENQUIRY INTO THE SOCIAL CONTEXT OF LITERACY IN THE EARLY MODERN WEST. New York: Norton, 1974. 164 p.

1085 Lovell, Robert W. "William Croswell: Eccentric Scholar." NEW EN-GLAND QUARTERLY 38 (1965): 35-53.

1086 Lovett, Robert W. HARVARD UNIVERSITY ARCHIVES, 1638-1750. 2 vols. Boston: Colonial Society of Massachusetts, 1975.

Also identifiable as volumes 49 and 50 of the Colonial Society documents series.

1087 Ludwell Papers. Virginia Historical Society Collection. "Proceedings of the Visitors of William and Mary College, 1716." VIRGINIA MAGAZINE OF HISTORY AND BIOGRAPHY 4 (1896): 161-75.

> In that era the trustees of the college were known as the visitors.

1088 McAnear, B. "College Founding in the American Colonies, 1745-1775." MISSISSIPPI VALLEY HISTORICAL REVIEW 42 (1955): 24-44.

1089 _____. "The Selection of an Alma Mater by Pre-Revolutionary Students." PENNSYLVANIA MAGAZINE OF HISTORY AND BIOGRAPHY 73 (1949): 429-40.

1090 _____. "The Charter of the Academy of Newark." DELAWARE HISTORY 4 (1950): 149-56.

1091 _____. "The Raising of Funds by the Colonial Colleges." MISSISSIPPI VALLEY HISTORICAL REVIEW 38 (1952): 591-612.

1092 McCaul, Robert L. "Education in Georgia During the Period of Royal Government, 1752-1776: Financial Support of Schools and Schoolmasters." GEORGIA HISTORICAL QUARTERLY 42 (1956): 103-12.

1093 _____. "Education in Georgia During the Period of Royal Government, 1752-1776: Public School Masters and Private Venture Teachers." GEORGIA HISTORICAL QUARTERLY 40 (1956): 248-59.

1094 _____. "Whitfield's Bethesda College Projects and Other Major Attempts to Found Colonial Colleges." GEORGIA HISTORICAL QUARTERLY 44 (1960): 263-77, 381-98.

1095 McKeehan, Louis W. YALE SCIENCE: THE FIRST HUNDRED YEARS, 1701-1801. New York: Schuman, 1947. 82 p.

> See bibliographical notes: pp. 61-77.

1096 MacLenny, W.E. "Yeates Free Schools." WILLIAM AND MARY COLLEGE QUARTERLY HISTORICAL MAGAZINE 5 (1925): 30-38.

1097 Matthews, Albert. "Harvard Commencement Days, 1642-1916." PUBLICATIONS, COLONIAL SOCIETY OF MASSACHUSETTS 18 (1916): 309-85.

1098 Matthews, Albert. "The Teaching of French at Harvard College Before 1750." PUBLICATIONS, COLONIAL SOCIETY OF MASSACHUSETTS 17 (1914): 216-31.

1099 _____. "The Harvard College Charter of 1672." PUBLICATIONS, COLONIAL SOCIETY OF MASSACHUSETTS 21 (1919): 363-409.

1100 _____. "Comenius and Harvard College." PUBLICATIONS, COLONIAL SOCIETY OF MASSACHUSETTS 21 (1920): 146-90.

   Suggests an explanation of Cotton Mather's rationale in the offering of the Harvard presidency to John Comenius, of Bohemia, in 1654.

1101 Matthews, Albert, et al., eds. "Corporation Records of Harvard College, 1636-1774." PUBLICATIONS, COLONIAL SOCIETY OF MASSACHUSETTS 15, 16 (1925): entire issues.

1102 Mau, Clayton C. "Pity the Pupil." NEW YORK FOLKLORE QUARTERLY 15 (1959): 93-98.

   Deals with the use of Noah Webster's spelling book and "scribblings" found in early schoolbooks.

1103 Mayo, Amory D. "Public Schools During the Colonial and Revolutionary Period in the United States. In UNITED STATES BUREAU OF EDUCATION, REPORT OF THE COMMISSIONER, 1893-1894. Vol. 1, pp. 639-738. Washington, D.C.: Government Printing Office, 1896.

1104 Messerli, Jonathan. "Benjamin Franklin: Colonial and Cosmopolitan Educator." BRITISH JOURNAL OF EDUCATIONAL STUDIES 16 (1968): 43-59.

1105 Middlekauf, Robert. ANCIENTS AND AXIOMS: SECONDARY EDUCATION IN EIGHTEENTH CENTURY NEW ENGLAND. New Haven, Conn.: Yale University Press, 1963. 218 p.

1106 Middleton, Arthur P. "Anglican Contributions to Higher Education in Colonial America." PENNSYLVANIA HISTORY 25 (1958): 251-68.

1107 Miles, Richard D. "The American Image of Benjamin Franklin." AMERICAN QUARTERLY 9 (1957): 117-43.

1108 "Minutes of the College Faculty, 1758." WILLIAM AND MARY COLLEGE QUARTERLY HISTORICAL MAGAZINE 1 (1921): 24-26.

1109 Moore, Kathryn McDaniel. "The Dilemma of Corporal Punishment at Harvard College." HISTORY OF EDUCATION QUARTERLY 14 (1974): 335-46.

   The old Harvard practice of admonition or corporal punishment was abolished in 1734.

1110 Morgan, Edmund S. "Ezra Stiles: The Education of a Yale Man, 1742-1746." HUNTINGTON LIBRARY QUARTERLY 17 (1954): 251-68.

1111 _____. THE GENTLE PURITAN: A LIFE OF EZRA STILES, 1727-1795. Chapel Hill: University of North Carolina Press, 1962. 408 p.

1112 Morgan, Morris H. "The First Harvard Doctors of Medicine." PUBLICATIONS, COLONIAL SOCIETY OF MASSACHUSETTS 12 (1909): 312-24.

1113 Morison, Samuel E. "Harvard in the Colonial Wars, 1675-1748." HARVARD GRADUATES MAGAZINE 26 (1918): 554-74.

1114 _____. "Precedence at Harvard College in the Seventeenth Century." PROCEEDINGS, AMERICAN ANTIQUARIAN SOCIETY 42 (1932): 371-431.

1115 _____. "College Laws and Customs." PUBLICATIONS, COLONIAL SOCIETY OF MASSACHUSETTS 31 (1935): 322-401.

1116 _____. "Urian Oakes Salutary Oration: Commencement, 1677." PUBLICATIONS, COLONIAL SOCIETY OF MASSACHUSETTS 31 (1935): 405-36.

1117 _____. "American Colonial Colleges." RICE INSTITUTE PAMPHLETS 33 (1936): 246-82.

1118 _____. "Old School and College Books in the Prince Library." MORE BOOKS 11 (1936): 77-93.

      A bibliographical essay on the Prince collection of books (mostly Latin, Greek, and Hebrew) used in New England colleges in the seventeenth century.

1119 _____. THE INTELLECTUAL LIFE OF COLONIAL NEW ENGLAND. 2d ed. New York: New York University Press, 1956. 288 p.

1120 Morton, Charles. COMPENDIUM PHYSICAE. Boston: Colonial Society of Massachusetts, 1940. 237 p.

      Appears as volume thirty-three of the Colonial Society volume series. Morison, in the prefaces points out Morton's influence on the Harvard curriculum (ca. 1687-1723) as a consequence of it. Morton was pastor of the Charlestown, Massachusetts, church and later vice-president of Harvard. It laid foundation of experimental philosophy.

1121 Mulhern, James. "Manuscript School Books." BIBLIOGRAPHY SOCIETY OF AMERICA PAPERS 33 (1936): 17-37.

 Covers their use in the eighteenth and nineteenth centuries. Includes printed works, exercise books, notebooks, student journals, and records of student societies.

1122 Murdock, Kenneth B. "Cotton Mather and the Rectorship of Yale College." PUBLICATIONS, COLONIAL SOCIETY OF MASSACHUSETTS 36 (1926): 388-401.

1123 _____. "The Teaching of Latin and Greek at the Boston Latin Schools in 1712." PUBLICATIONS, COLONIAL SOCIETY OF MASSACHUSETTS 27 (1927): 21-29.

1124 Nash, G. "The Image of the Indian in the Southern Colonial Mind." WILLIAM AND MARY QUARTERLY 29 (1972): 197-230.

 Mostly about Anglo-Indian interactions in the colonial South.

1125 Nicholson, Francis, and Blair, James. "Papers Relating to the Administration of Governor Nicholson and to the Founding of William and Mary College." VIRGINIA MAGAZINE OF HISTORY AND BIOGRAPHY 7 (1899-1900): 153-72, 275-86, 386-401; 8 (1900-91): 46-64, 126-46, 366-85; 9 (1901-02): 18-29, 152-62, 251-62.

1126 Noble, John. "Comments on an Old Harvard Commencement Program of 1730." PUBLICATIONS, COLONIAL SOCIETY OF MASSACHUSETTS 6 (1899): 265-78.

1127 Noble, Stuart G., and Nuhrah, Arthur G. "Education in Colonial Louisiana." LOUISIANA HISTORICAL QUARTERLY 32 (1949): 759-76.

1128 Norton, Arthur O. "Harvard Textbooks and Reference Books of the Seventeenth Century." PUBLICATIONS, COLONIAL SOCIETY OF MASSACHUSETTS 38 (1933): 361-438.

1129 "Notes Relative to Some of the Students Who Attended the College of William and Mary, 1753-1778." WILLIAM AND MARY COLLEGE QUARTERLY HISTORICAL MAGAZINE 1 (1921): 27-41, 116-30.

1130 O'Brien, Michael J. "Early Irish Schoolmasters in New England." CATHOLIC HISTORICAL REVIEW 3 (1917): 52-71.

1131 Olson, Alison B. "The Founding of Princeton University: Religion and Politics in Eighteenth Century New Jersey." NEW JERSEY HISTORY 87 (1969): 133-50.

1132 "Papers Concerning the College of William and Mary." WILLIAM AND MARY COLLEGE QUARTERLY HISTORICAL MAGAZINE 2 (1893): 36-37.

1133 "Papers Relating to the College." WILLIAM AND MARY COLLEGE QUARTERLY HISTORICAL MAGAZINE 16 (1908): 162-80.

1134 "Papers Relating to the Founding of William and Mary College." WILLIAM AND MARY COLLEGE QUARTERLY HISTORICAL MAGAZINE 7 (1899): 158-74.

1135 Parsons, Elsie W. [Clewes]. EDUCATIONAL LEGISLATION AND AD-MINISTRATION OF THE COLONIAL GOVERNMENTS. New York: Macmillan, 1899. 524 p.

1136 Parsons, Francis. "Elisha Williams, Minister, Soldier, President of Yale." PAPERS, NEW HAVEN COLONY HISTORICAL SOCIETY 7 (1908): 188-214.

1137 _____. "Ezra Stiles of Yale." NEW ENGLAND QUARTERLY 9 (1936): 286-316.

1138 Pennington, E.L. "Thomas Bray's Associates and Their Work Among the Negroes." PROCEEDINGS, AMERICAN ANTIQUARIAN SOCIETY 48 (1939): 311-403.

   Deals with the establishment of schools for black children in colonial America.

1139 Pike, Nicholas. A NEW AND COMPLETE SYSTEM OF ARITHMETIC. Worcester, Mass.: Press of Isaiah Thomas, 1797. 516 p.

1140 Plimpton, George A. "The Hornbook and Its Use in America." PRO-CEEDINGS, AMERICAN ANTIQUARIAN SOCIETY 25 (1916): 264-72.

1141 Pool, Rev. David de Sola. "Hebrew Learning Among the Puritans of New England Prior to 1700." PUBLICATIONS, AMERICAN JEWISH HIS-TORICAL SOCIETY 20 (1911): 31-83.

1142 Potter, Alfred C. "The Harvard College Library, 1723-1735." PUBLI-CATIONS, COLONIAL SOCIETY OF MASSACHUSETTS 25 (1922): 1-13.

1143 Powell, William S. "Books in the Virginia Colony Before 1624." WIL-LIAM AND MARY QUARTERLY 5 (1948): 177-84.

1144 Rand, Edward K. "Liberal Education in Seventeenth Century Harvard." NEW ENGLAND QUARTERLY 6 (1933): 525-51.

1145 Richardson, Leon Burr, ed. AN INDIAN PREACHER IN ENGLAND.
Hanover, N.H.: Dartmouth College Publications, 1933. 376 p.

> A facsimile reproduction of letters and diaries of Rev. Samson
> Occum and Rev. Nathaniel Whittaker and their mission to
> England to raise funds for Eleazar Wheelock's Indian Charity
> School, precursor to Dartmouth College.

1146 Robinson, W. Stitt. "Indian Education and Missions in Colonial Virginia."
JOURNAL OF SOUTHERN HISTORY 18 (1952): 152-68.

1147 Rothman, David [J.]. "A Note on the Study of the Colonial Family."
WILLIAM AND MARY QUARTERLY 23 (1966): 627-34.

1148 Rothman, David J., and Rothman, Sheila A., eds. THE COLONIAL
AMERICAN FAMILY. New York: Arno Press, New York Times, 1972.

> A collection of essays separately paginated. Reproductions of
> earlier essays on the subject. The final essay is an educa-
> tional directory by Amos Weed, ca. 1803, on desirable edu-
> cational practices as then perceived. All facsimile reprints.

1149 Sack, Saul. "The Birth of American Medical Education." PAEDAGO-
GICA HISTORICA 3 (1963): 97-132.

1150 Salisbury, Stephen. "Early Books and Libraries in America." PROCEED-
INGS, AMERICAN ANTIQUARIAN SOCIETY 5 (1884): 171-215.

1151 Savin, Marion B., and Abrahams, Harold J. "The Young Ladies' Academy
of Philadelphia." HISTORY OF EDUCATION JOURNAL 8 (1956): 58-67.

1152 Schlesinger, Elizabeth B. "Cotton Mather and His Children." WILLIAM
AND MARY QUARTERLY 10 (1953): 181-89.

1153 Schmidt, George P. PRINCETON AND RUTGERS: THE TWO COLONIAL
COLLEGES OF NEW JERSEY. Princeton, N.J.: Van Nostrand, 1964.
137 p.

> Also appears as volume five of the New Jersey Historical
> Series.

1154 Scott, Kenneth. "A 'Dust' at Yale and a 'Blessing' for President Clapp."
BULLETIN, CONNECTICUT HISTORICAL SOCIETY 33 (1958): 46-49.

1155 Seybolt, Robert F. APPRENTICESHIP AND APPRENTICESHIP EDUCATION
IN COLONIAL NEW ENGLAND AND NEW YORK. New York: Teachers
College, Columbia University Press, 1917. 121 p.

> Includes documents and sources, as well as a survey of the subject.

1156 _____. THE EVENING SCHOOL IN COLONIAL AMERICA. Bulletin No. 24. Bureau of Educational Research, College of Education, University of Illinois, 1925. Reprint. New York: Arno Press, New York Times, 1971. 68 p.

> Explains in detail how they were essentially schools of continuing education.

1157 _____. "The Grammar School at Brown University in 1772." RHODE ISLAND HISTORICAL SOCIETY COLLECTIONS 23 (1930): 73 p.

1158 _____. THE PRIVATE SCHOOLS OF COLONIAL BOSTON. Cambridge, Mass.: Harvard University Press, 1935. 250 p.

> Covers subjects listed, as well as sample newspaper advertisements of the schools: 1706-76.

1159 _____. "The Private Schools of Seventeenth Century Boston." NEW ENGLAND QUARTERLY 8 (1935): 418-24.

1160 _____. THE PUBLIC SCHOOLS OF COLONIAL BOSTON, 1635-1775. Cambridge, Mass.: Harvard University Press, 1935. 101 p.

1161 _____. "Notes on the Curriculum in Colonial America." JOURNAL OF EDUCATIONAL RESEARCH 12 (1925): 275-81, 370-78.

1162 _____. "Schoolmasters of Colonial Boston." PUBLICATIONS, COLONIAL SOCIETY OF MASSACHUSETTS 27 (1928): 130-56.

1163 _____. SOURCE STUDIES IN AMERICAN COLONIAL EDUCATION: THE PRIVATE SCHOOL. Urbana: University of Illinois Press, 1925. Reprint. New York: Arno Press, 1971. 350 p.

> Deals with the teaching of math, geography, history, and foreign languages. One chapter deals especially with girls' education.

1164 _____. SOURCE STUDIES IN AMERICAN COLONIAL EDUCATION: THE PRIVATE SCHOOL. Urbana: University of Illinois Press, 1925. 350 p.

> See entry no. 1163.

1165 _____. "South Carolina's Schoolmasters of 1744." SOUTH CAROLINA HISTORICAL MAGAZINE 31 (1930): 314-15; 38 (1937): 64-65.

1166 _____. "The S.P.G. Myth: A Note on Education in Colonial New York (1770-1776)." JOURNAL OF EDUCATIONAL RESEARCH 12 (1926): 129-37.

"S.P.G." stands for: Society for the Propagation of the Gospel in Foreign Parts. Takes exception that all or most of the schools in New York, 1770-76, were S.P.G. maintained.

1167 _____. "Student Libraries at Harvard, 1763-1764." PUBLICATIONS, COLONIAL SOCIETY OF MASSACHUSETTS 28 (1935): 449-61.

1168 Seyler, Harry. "Pennsylvania's First Loyalty Oath." HISTORY OF EDUCATION JOURNAL 3 (1952): 114-26.

In 1776 Pennsylvania required that all teachers swear loyalty to the political ideas set forth in its Constitution of 1776.

1169 Shipton, Clifford K. "Secondary Education in the Puritan Colonies." NEW ENGLAND QUARTERLY 7 (1934): 646-61.

1170 _____. "The New England Clergy of the 'Glacial Age.'" PUBLICATIONS, COLONIAL SOCIETY OF MASSACHUSETTS 32 (1937): 24-54.

1171 _____. "Ye Mystery of Ye Ages Solved, or How Placing Worked at Colonial Harvard and Yale." HARVARD ALUMNI BULLETIN 57 (1954-55): 258-59, 262-63, 417.

1172 _____. "The Puritan Influence on Education." PENNSYLVANIA HISTORY 25 (1958): 223-33.

1173 Shouse, J.B. "If Comenius Had Come to America." EDUCATION 58 (1938): 361-68.

Speculates on the effect Comenius would have had on American education had he accepted the Harvard presidency in 1654.

1174 Sidwell, Robert T. "'An Odd Fish'--Samuel Keimer and a Footnote to American Educational History." HISTORY OF EDUCATION QUARTERLY 6 (1966): 16-30.

1175 _____. "Writers, Thinkers and Fox Hunters." HISTORY OF EDUCATION QUARTERLY 8 (1968): 275-88.

Surveys colonial American educational theory as espoused in almanacs of the era.

1176 Simons, Lao G. INTRODUCTION OF ALGEBRA INTO AMERICAN SCHOOLS IN THE EIGHTEENTH CENTURY. U.S. Bureau of Education, Bulletin No. 18, 1924. Washington, D.C.: Government Printing Office, 1924. 80 p.

1177 Simpson, William S. "A Comparison of the Libraries of Seven Colonial Virginians, 1754-1789." JOURNAL OF LIBRARY HISTORY 9 (1974): 54-65.

1178 Sloan, Douglas. THE SCOTTISH ENLIGHTENMENT AND THE AMERICAN COLLEGE IDEAL. New York: Teachers College, Columbia University Press, 1971. 298 p.

1179 Smart, George K. "Private Libraries in Colonial Virginia." AMERICAN LITERATURE 10 (1938): 24-52.

1180 Smith, David Eugene. "A Glimpse at Early Colonial Algebra." SCHOOL AND SOCIETY 7 (1918): 8-11.

1181 Smith, Edgar F. "Early Scientists of Philadelphia." PENNSYLVANIA MAGAZINE OF HISTORY AND BIOGRAPHY 47 (1923): 1-27.

1182 Smith, L.A.H. "Three Spelling Books of American Schools, 1740-1800." HARVARD LIBRARY REVIEW 16 (1968): 72-93.

    Essentially a content analysis of the spellers involved.

1183 Smith, Perry W. "'Exercises' Presented During the Commencement of the College of Philadelphia and Other Colonial Colleges." PAEDAGOGICA HISTORICA 7 (1967): 182-222.

1184 Smith, W. "The Teacher in Puritan Culture." HARVARD EDUCATIONAL REVIEW 36 (1966): 394-411.

    Traces the sources of American attitudes towards teachers to the influence of the Puritan ideology and of Harvard College.

1185 Smith, Willard W. THE RELATIONS OF COLLEGE AND STATE IN CO-LONIAL AMERICA, 1636-1819. Ann Arbor, Mich.: Xerox University Microfilms International, 1949. 175 p.

    A positive microfilm of a 175-page manuscript. Publication no. 1654.

1186 Speare, Elizabeth G. "Old-Time Schoolmasters and Scholars." NEW ENGLAND GALAXY 1 (1960): 6-15.

1187 "The Statutes of the College of William and Mary, Codified in 1736." WILLIAM AND MARY COLLEGE QUARTERLY HISTORICAL MAGAZINE 32 (1914): 281-96.

1188 "The Statutes of the College of William and Mary in Virginia." WILLIAM AND MARY COLLEGE QUARTERLY HISTORICAL MAGAZINE 16 (1908): 239-56.

1189 Stearns, Raymond P. "James Petiver, Seventeenth Century Promoter of Natural Science." PROCEEDINGS, AMERICAN ANTIQUARIAN SOCIETY 62 (1952): 243-365.

1190 Steiner, Bernard C. "Rev. Thomas Bray and His American Libraries." AMERICAN HISTORICAL REVIEW 2 (1896-97): 59-75.

1191 Stephenson, Martha. "The Pioneer Child's Education." REGISTER OF KENTUCKY STATE HISTORICAL SOCIETY 7 (1909): 41-43.

1192 Stout, Harry S. "University Men in New England 1620-1660: A Demographic Analysis." JOURNAL OF INTERDISCIPLINARY HISTORY 4 (1974): 375-400.

1193 Straub, Jean S. "Quaker School Life in Philadelphia Before 1800." PENNSYLVANIA MAGAZINE OF HISTORY AND BIOGRAPHY 89 (1965): 447-58.

1194 Studer, Gerald C. CHRISTOPHER DOCK: COLONIAL SCHOOLMASTER: THE BIOGRAPHY AND WRITINGS OF CHRISTOPHER DOCK. Scottsdale, Pa.: Herald Press, 1967. 445 p.

   Also contains genealogical and personal documents and a bibliography.

1195 Swem, Earl G. "The Lee Free School and the College of William and Mary." WILLIAM AND MARY QUARTERLY 16 (1959): 207-13.

1196 Tanis, Norman E. "Education in John Eliot's Indian Utopia, 1646-1675." HISTORY OF EDUCATION QUARTERLY 10 (1970): 308-22.

   Explains how he sought to make the Indians into Puritans. Cites details of such Utopias in Massachusetts.

1197 Teaford, Jon. "The Transformation of Massachusetts Education, 1670-1780." HISTORY OF EDUCATION QUARTERLY 10 (1970): 287-307.

   Describes changeover from the classical grammar school to the English and vocational school instead.

1198 Thomson, Robert P. "Colleges in the Revolutionary South: The Shaping of a Tradition." HISTORY OF EDUCATION QUARTERLY 10 (1970): 399-412.

   Describes the great outburst of college foundings and failures from lack of support.

1199 Thorpe, Francis N., ed. BENJAMIN FRANKLIN AND THE UNIVERSITY OF PENNSYLVANIA. U.S. Bureau of Education Information Circular no.

2, 1892. Washington, D.C.: Government Printing Office, 1893. 450 p.

1200 Tolles, Frederick B. "Philadelphia's First Scientist, James Logan." ISIS 47 (1956): 20-30.

1201 Tucker, Leonard. "President Thomas Clap of Yale College: Another 'Founding Father' of American Science." ISIS 52 (1961): 55-77.

1202 Tucker, Louis L. "The Church of England and Religious Liberty at Pre-Revolutionary Yale." WILLIAM AND MARY QUARTERLY 17 (1960): 314-28.

1203 _____. PURITAN PROTAGONIST: PRESIDENT THOMAS CLAP OF YALE COLLEGE. Chapel Hill: University of North Carolina Press, 1962. 240 p.

1204 Tully, Alan. "Literacy Levels and Educational Development in Rural Pennsylvania." PENNSYLVANIA HISTORY 39 (1972): 301-02.

Essentially a negative assessment for the period 1729-1775.

1205 Turnbull, L. Minerva. "The Southern Educational Revolt." WILLIAM AND MARY QUARTERLY 14 (1934): 60-76.

1206 Tyack, David. "Education as Artifact: Benjamin Franklin and Instruction of a Rising People." HISTORY OF EDUCATION QUARTERLY 6 (1966): 3-15.

A discussion of Franklin's thoughts on education as appears in his: PROPOSALS RELATING TO THE EDUCATION OF YOUTH IN PENNSYLVANIA, and his: IDEA OF THE ENGLISH SCHOOL, SKETCHED OUT FOR THE CONSIDERATION OF THE TRUSTEES OF THE PHILADELPHIA ACADEMY.

1207 Tyler, Lyong G. "A Few Facts from the Records of William and Mary College." PAPERS, AMERICAN HISTORICAL ASSOCIATION 4 (1890): 129-41.

1208 _____. "Early Presidents of William and Mary." WILLIAM AND MARY COLLEGE QUARTERLY HISTORICAL MAGAZINE 1 (1892): 63-75.

1209 _____. "Grammar and Model School, Founded by Mrs. Mary Whaley in 1706." WILLIAM AND MARY COLLEGE QUARTERLY HISTORICAL MAGAZINE 4 (1895): 3-14.

1210 _____. "Education in Colonial Virginia: Free Schools." WILLIAM AND MARY COLLEGE QUARTERLY HISTORICAL MAGAZINE 6 (1897): 71-85.

1211 _____. "Education in Colonial Virginia: Poor Children and Orphans." WILLIAM AND MARY COLLEGE QUARTERLY HISTORY MAGAZINE 5 (1897): 219-23.

1212 _____. "Education in Colonial Virginia: Private Schools and Tutors." WILLIAM AND MARY COLLEGE QUARTERLY HISTORICAL MAGAZINE 6 (1897): 1-6.

1213 _____. "Education in Colonial Virginia: Comparative Results." WILLIAM AND MARY COLLEGE QUARTERLY HISTORICAL MAGAZINE 7 (1898): 65-76.

1214 _____. "Education in Colonial Virginia: The Higher Education." WILLIAM AND MARY COLLEGE QUARTERLY HISTORICAL MAGAZINE 6 (1898): 171-87.

1215 _____. "Education in Colonial Virginia: The Influence of William and Mary College." WILLIAM AND MARY COLLEGE QUARTERLY HISTORICAL MAGAZINE 7 (1898): 1-9.

1216 _____. "Early Courses and Professors at William and Mary College." WILLIAM AND MARY COLLEGE QUARTERLY HISTORICAL MAGAZINE 14 (1905): 71-83.

1217 _____. "William and Mary College and Its Influence on the Founding of the Republic." WILLIAM AND MARY COLLEGE QUARTERLY HISTORICAL MAGAZINE 15 (1935): 324-33.

1218 _____. "William and Mary College as Expressing the American Principle of Democracy." WILLIAM AND MARY COLLEGE QUARTERLY HISTORICAL MAGAZINE 15 (1935): 282-93.

1219 Vassar, Rena. "The College Battle: Political Factionalism in the Founding of the College of William and Mary." PAEDAGOGICA HISTORICA 4 (1964): 444-56.

1220 Walsh, James J. EDUCATION OF THE FOUNDING FATHERS OF THE REPUBLIC: SCHOLASTICISM IN THE COLONIAL COLLEGES. New York: Fordham University Press, 1935. 377 p.

   For a shorter version of this thesis also see: James J. Walsh. "Scholasticism in the Colonial Colleges." NEW ENGLAND QUARTERLY 5 (1932): 443-532.

1221 Walsh, Louise A., and Walsh, Matthew J. HISTORY AND ORGANIZATION OF EDUCATION IN PENNSYLVANIA. Indiana, Pa.: Grosse Print Shop, 1930. 412 p.

A general survey of educational development in Pennsylvania from the founding of the colony.

1222 Waring, Martha G. "Savannah's Earliest Private Schools, 1733-1800." GEORGIA HISTORICAL QUARTERLY 14 (1930): 324-34.

1223 Weaver, Glenn. "Benjamin Franklin and the Pennsylvania Germans." WILLIAM AND MARY QUARTERLY 14 (1957): 535-59.

1224 Wechsler, Louis K. BENJAMIN FRANKLIN: AMERICAN AND WORLD EDUCATOR. Boston: G.K. Hall and Co., 1976. 206 p.

1225 Wertenbaker, Thomas J. THE GOLDEN AGE OF COLONIAL CULTURE. New York: New York University Press, 1942. 171 p.

1226 "William and Mary College, 1771." WILLIAM AND MARY COLLEGE QUARTERLY HISTORICAL MAGAZINE 4 (1924): 277-79.

1227 "William and Mary College in 1774." WILLIAM AND MARY COLLEGE QUARTERLY HISTORICAL MAGAZINE 2 (1922): 101-13.

1228 Woody, Thomas. EARLY QUAKER EDUCATION IN PENNSYLVANIA. New York: Teachers College, Columbia University Press, 1920. 287 p.

Insightfully reviewed in AMERICAN HISTORICAL REVIEW 26 (1921): 838-39.

1229 _____, ed. EDUCATIONAL VIEWS OF BENJAMIN FRANKLIN. New York: McGraw-Hill, 1931. 270 p.

1230 Wright, Louis B. "Intellectual History and the Colonial South." WILLIAM AND MARY QUARTERLY 16 (1959): 214-27.

Chapter 7

THE GROWTH OF THE AMERICAN REPUBLIC: 1783-1865

1231 Abbott, Martin. "The Freedmen's Bureau and Negro Schooling in South Carolina." SOUTH CAROLINA HISTORICAL MAGAZINE 57 (1956): 65-81.

1232 Adams, Herbert B. THOMAS JEFFERSON AND THE UNIVERSITY OF VIRGINIA. U.S. Bureau of Education Information Circular No. 1, 1888. Washington, D.C.: Government Printing Office, 1888. 308 p.

1233 Akers, Charles N. "The Ebenezer Manual Labor School and Its Indian Pupils." ILLINOIS STATE HISTORICAL SOCIETY JOURNAL 3 (1911): 74-79.

1234 Alcott, William A. CONFESSIONS OF A SCHOOLMASTER. Andover, Mass.: Gould, Newman and Saxton, 1839. 316 p.

1235 Aldrich, F.R. "Industrial Education in the Early Nineteenth Century." ELEMENTARY SCHOOL TEACHER 13 (1913): 478-85.

An overview of the programs in this field in the nineteenth century in the United States.

1236 Allmendinger, David F., Jr. "New England Students and the Revolution in Higher Education, 1800-1900." HISTORY OF EDUCATION QUARTERLY 11 (1971): 381-89.

1237 _____. "The Strangeness of the American Education Society: Indigent Students and the New Charity, 1815-1840." HISTORY OF EDUCATION QUARTERLY 11 (1971): 3-22.

Examines how the society irrevocably established the material and administrative changes which greatly expanded the options of indigent students between 1815 and 1840.

1238 _____. "The Dangers of Ante-Bellum Student Life." JOURNAL OF SOCIAL HISTORY 7 (1973): 75-85.

1239 _____. PAUPERS AND SCHOLARS: THE TRANSFORMATION OF STU-
DENT LIFE IN NINETEENTH CENTURY NEW ENGLAND. New York:
St. Martin's Press, 1975. 160 p.

Suggests a great transformation took place in New England
student life: 1800-1860. Drawn from data mostly with regard
to: Amherst, Bowdoin, Dartmouth, Harvard, Middlebury, Vermont, and Yale.

1240 Ambrose, Stephen E. "Public Education in the Post-War South." EDU-
CATIONAL FORUM 26 (1962): 353-62.

Refers to the Reconstruction period in American history (ca.
1867-77).

1241 Anderson, Lewis F. "The Manual Labor School Movement." EDUCA-
TIONAL REVIEW 46 (1913): 369-86.

1242 Anderson, William T., Jr. "The Freedmen's Bureau and Negro Education
in Virginia." NORTH CAROLINA HISTORICAL REVIEW 29 (1952): 64-
90.

1243 Andress, J. Mace. "The Last Vestige of Puritanism in the Public Schools
of Massachusetts." SCHOOL REVIEW 20 (1912): 161-69.

Examines the public law in Massachusetts that required the
reading of a portion of the Bible "without written note or oral
comment," as enacted in 1862.

1244 Andrews, Benjamin F. THE LAND GRANT OF 1862 AND THE LAND
GRANT COLLEGES. U.S. Bureau of Education Bulletin No. 13, 1918.
Washington, D.C.: Government Printing Office, 1918. 63 p.

1245 Andrews, Edward D. "The County Grammar Schools and Academies of
Vermont." PROCEEDINGS, VERMONT HISTORICAL SOCIETY 4 (1936):
117-211.

Deals with the period: 1724-1860.

1246 Ashe, Samuel A. "Memories of Annapolis." SOUTH ATLANTIC QUAR-
TERLY 18 (1919): 197-210.

1247 Asher, Helen D. "A Frontier College of the Middle West: Hamline University, 1854-1869." MINNESOTA HISTORY 9 (1928): 363-78.

1248 Atherton, Lewis E. "Mercantile Education in the Ante-Bellum South."
MISSISSIPPI VALLEY HISTORICAL REVIEW 39 (1952-53): 623-41.

1249 Aurner, Clarence R. "Some Early Educational Leaders in Iowa." IOWA JOURNAL OF HISTORY 22 (1924): 532-68.

1250 _____. "The Founding of Iowa College." PALIMPSEST 25 (1944): 65-77.

1251 Badger, Henry G. "Colleges That Did Not Survive." JOURNAL OF NEGRO EDUCATION 35 (1966): 306-12.

1252 Bahney, Robert S. "Generals and Negroes: Education of Negroes by the Union Army, 1861-1865." Ph.D. dissertation, University of Michigan, 1965. 342 p.

1253 Bail, Hamilton V. "Harvard's Commemoration Day, July Twenty-First, 1865." NEW ENGLAND QUARTERLY 15 (1942): 256-79.

1254 Baker, Gordon E. "Thomas Jefferson and Academic Freedom." BULLETIN, AMERICAN ASSOCIATION OF UNIVERSITY PROFESSORS 39 (1953): 377-87.

1255 Barnard, Henry. LEGAL PROVISION RESPECTING THE EDUCATION AND EMPLOYMENT OF CHILDREN IN FACTORIES. Hartford, Conn.: Case, Tiffany and Burnham, 1842. 32 p.

1256 _____. SCHOOL ARCHITECTURE: OR CONTRIBUTIONS TO THE IMPROVEMENT OF SCHOOL HOUSES IN THE UNITED STATES. 5th ed. New York: Norton, 1854. 464 p.

Also includes information on school furniture, "apparatus," and the library.

1257 Baxter, Maurice. "Should the Dartmouth College Case Have Been Reargued?" NEW ENGLAND QUARTERLY 33 (1960): 19-36.

1258 Beckmer, Lucian. "Abraham Lincoln, Influences That Produced Him." FILSON CLUB (Kentucky) 33 (1959): 125-38.

1259 Belok, Michael V. "The Courtesy Tradition and Early Schoolbooks." HISTORY OF EDUCATION QUARTERLY 8 (1968): 306-18.

Deals with the attributes of a gentleman, such as: justice, prudence, temperance, fortitude, courtesy, and liberality.

1260 _____. FORMING THE AMERICAN MINDS: EARLY SCHOOL BOOKS AND THEIR COMPILERS (1783-1837). Moti Katra, India: Satish Book Enterprise, 1973. 248 p.

Examines whether or not there was a hidden, but definite, effort to forge a distinctive "American mind" after the Revolution.

1261 Belting, Paul E. "The Development of the Free Public High School in Illinois to 1860." JOURNAL OF THE ILLINOIS STATE HISTORICAL SOCIETY 11 (1918): 269-370.

1262 Bidwell, Charles E. "The Moral Significance of the Common School." HISTORY OF EDUCATION QUARTERLY 6 (1966): 50-91.

1263 Binder, Frederick M. THE AGE OF THE COMMON SCHOOL: 1860-1865. New York: Wiley, 1974. 191 p.

1264 Birnie, C.W. "The Education of the Negro in Charleston, South Carolina, Before the Civil War." JOURNAL OF NEGRO HISTORY 12 (1927): 13-21.

1265 Bixler, Paul. "Horace Mann: Mustard Seed." AMERICAN SCHOLAR 7 (1938): 24-38.

1266 Blassingame, John W. "The Union Army as an Education Institution for Negroes, 1862-1865." JOURNAL OF NEGRO EDUCATION 34 (1965): 152-59.

1267 Blaunch, L.E. "The First Uniform School System of Maryland, 1865-1868." MARYLAND HISTORICAL MAGAZINE 26 (1931): 205-27.

1268 Bone, Robert G. "Education in Illinois Before 1857." JOURNAL, ILLINOIS STATE HISTORICAL SOCIETY 50 (1957): 119-40.

1269 Borrowman, Merle. "The False Dawn of the State University." HISTORY OF EDUCATION QUARTERLY 1 (1961): 6-22.

1270 Boskin, Joseph. "The Origin of American Slavery: Education as an Index of Early Differentiation." JOURNAL OF NEGRO EDUCATION 35 (1966): 125-33.

1271 Boyd, W.W. "Secondary Education in Ohio Previous to the Year 1840." OHIO HISTORICAL QUARTERLY 25 (1916): 118-34.

1272 Brigham, R.I. "Negro Education in Ante-Bellum Missouri." JOURNAL OF NEGRO HISTORY 30 (1945): 405-20.

1273 Brockett, Limus P. HISTORY OF PROGRESS OF EDUCATION FROM THE

EARLIEST TIMES TO THE PRESENT. New York: A.S. Barnes and Burr, 1860. 310 p.

> Intended as a manual for students and teachers, c. 1860.
> Appeared under the pseudonym of "Philobiblius" with an intro-
> duction by Henry Barnard.

1274 Brooks, Harold C. "Founding of the Michigan Public School System." MICHIGAN HISTORY 33 (1949): 291-306.

1275 Brown, R.M. "Agricultural Science and Education in Virginia Before 1860." WILLIAM AND MARY COLLEGE QUARTERLY HISTORICAL MAGAZINE 19 (1939): 197-213.

1276 Browne, C.A. "History of Chemical Education in America, 1820-1870." JOURNAL OF CHEMICAL EDUCATION 9 (1932): 718-20.

1277 Browne, Henry J. "Public Support of Catholic Education in New York, 1825-1842: Some Aspects." CATHOLIC HISTORICAL REVIEW 39 (1953): 1-27.

1278 Bruce, Phillip A. "Recollections of My Plantation Teachers." SOUTH ATLANTIC QUARTERLY 16 (1917): 1-13.

1279 Bunkle, Phillida. "Sentimental Womanhood and Domestic Education, 1830-1870." HISTORY OF EDUCATION QUARTERLY 14 (1974): 13-30.

> An antifeminist ideology as extant in the North, 1830-1870.
> Defined women as essentially spiritual, emotional, and depen-
> dent beings.

1280 Burgess, Charles O. "William Maclure and Education for a Good Society." HISTORY OF EDUCATION QUARTERLY 3 (1963): 58-76.

1281 _____. "Two Tendencies of Educational Thought in the New Nation: America as a Presbyterian City on a Hill or As a Deist's Island in the Sea." PAEDAGOGICA HISTORICA 4 (1964): 326-42.

1282 Burnett, Howard R. "Early History of Vincennes University." INDIANA MAGAZINE OF HISTORY 29 (1933): 114-21.

1283 Burrage, Henry S. BROWN UNIVERSITY IN THE CIVIL WAR. Provi-dence: Providence Press Company Printers, 1868. 380 p.

1284 Butts, R. Freeman. "James Madison, the Bill of Rights, and Education." TEACHERS COLLEGE RECORD 60 (1958): 121-28.

1285 Calhoun, F.P. "The Founding and the Early History of the Atlanta Medical College." GEORGIA HISTORICAL QUARTERLY 9 (1925): 34–54.

1286 Calkins, Earnest E. THEY BROKE THE PRAIRIE; BEING SOME ACCOUNT OF THE SETTLEMENT OF THE UPPER MISSISSIPPI VALLEY BY RELIGIOUS AND EDUCATIONAL PIONEERS, TOLD IN TERMS OF ONE CITY, GALESBURG, AND OF ONE COLLEGE, KNOX. New York: Charles Scribner's Sons, 1937. 451 p.

1287 Capen, Eliza P. "Zilpah Grant and the Art of Teaching: 1829." NEW ENGLAND QUARTERLY 20 (1947): 347–64.

> About Ipswich Female Academy in Massachusetts in the days of Mary Lyon.

1288 Carlton, Frank T. ECONOMIC INFLUENCES UPON EDUCATIONAL PROGRESS IN THE UNITED STATES, 1820–1850. New York: Teachers College, Columbia University Press, 1966. 165 p.

> An influential Ph.D. dissertation (University of Wisconsin, 1908) which stressed economic determinism.

1289 Carrier, Lyman. "The United States Agricultural Society, 1852–1860: Its Relation to the Origin of the United States Department of Agriculture and the Land Grant Colleges." AGRICULTURAL HISTORY 11 (1937): 278–88.

1290 Carroll, J.C. "The Beginnings of Public Education for Negroes in Indiana." JOURNAL OF NEGRO EDUCATION 8 (1939): 649–58.

1291 Castel, Albert. "The Founding Fathers and the Vision of a National University." HISTORY OF EDUCATION QUARTERLY 4 (1964): 280–302.

1292 Chinard, Gilbert. "Thomas Jefferson as a Classical Scholar." AMERICAN SCHOLAR 1 (1932): 133–43.

1293 Churchill, Alfred V. "The Founding of Oberlin." NORTHWEST OHIO QUARTERLY 23 (1951): 107–32, 158–78.

1294 Clark, Thomas D. "Arts and Sciences on the Early American Frontier." NEBRASKA HISTORY MAGAZINE 37 (1956): 247–68.

1295 Coburn, Frank E. "The Educational Level of the Jacksonians." HISTORY OF EDUCATION QUARTERLY 7 (1967): 515–20.

> Rejects assumption that the Jacksonians were educationally inferior to their predecessors in political office.

1296 Colbourn, H. Trevor. "Thomas Jefferson's Use of the Past." WILLIAM
      AND MARY QUARTERLY 15 (1958): 56-70.

1297 Collacott, Mary H. "Education of Women in the United States in the
      Period of the Young Ladies' Seminary." WESTERN RESERVE UNIVERSITY
      BULLETIN 16 (1913): 43-50.

1298 Come, Donald R. "The Influence of Princeton on Higher Education in
      the South Before 1825." WILLIAM AND MARY QUARTERLY 2 (1945):
      359-96.

1299 Constantine, Robert. "Minutes of the Board of Trustees for Vincennes
      University, 1801-1824." INDIANA MAGAZINE OF HISTORY 54 (1956):
      313-64; 55 (1959): 247-92; 57 (1961): 311-68.

1300 Coulter, E. Merton. "The Ante-Bellum Academy Movement in Georgia."
      GEORGIA HISTORICAL QUARTERLY 5 (1921): 11-42.

1301 _____. "A Georgia Educational Movement During the Eighteen Hundred
      Fifties." GEORGIA HISTORICAL QUARTERLY 9 (1925): 1-33.

1302 _____. "Why John and Joseph LeConte Left the University of Georgia,
      1855-1856." GEORGIA HISTORICAL QUARTERLY 53 (1969): 18-40.

1303 Crabb, A.L. "The Rise of the Normal School." NATIONAL EDUCA-
      TION ASSOCIATION JOURNAL 19 (1930): 239-40.

          A brief sketch of the first normal schools in early nineteenth-
          century America.

1304 Crandall, John C. "Patriotism and Humanitarian Reform in Children's
      Literature, 1825-1860." AMERICAN QUARTERLY 21 (1969): 3-22.

1305 Farmer, Fannie M. "Legal Education in North Carolina, 1820-1860."
      NORTH CAROLINA HISTORICAL REVIEW 38 (1951): 271-97.

1306 Farrell, Emma L. "The New Harmony Experiment, An Origin of Progres-
      sive Education." PEABODY JOURNAL OF EDUCATION 15 (1938): 357-
      61.

          An account of Joseph Neef's Socialist experiments at New
          Harmony, Indiana, in the early nineteenth century.

1307 FEDERAL LAWS AND RULINGS RELATING TO MORRILL AND SUPPLE-
      MENTARY MORRILL FUNDS FOR LAND-GRANT COLLEGES AND UNI-
      VERSITIES. U.S. Office of Education Pamphlet No. 91, 1940. Wash-
      ington, D.C.: Government Printing Office, 1940. 16 p.

1308 Fen, Sing-Nan. "Notes on the Education of Negroes in North Carolina During the Civil War." JOURNAL OF NEGRO EDUCATION 36 (1967): 24-31.

1309 Filler, Louis, ed. HORACE MANN ON THE CRISIS IN EDUCATION. Yellow Springs, Ohio: Antioch Press, 1965. 340 p.

   Extensive extracts from Mann on the aims and problems of education, with notes by the editor.

1310 Fisher, Berenice M. "Public Education and Special Interest: An Example from the History of Mechanical Engineering." HISTORY OF EDUCATION QUARTERLY 6 (1966): 31-40.

1311 Fitsgerald, Virginia. "A Southern College Boy Eighty Years Ago." SOUTH ATLANTIC QUARTERLY 20 (1921): 236-46.

1312 Fleming, Walter L. "William Tecumseh Sherman as College President." SOUTH ATLANTIC QUARTERLY 11 (1912): 33-54.

1313 Fletcher, Robert S. "Oberlin and Co-Education." NORTHWEST OHIO QUARTERLY 47 (1938): 1-19.

1314 Florer, John H. "Major Issues in the Congressional Debate on the Morrill Act of 1862." HISTORY OF EDUCATION QUARTERLY 8 (1968): 459-78.

1315 Ford, Paul M. "Calvin Wiley's View of the Negro." NORTH CAROLINA HISTORICAL REVIEW 41 (1964): 1-20.

1316 Foster, Ashley. "An 1803 Proposal to Improve the American Teaching Profession." SCHOOL AND SOCIETY 80 (1954): 69-73.

1317 Foster, Frank C. "Horace Mann as Philosopher." EDUCATIONAL THEORY 10 (1960): 9-25.

1318 Freidel, Frank. "A Plan for Modern Education in Early Philadelphia." PENNSYLVANIA HISTORY 14 (1947): 175-84.

   Refers to Girard College in Philadelphia.

1319 Freimarck, Vincent. "Rhetoric at Yale in 1807." PROCEEDINGS, AMERICAN PHILOSOPHICAL SOCIETY 110 (1966): 235-55.

1320 Fuller, Edmund. PRUDENCE CRANDALL: AN INCIDENT OF RACISM IN NINETEENTH-CENTURY CONNECTICUT. Middletown, Conn.: Wesleyan University Press, 1971. 113 p.

Deals with violence directed against Crandall's school for
black girls at Canterbury, Connecticut, in 1831-1833 era.
This incident is also treated in L.L. Richards's 1970 study on:
GENTLEMEN OF PROPERTY AND STANDING: ANTI-ABOLI-
TION MOBS IN JACKSONIAN AMERICA.

1321 Fulton, C.J. "The Beginnings of Education in Iowa." IOWA JOURNAL
OF HISTORY 23 (1925): 171-91.

1322 Garrett, Jane N. "The Delaware College Lotteries, 1818-1845." DELA-
WARE HISTORY 7 (1957): 299-318.

1323 Gatke, Robert M. "The First Indian School of the Pacific Northwest."
OREGON HISTORICAL SOCIETY QUARTERLY 23 (1922): 70-83.

About the Oregon Mission of the Methodist Episcopal Church:
1835-1844.

1324 Good, Harry G. "Who First Proposed a National University?" SCHOOL
AND SOCIETY 3 (1916): 387-91.

It was Benjamin Rush.

1325 _____. "New Data on Early Engineering Education." JOURNAL OF
EDUCATIONAL RESEARCH 29 (1935-36): 37-46.

1326 _____. "Emerson, An Educational Liberal." HISTORY OF EDUCA-
TIONAL JOURNAL 1 (1949): 7-20.

1327 Goode, G. Brown. "The Origin of the National Scientific and Educational Institutions of the United States." ANNUAL REPORT, AMERICAN
HISTORICAL ASSOCIATION, 1889 (1890): 53-161.

1328 Goodfellow, Donald M. "The First Boylston Professor of Rhetoric and
History." NEW ENGLAND QUARTERLY 19 (1946): 372-89.

It was John Quincy Adams who was so appointed in 1805.

1329 Goodsell, Willystine, ed. PIONEERS OF WOMEN'S EDUCATION IN
THE UNITED STATES: EMMA WILLARD, CATHERINE BEECHER, MARY
LYON. New York: McGraw-Hill, 1931. 311 p.

Essentially educational biographies of these three, together
with some of their writings on education.

1330 Greene, Evarts B. "Some Educational Values of the American Revolution."
PROCEEDINGS, AMERICAN PHILOSOPHICAL SOCIETY 68 (1920): 85-
194.

1331 Gresham, Luveta W. "Colonization Proposals for Free Negroes and Con-
trabands During the Civil War." JOURNAL OF NEGRO EDUCATION
16 (1947): 28-33.

1332 Guralnick, Stanley M. SCIENCE AND THE ANTEBELLUM AMERICAN
COLLEGE. Philadelphia: American Philosophical Society, 1975. 340 p.

1333 Haar, Charles M. "E.L. Youmans: A Chapter in the Diffusion of Science
in America." JOURNAL OF THE HISTORY OF IDEAS 9 (1948): 193-213.

1334 Hall, D.D. "A Yankee Tutor in the Old South." NEW ENGLAND
QUARTERLY 33 (1960): 82-91.

1335 Hamilton, J.G. deRoulhac. "The Freedmen's Bureau in North Carolina."
SOUTH ATLANTIC QUARTERLY 8 (1909): 154-63.

1336 Hammond, William G. REMEMBRANCE OF AMHERST. New York:
Columbia University Press, 1946. 210 p.

    Reprint of a diary of an Amherst undergraduate, 1846-1848.

1337 Harding, Thomas S. COLLEGE LITERARY SOCIETIES: THEIR CONTRI-
BUTION TO HIGHER EDUCATION IN THE UNITED STATES, 1815-1876.
New York: Pageant Press, 1971. 537 p.

    Essentially a collection of data that appeared before 1956
    with a survey discussion of the societies and their libraries.

1338 Harding, Walter. "Henry D. Thoreau, Instructor." EDUCATIONAL
FORUM 29 (1964): 89-97.

1339 Hargrell, Lester. "Student Life at the University of Georgia in the
1840s." GEORGIA HISTORICAL QUARTERLY 8 (1924): 49-59.

1340 Harlan, Louis R. "Desegregation in New Orleans Public Schools During
Reconstruction." AMERICAN HISTORICAL REVIEW 67 (1962): 663-75.

1341 Harris, William T. "On Horace Mann." In U.S. BUREAU OF EDUCA-
TION, REPORT OF THE COMMISSIONER, 1895-1896. Washington, D.C.:
Government Printing Office, 1897. Vol. 1, pp. 887-97.

    Also appears in: EDUCATIONAL REVIEW 12 (1896): 105-19.

1342 Harrison, Lowell H. "William Duane on Education: A Letter to the Kentucky Assembly, 1822." PENNSYLVANIA MAGAZINE OF HISTORY AND
BIOGRAPHY 73 (1949): 316-25.

1343 Hatch, Richard A., comp. SOME FOUNDING PAPERS ON THE UNI-
VERSITY OF ILLINOIS. Urbana: University of Illinois Press, 1967. 139 p.

Includes: speeches of Jonathan B. Turner: 1850-1871, text of
Morrill Act, and Illinois enabling legislation among other miscellaneous documents relevant to this period.

1344 Haunton, Richard H. "Education and Democracy: The Views of Philip
Lindsley." TENNESSEE HISTORICAL QUARTERLY 21 (1962): 131-39.

1345 Hayes, Cecil B. THE AMERICAN LYCEUM, ITS HISTORY AND CON-
TRIBUTION TO EDUCATION. Office of Education Bulletin No. 12,
1932. Washington, D.C.: Government Printing Office, 1932. 72 p.

1346 Heimstra, William L. "Presbyterian Mission Schools Among the Choctaws
and Chickesaws (1845-1860)." CHRONICLES OF OKLAHOMA 27 (1949):
33-40.

1347 "Henry Barnard." In THE UNITED STATES BUREAU OF EDUCATION,
REPORT OF THE COMMISSIONER, 1902, pp. 887-928. Washington,
D.C.: Government Printing Office, 1903.

1348 Heslep, Robert D. "Thomas Jefferson's View of Equal Social Opportunity."
EDUCATIONAL THEORY 13 (1963): 142-48.

1349 Hewitt, John H. "Contributions to the History of American Teaching:
College Education Fifty Years Ago." EDUCATIONAL REVIEW 39 (1910):
227-37.

1350 Hill, Benjamin T. "Life at Harvard a Century Ago as Illustrated by the
Papers of Stephen Salisbury, Class of 1817." PROCEEDINGS, AMERICAN
ANTIQUARIAN SOCIETY 20 (1910): 197-248.

1351 Hinsdale, Burke A. "The History of Popular Education on the Western
Reserve." OHIO HISTORICAL QUARTERLY 6 (1898): 35-59.

1352 Hislop, Codman. ELIPHALET NOTT. Middletown, Conn.: Wesleyan
University Press, 1971. 680 p.

An educational biography of Nott, who was president of Union
College (1804-66), and who was noted as an educational innovator.

1353 Hobson, Elsie G. EDUCATIONAL LEGISLATION AND ADMINISTRATION
IN THE STATE OF NEW YORK FROM 1777 TO 1850. Chicago: University of Chicago Press, 1918. 267 p.

Published in conjunction with the SCHOOL REVIEW AND
ELEMENTARY SCHOOL JOURNAL 3 (1918): entire issue.
See review in: AMERICAN HISTORICAL REVIEW 24 (1919):
486-88.

1354 Hollingsworth, R.R. "Education and Reconstruction in Georgia." GEOR-
GIA HISTORICAL QUARTERLY 19 (1935): 112-33, 229-50.

1355 Honeywell, Roy J. THE EDUCATIONAL WORK OF THOMAS JEFFERSON.
Cambridge, Mass.: Harvard University Press, 1931. 295 p.

1356 _____. "A Note on the Educational Work of Thomas Jefferson." HIS-
TORY OF EDUCATION QUARTERLY 9 (1969): 64-72.

Based on his earlier book (see entry no. 1355) about Jefferson
as the father of the University of Virginia and of his proposals
on education systems.

1357 Hoover, Thomas N. "The Beginnings of Higher Education in the Northwest Territory." NORTHWEST OHIO QUARTERLY 50 (1941): 244-60.

1358 Howison, G.H. "Contributions to the History of American Teaching:
Academy and College in Early Ohio." EDUCATIONAL REVIEW 40 (1910):
455-72.

1359 Hoyl, William D., Jr. "Richard Henry Dana and the Lecture System,
1841." NEW ENGLAND QUARTERLY 18 (1945): 93-96.

1360 Hubbell, George A. "Horace Mann and Antioch College." OHIO HIS-
TORICAL QUARTERLY 14 (1905): 12-28.

1361 Hutcheson, James M. "Virginia's 'Dartmouth College Case.'" VIRGINIA
MAGAZINE OF HISTORY AND BIOGRAPHY 51 (1943): 134-40.

1362 Hutchison, Keith R. "James Gordon Carter, Educational Reformer."
NEW ENGLAND QUARTERLY 16 (1943): 376-96.

1363 Isbell, Egbert R. "The Universities of Virginia and Michigania." MICHI-
GAN HISTORY 26 (1942): 39-52.

1364 Jackson, L.P. "The Educational Efforts of the Freedmen's Bureau and
Freedmen's Aid Societies in South Carolina, 1862-1872." JOURNAL OF
NEGRO HISTORY 8 (1923): 1-40.

1365 Jackson, Sidney L. "Labor, Education and Politics in the 1830's."
PENNSYLVANIA MAGAZINE OF HISTORY AND BIOGRAPHY 66 (1942):
279-93.

1366 _____. "Some Ancestors of the 'Extension Course.'" NEW ENGLAND QUARTERLY 14 (1941): 505-18.

1367 _____. "An Unknown Ben Franklin." HARVARD EDUCATIONAL RE-VIEW 11 (1941): 102-11.

About Joseph Curtis, a somewhat unknown New York educational pioneer (1782-1856).

1368 [Jefferson, Thomas]. "Letters from Thomas Jefferson to William B. Giles in Regard to Central College [4 August 1817]." VIRGINIA MAGAZINE OF HISTORY AND BIOGRAPHY 29 (1921): 445-47.

Central College was the precursor of the University of Virginia.

1369 Jenkins, Elizabeth. "How the Kindergarten Found its Way to America." WISCONSIN MAGAZINE OF HISTORY 14 (1930): 48-62.

Mrs. Carl Schurz founded the first kindergarten in America at Watertown, Wisconsin, in 1856.

1370 _____. "Froebel's Disciples in America." AMERICAN-GERMAN REVIEW 3 (1937): 15-18.

About the work of Mrs. Carl Schurz, Caroline L. Frankenberg, and Emma Marwedel, founders of the earliest kindergartens in the United States (on the German model).

1371 Jewett, James P. "Moral Education in American Secondary Schools Before the Civil War." HISTORY OF EDUCATION JOURNAL 3 (1951): 18-26.

Predicated upon William Paley's PRINCIPLES OF MORAL AND POLITICAL PHILOSOPHY, and Francis Wayland's, THE ELEMENTS OF INTELLECTUAL PHILOSOPHY AND THE ELEMENTS OF MORAL SCIENCE.

1372 _____. "The Fight Against Corporal Punishment in American Schools." HISTORY OF EDUCATION JOURNAL 4 (1952): 1-10.

1373 Johnson, Richard M. "Early Educational Life in Middle Georgia." In UNITED STATES BUREAU OF EDUCATION, REPORT OF THE COMMISSIONER, 1894-1895. Washington, D.C.: Government Printing Office, 1896-97.

In two parts: (1896): 1699-1733, and (1897): 839-86.

1374 Johnson, T. Walter. "Peter Akers, Methodist Circuit Rider and Educator, 1790-1886." JOURNAL OF THE ILLINOIS STATE HISTORICAL SOCIETY 32 (1939): 417-41.

1375 Jones, Edgar D. "Educational Pathfinders of Illinois." JOURNAL OF THE ILLINOIS STATE HISTORICAL SOCIETY 24 (1931): 1-11.

1376 Jones, Lewis W. "The Agent as a Factor in the Education of Negroes in the South." JOURNAL OF NEGRO EDUCATION 19 (1950): 28-37.

1377 Juettner, Otto. "Rise of Medical Colleges in the Ohio Valley." OHIO HISTORICAL QUARTERLY 22 (1913): 481-91.

1378 Kaplan, Sidney. "The Reduction of Teachers' Salaries in Post-Revolutionary Boston." NEW ENGLAND QUARTERLY 21 (1948): 373-79.

1379 Kelly, Alfred H. "The Congressional Controversy over School Segregation, 1867-1875." AMERICAN HISTORICAL REVIEW 64 (1959): 537-63.

1380 Kerr, Robert V. "The Wittenberg Manual Labor College." IOWA JOURNAL OF HISTORY 24 (1926): 290-304.

1381 Kilpatrick, William H. "The Beginnings of the Public School System in Georgia." GEORGIA HISTORICAL QUARTERLY 5 (1921): 3-19.

1382 King, Emma. "Some Aspects of the Work of the Society of Friends for Negro Education in North Carolina." NORTH CAROLINA HISTORICAL REVIEW 1 (1924): 403-11.

1383 Klatt, Albert G. "A Brief Survey of the Events Pertaining to Education Previous to the Organization of Minnesota as a Territory." SCHOOL REVIEW 24 (1916): 603-09.

1384 Knauss, J.O. "Education in Florida, 1821-1829." FLORIDA HISTORICAL QUARTERLY 3 (1925): 22-35.

1385 Knight, Edgar W. "Some Fallacies Concerning the History of Public Education in the South." SOUTH ATLANTIC QUARTERLY 13 (1914): 371-81.

1386 _____. "The Peabody Fund and Its Early Operation in North Carolina." SOUTH ATLANTIC QUARTERLY 14 (1915): 186-80.

1387 _____. "Reconstruction and Education in Virginia." SOUTH ATLANTIC QUARTERLY 15 (1916): 25-40, 157-74.

1388 _____. "Manual Labor Schools in the South." SOUTH ATLANTIC QUARTERLY 16 (1917): 209-21.

1389 _____. "Some Evidence of Horace Mann's Influence in the South."
SCHOOL AND SOCIETY 65 (1947): 33-37.

1390 _____. "More Evidence of Horace Mann's Influence in the South."
EDUCATIONAL FORUM 12 (1948): 167-84.

1391 _____. "North Carolina's Dartmouth College Case." JOURNAL OF
HIGHER EDUCATION 19 (1948): 116-22.

1392 _____. "Some Evidence of Henry Barnard's Influence in the South."
EDUCATIONAL FORUM 13 (1949): 301-12.

1393 _____. "Southern Opposition to Northern Education." EDUCATIONAL
FORUM 14 (1949): 47-58.

1394 Knight, George W. "Higher Education in the North West Territory."
In UNITED STATES BUREAU OF EDUCATION, REPORT OF THE COMMIS-
SIONER, 1887-1888, pp. 1039-47. Washington, D.C.: Government
Printing Office, 1889.

1395 Kurwitz, "Benjamin Rush: His Theory of Republican Education." HISTORY
OF EDUCATION QUARTERLY 7 (1969): 432-51.

1396 Lannie, Vincent P. "William Seward and Common School Education."
HISTORY OF EDUCATION QUARTERLY 4 (1964): 181-92.

1397 _____. "William Seward and the New York School Controversy, 1840-
1842: A Problem in Historical Motivation." HISTORY OF EDUCATION
QUARTERLY 6 (1966): 52-71.

1398 _____. PUBLIC MONEY AND PAROCHIAL EDUCATION. Cleveland:
Press of Case Western Reserve University, 1968. 282 p.

    Deals with the bitter conflict, in 1840-1842, between Roman
    Catholic Bishop Hughes and the Public School Society over the
    form of public education that shaped both American public
    and Catholic education for years to come.

1399 Lannie, Vincent P., and Diethorn, Bernard C. "For the Honor and Glory
of God: The Philadelphia Bible Riots of 1840." HISTORY OF EDUCA-
TION QUARTERLY 8 (1968): 44-106.

1400 Laqueur, Thomas W. RELIGION AND RESPECTABILITY: SUNDAY
SCHOOLS AND WORKING CLASS CULTURE, 1780-1850. New Haven,
Conn.: Yale University Press, 1976. 293 p.

1401 Lauderdale, Virginia E. "Tullahassee Mission." CHRONICLES OF OKLA-
HOMA 26 (1948): 285-300.

About the Presbyterian missions in Creek Indian territory in
1850.

1402 Lazerson, Marvin. "F.A.P. Bernard and Columbia College: Prologue to
a University." HISTORY OF EDUCATION QUARTERLY 6 (1966): 49-64.

1403 Lee, Gordon C. "The Morrill Act and Education." BRITISH JOURNAL
OF EDUCATIONAL STUDIES 12 (1963): 19-40.

1404 Levy, Leonard W., and Phillips, Harlan B. "The Roberts Case: Source
of the Separate But Equal Doctrine." AMERICAN HISTORICAL REVIEW
56 (1951): 510-18.

1405 Lewis, Albert. "Emerson and Educational Reconstruction." EDUCATION-
AL FORUM 8 (1944): 449-57.

1406 Lewis, Miriam E. "The Mutiny of the Wilmington Academy, 1777-1802."
DELAWARE HISTORY 3 (1949): 181-226.

1407 Littell, Harold. "Development of the City School System of Indiana."
INDIANA MAGAZINE OF HISTORY 12 (1916): 193-213, 299-325.

1408 Lockard, E. Kidd. "The Influence of New England in Denominational
Colleges in the Northwest (1830-1860)." NORTHWEST OHIO QUARTER-
LY 53 (1944): 1-14.

1409 Lottich, Kenneth V. "The Oldest University in the West." SCHOOL
AND SOCIETY 73 (1951): 193-96.

1410 _____. "Democracy and Education in the Early American Northwest."
PAEDAGOGICA HISTORICA 2 (1962): 234-54.

1411 _____. "Educational Leadership in Early Ohio." HISTORY OF EDUCA-
TION QUARTERLY 2 (1962): 52-61.

1412 Low, W.A. "The Freedmen's Bureau and Education in Maryland." MARY-
LAND HISTORICAL MAGAZINE 47 (1952): 29-39.

1413 Lyman, Rollo L. ENGLISH GRAMMAR IN AMERICAN SCHOOLS BEFORE
1850. U.S. Bureau of Education Bulletin No. 12, 1921. Washington,
D.C.: Government Printing Office, 1922. 170 p.

1414 Mabee, Carleton. "A Negro Boycott to Integrate Boston Schools." NEW ENGLAND QUARTERLY 41 (1968): 341-61.

1415 McAlpina, William. "The Origin of Public Education in Ohio." NORTHWEST OHIO QUARTERLY 38 (1929): 409-47.

1416 McCadden, Joseph J. "Joseph Lancaster and the Philadelphia Schools." PENNSYLVANIA HISTORY 33 (1936): 225-39; 4 (1937): 241-47.

1417 _____. "Bishop Hughes Versus the Public School Society of New York." CATHOLIC HISTORICAL REVIEW 50 (1964): 188-207.

1418 McCain, William D. "Education in Mississippi in 1860." JOURNAL OF MISSISSIPPI HISTORY 22 (1960): 156-66.

1419 McCaughey, Robert A. "The Transformation of American Academic Life: Harvard University, 1821-1892." PERSPECTIVES IN AMERICAN HISTORY 8 (1974): 237-332.

1420 McDermott, John F. "Private Schools in St. Louis, 1809-1821." MID-AMERICA 9 (1940): 96-119.

1421 McGroarty, W.B. "Alexandria's Lancasterian Schools." WILLIAM AND MARY COLLEGE QUARTERLY HISTORICAL MAGAZINE 21 (1941): 111-18.

1422 MacLear, Martha. THE HISTORY OF THE EDUCATION OF GIRLS IN NEW YORK AND IN NEW ENGLAND, 1800-1870. Washington, D.C.: Howard University Press, 1926. 123 p.

1423 Madsen, David. EARLY NATIONAL EDUCATION, 1776-1830. New York: Wiley, 1974. 162 p.

1424 Manly, John M. "Educational Ideals of 1850." SCHOOL REVIEW 24 (1916): 746-51.

1425 Martin, Asa E. "Pennsylvania's Land Grant Under the Morrill Act of 1862." PENNSYLVANIA HISTORY 9 (1942): 85-117.

1426 Martin, George H. "Horace Mann and the Revival of Education in Massachusetts." EDUCATIONAL REVIEW 5 (1893): 434-50.

1427 Martin, William J. "The Old Log School, A Chronicle of Rural Education." WESTERN PENNSYLVANIA HISTORICAL MAGAZINE 16 (1933): 163-73.

1428 Mattingly, Paul H. "Educational Rivals in Ante-Bellum New England." HISTORY OF EDUCATION QUARTERLY 11 (1971): 39-71.

> Deals with the Teacher's Institute's origins, decline and eclipse, as well as shifts in educational policy prior to the Civil War in conceptual terms.

1429 Mayo, Amory D. "The American Common School in New England from 1790 to 1840." In UNITED STATES BUREAU OF EDUCATION, REPORT OF THE COMMISSIONER, 1894-1895, Vol. 2, pp. 1551-615. Washington, D.C.: Government Printing Office, 1896.

1430 _____. "Education in the Northwest During the First Half Century of the Republic, 1790-1840." In UNITED STATES BUREAU OF EDUCATION, REPORT OF THE COMMISSIONER, 1894-1895. Vol. 2, pp. 1513-50. Washington, D.C.: Government Printing Office, 1896.

1431 _____. "The American Common School in New York, New Jersey, and Pennsylvania During the First Half Century of the Republic." In UNITED STATES BUREAU OF EDUCATION, REPORT OF THE COMMISSIONER, 1895-1896. Vol. 1, pp. 219-66. Washington, D.C.: Government Printing Office, 1897.

1432 _____. "The American School in the Southern States During the First Half Century of the Republic, 1790-1840." In UNITED STATES BUREAU OF EDUCATION, REPORT OF THE COMMISSIONER, 1895-1896. Vol. 1, pp. 267-338. Washington, D.C.: Government Printing Office, 1897.

1433 _____. "Henry Barnard." In UNITED STATES BUREAU OF EDUCATION, REPORT OF THE COMMISSIONER, 1896-1897. Vol. 1, pp. 769-810. Washington, D.C.: Government Printing Office, 1898.

1434 _____. "Horace Mann and the American Common School." In UNITED STATES BUREAU OF EDUCATION, REPORT OF THE COMMISSIONER, 1896-1897, pp. 715-67. Washington, D.C.: Government Printing Office, 1898.

1435 _____. "The Development of the Common School in the Western States from 1830 to 1865." In UNITED STATES BUREAU OF EDUCATION, REPORT OF THE COMMISSIONER, 1899. Vol. 1, pp. 1367-71. Washington, D.C.: Government Printing Office, 1900.

1436 _____. "The Organization and Development of the American Common School in the Atlantic and Central States of the South, 1830 to 1860." In UNITED STATES BUREAU OF EDUCATION, REPORT OF THE COMMISSIONER, 1899-1900." Vol. 1, pp. 65-69. Washington, D.C.: Government Printing Office, 1901.

1437 _____. "Common School Education in the South from the Beginning of the Civil War to 1870-1876." In UNITED STATES BUREAU OF EDUCATION, REPORT OF THE COMMISSIONER, 1900-1901. Vol. 1, pp. 429-541. Washington, D.C.: Government Printing Office, 1902.

1438 _____. "The Common School in the Southern States Beyond the Mississippi River From 1830 to 1860." In UNITED STATES BUREAU OF EDUCATION, REPORT OF THE COMMISSIONER, 1900-1901. Vol. 1, pp. 285-314. Washington, D.C.: Government Printing Office, 1902.

1439 Messerli, Jonathan C. "Horace Mann at Brown." HARVARD EDUCATIONAL REVIEW 33 (1963): 285-311.

1440 _____. "James G. Carter's Liabilities as a Common School Reformer." HISTORY OF EDUCATION QUARTERLY 5 (1965): 14-25.

1441 _____. "Localism and State Control in Horace Mann's Reform of the Common Schools." AMERICAN QUARTERLY 17 (1965): 104-18.

1442 _____. "Horace Mann's Childhood: Myth and Reality." EDUCATIONAL FORUM 30 (1966): 159-68.

1443 _____. "The Columbia Complex: The Impulse to National Consolidation." HISTORY OF EDUCATION QUARTERLY 7 (1967): 417-31.

1444 Meyers, Mary A. "The Children's Crusade: Philadelphia Catholics and the Public Schools, 1840-1844." RECORDS, AMERICAN CATHOLIC HISTORICAL SOCIETY OF PHILADELPHIA 75 (1964): 103-27.

1445 Miles, Edwin A. "The Old South and the Classical World." NORTH CAROLINA HISTORICAL REVIEW 48 (1971): 258-75.

1446 _____. "The Young American Nation and the Classical World." JOURNAL OF THE HISTORY OF IDEAS 35 (1974): 259-74.

1447 Miller, Edward A. "High Schools in Ohio Prior to 1850." SCHOOL REVIEW 38 (1920): 454-69.

1448 _____. THE HISTORY OF EDUCATIONAL LEGISLATION IN OHIO FROM 1803 TO 1850. Chicago: n.p., 1920. 271 p.

　　　　Also appears in: NORTHWESTERN OHIO QUARTERLY 37 (1918): 1-271.

1449 Miller, James L., Jr. "Transylvania University as the Nation Saw It, 1818-1820." FILSON CLUB 34 (1960): 305-18.

1450 Mills, Edward C. "Dental Education in Ohio (1838-1858). NORTHWEST OHIO QUARTERLY 51 (1942): 332-40; 52 (1943): 356-72.

1451 Mintz, Max M. "Robert Morris and John Jay on Education: Two Letters." PENNSYLVANIA MAGAZINE OF HISTORY AND BIOGRAPHY 74 (1950): 340-47.

1452 Moffat, Walter. "Arkansas Schools, 1819-1840." ARKANSAS HISTORICAL QUARTERLY 12 (1953): 91-105.

1453 Mohl, Raymond A. "Education as Social Control in New York City, 1784-1825." NEW YORK HISTORY 51 (1970): 219-37.

1454 Mohr, James C. "New York State's Free School Law of 1867: A Chapter in the Reconstruction of the North." NEW YORK HISTORICAL SOCIETY QUARTERLY 53 (1969): 230-40.

1455 Morison, Samuel E. "The Great Rebellion in Harvard College and the Resignation of President Kirkland." PUBLICATIONS, COLONIAL SOCIETY OF MASSACHUSETTS 27 (1927-30): 54-112.

1456 Mosier, Richard D. "Educational Theories of the American Transcendentalists." HISTORY OF EDUCATION JOURNAL 3 (1952): 33-42.

On how they rediscovered, in a different context, the Socratic admonition that man should know himself, and that such self-knowledge should be valued above all other kinds of knowledge.

1457 Nash, Paul. "Innocents Abroad: American Students at British Universities in the Early Nineteenth Century." HISTORY OF EDUCATION QUARTERLY 1 (1961): 32-44.

1458 Naylor, Natalie. "The Ante-Bellum College Movement: A Reappraisal of Tewkesbury's THE FOUNDING OF AMERICAN COLLEGES AND UNIVERSITIES." HISTORY OF EDUCATION QUARTERLY 13 (1973): 261-74.

1459 Newman, Otto L. "Development of the Common Schools of Indiana." INDIANA MAGAZINE OF HISTORY 22 (1926): 216-29.

1460 Nietz, John A. "Horace Mann's Ideas on General Methods in Education." ELEMENTARY SCHOOL JOURNAL 37 (1937): 742-51.

1461 _____. "Some Findings From Analyses of Old Textbooks." HISTORY OF EDUCATION JOURNAL 3 (1952): 79-87.

1462 _____. "Why the Longevity of the McGuffey Readers?" HISTORY OF EDUCATION QUARTERLY 4 (1964): 119-25.

1463 _____. THE EVOLUTION OF AMERICAN SECONDARY SCHOOL TEXT-BOOKS . . . BEFORE 1900. Rutland, Vt.: Charles E. Tuttle, 1965. 265 p.

Textbooks from American secondary schools before 1900 in rhetoric, literature, algebra, geometry, zoology, botany, physics, chemistry, Latin, Greek, French, German, and world history.

1464 Nolan, Val, Jr. "Caleb Mills and the Indiana Free School Law." INDIANA MAGAZINE OF HISTORY 49 (1953): 81-90.

1465 North, Sue. "Damyankees in Negro Schools." AMERICAN HISTORY 35 (1935): 198-204.

On the continued employment of Yankee school teachers in Negro schools in the South prior to the Civil War.

1466 North, William G. "The Political Background of the Dartmouth College Case." NEW ENGLAND QUARTERLY 18 (1945): 181-203.

1467 O'Brien, Michael J. "Early Schoolmasters in New England." CATHOLIC HISTORY REVIEW 3 (1917): 52-71.

1468 Parker, Francis W. "Horace Mann." EDUCATIONAL REVIEW 12 (1896): 65-74.

1469 Parker, Marjorie H. "Some Educational Activities of the Freedmen's Bureau." JOURNAL OF NEGRO EDUCATION 23 (1954): 9-21.

1470 Paulson, Arthur C., and Bjork, Kenneth, trans. and eds. "A School and Language Controversy in 1858: A Documentary Study." NORWEGIAN AMERICAN STUDIES AND RECORDS 10 (1938): 76-106.

Deals with educational conditions among Norwegian immigrants in Wisconsin in 1858.

1471 Paulston, Roland G. "French Influence in American Institutions of Higher Learning, 1784-1825." HISTORY OF EDUCATION QUARTERLY 8 (1968): 229-45.

1472 Payton, Phillip W. "Origins of the Terms 'Major' and 'Minor' in American Higher Education." HISTORY OF EDUCATION QUARTERLY 1 (1961): 57-63.

1473 Pedrick, Samuel M. "Early History of Ripon College, 1850-1864." WIS-CONSIN MAGAZINE OF HISTORY 8 (1924): 22-37.

1474 Petersen, William J. "Iowa in 1858: Education for All." THE PALIMP-SET (IOWA STATE HISTORICAL SOCIETY) 39 (1958): 545-55.

1475 Pleasants, Samuel A. "Thomas Jefferson: Educational Philosopher." PROCEEDINGS, AMERICAN PHILOSOPHICAL SOCIETY 111 (1967): 1-4.

1476 Polos, Nicholas C. "A Yankee Patriot: John Swett, the Horace Mann of the Pacific." HISTORY OF EDUCATION QUARTERLY 4 (1964): 17-32.

1477 Porter, Dorothy B. "The Organized Educational Activities of Negro Literary Societies, 1828-1846." JOURNAL OF NEGRO EDUCATION 5 (1936): 555-76.

1478 Potts, David B. "American Colleges in the Nineteenth Century: From Localism to Denominationalism." HISTORY OF EDUCATION QUARTERLY 11 (1971): 363-80.

1479 Pratt, John W. "Governor Seward and the New York City School Controversy, 1840-1842: A Milestone in the Advance of Nonsectarian Public Education." NEW YORK HISTORY 42 (1961): 351-64.

1480 _____. "Religious Conflict in the Development of the New York City Public School System." HISTORY OF EDUCATION QUARTERLY 5 (1965): 110-20.

1481 Preston, Emmett D., Jr. "The Development of Negro Education in the District of Columbia, 1800-1860." JOURNAL OF NEGRO EDUCATION 12 (1943): 189-98.

1482 Proctor, John C. "Joseph Lancaster and the Lancasterian Schools in the District of Columbia." COLUMBIA HISTORICAL SOCIETY RECORDS 25 (1923): 248-56.

1483 Pulliam, John. "Changing Attitudes Toward Free Public Schools in Illinois, 1825-1860." HISTORY OF EDUCATION QUARTERLY 7 (1967): 191-208.

1484 Pyburn, Nita K. "Public Schools in Mississippi Before 1860." JOURNAL OF MISSISSIPPI HISTORY 21 (1959): 113-30.

1485 Ravitz, Abe C. "Timothy Dwight: Professor of Rhetoric." NEW ENGLAND QUARTERLY 29 (1956): 63-72.

1486 Rawsford, George N. CONGRESS AND HIGHER EDUCATION IN THE NINETEENTH CENTURY. Knoxville: University of Tennessee Press, 1972. 156 p.

Suggests how the initial goal was to support the existing social structure in the colonial period to facilitate the sale of public land in the Civil War period, and to answer the demands of special interest groups later on.

1487 Reisner, Edward H. "Antecedents of the Federal Acts Concerning Education." EDUCATIONAL REVIEW 11 (1930): 196-207.

1488 Rezneck, Samuel. "A Schoolboy of 1830." NEW YORK HISTORY 17 (1936): 135-46.

As derived from papers, diaries, letters and compositions, and accounts of a student at Washington College, Hartford, Connecticut, 1828-32.

1489 _____. "The Emergence of a Scientific Community in New York State a Century Ago." NEW YORK HISTORY 43 (1962): 209-25.

1490 Richardson, Joe M. "The Freedmen's Bureau and Negro Education in Florida." JOURNAL OF NEGRO EDUCATION 31 (1962): 460-67.

1491 Richey, Herman G. "The Persistence of Educational Progress During the Decade of the Civil War." ELEMENTARY SCHOOL JOURNAL 42 (1942): 456-63.

1492 _____. "The Persistence of Educational Progress During the Decade of the Civil War." ELEMENTARY SCHOOL JOURNAL 42 (1942): 456-63.

1493 Riley, Herman M. "A History of Negro Elementary Education in Indiana." INDIANA MAGAZINE OF HISTORY 26 (1930): 288-305.

1494 Riley, Martin L. "The Development of Education in Louisiana Prior to Statehood." LOUISIANA HISTORICAL QUARTERLY 19 (1936): 595-634.

1495 Robbins, Gerald. "William F. Allen, Classical Scholar Among the Slaves." HISTORY OF EDUCATION QUARTERLY 5 (1965): 211-23.

1496 Roberts, Josephine. "Elizabeth Peabody and the Temple School." NEW ENGLAND QUARTERLY 15 (1942): 497-508.

1497 Robinson, Dale G. THE ACADEMIES OF VIRGINIA, 1776-1861. Richmond, Va.: Dietz Press, 1977. 76 p.

Essentially the story of education in Virginia on the secondary
level prior to the creation of the public school system in 1870.

1498 Roelker, William G. "Francis Wayland, 1796-1865, President of Brown
University and Citizen of Providence." COLLECTIONS, RHODE ISLAND
HISTORICAL SOCIETY 32 (1939): 33-55.

1499 _____. "Francis Wayland: A Neglected Pioneer of Higher Education."
PROCEEDINGS, AMERICAN ANTIQUARIAN SOCIETY 53 (1944): 27-98.

1500 Ross, Earle D. "The Father of the Land Grant College." AGRICULTUR-
AL HISTORY 12 (1938): 151-86.

1501 Ross, Elizabeth D. THE KINDERGARTEN CRUSADE: THE ESTABLISH-
MENT OF PRESCHOOL EDUCATION IN THE UNITED STATES. Athens:
Ohio University Press, 1976. 120 p.

1502 Rowland, Major T. "Letters of a Virginia Cadet at West Point, 1859-
1861." SOUTH ATLANTIC QUARTERLY 14 (1915): 201-19; 15 (1916):
1-17, 142-56, 201-15.

1503 Rudolph, Frederick. "Who Paid the Bills: An Inquiry into the Nature
of Nineteenth-Century College Finance." HARVARD EDUCATIONAL RE-
VIEW 31 (1961): 144-57.

1504 _____, ed. ESSAYS ON EDUCATION IN THE EARLY REPUBLIC. Cambridge, Mass.: Harvard University Press, 1965. 389 p.

Collects the full text of educational essays by: Benjamin Rush,
Noah Webster, Robert Coram, Simeon Doggett, Samuel Harrison Smith, de Lafitte du Courteil, and Samuel Knox.

1505 Ruggles, Alice McGuffey. "A Buckeye Boarding School in 1821."
NORTHWEST OHIO QUARTERLY 53 (1944): 251-68.

1506 Sack, Saul. "A Nineteenth Century Scheme for Financing Higher Education in Pennsylvania." HISTORY OF EDUCATION QUARTERLY 1 (1961):
50-54.

1507 Sahli, John R. "The Slavery Issue in Early Geography Textbooks." HIS-
TORY OF EDUCATION QUARTERLY 3 (1963): 153-58.

Notes how geography texts usually tended to take a marked
stand against slavery until about 1830. By 1860 this disap-
peared in the South.

1508 Salomon, Louis B. "The Straight-Cut Ditch: Thoreau on Education."
AMERICAN QUARTERLY 14 (1962): 52-61.

1509 Sargent, Walter. "The Evolution of the Little Red Schoolhouse." SCHOOL REVIEW 11 (1903): 435-55.

1510 Savage, W. Sherman. "Early Negro Education in the Pacific Coast States." JOURNAL OF NEGRO EDUCATION 15 (1946): 134-39.

1511 Schafer, Joseph. "Origins of Wisconsin's Free School System." WISCONSIN MAGAZINE OF HISTORY 9 (1925): 27-46.

1512 Schmidt, George P. "Intellectual Cross-Currents in American Colleges, 1825-1855." AMERICAN HISTORICAL REVIEW 42 (1936): 46-67.

1513 _____. "Colleges in Ferment." AMERICAN HISTORICAL REVIEW 59 (1953): 19-42.

1514 Scott, Roy V. "Early Agricultural Education in Minnesota: The Institute Phase." AGRICULTURAL HISTORY 38 (1963): 21-34.

1515 Seifman, Eli. "Education or Emigration: The Schism Within the African Colonization Movement, 1865-1875." HISTORY OF EDUCATION QUARTERLY 7 (1967): 36-57.

1516 Sellers, James B. "Student Life at the University of Alabama Before 1860." ALABAMA REVIEW 2 (1949): 269-93.

1517 Shaw, Henry K. "The Founding of Butler University, 1847-1855." INDIANA MAGAZINE OF HISTORY 58 (1962): 233-64.

1518 Shaw, Wilfred. "The Early Days of the University of Michigan." MICHIGAN HISTORY 16 (1932): 439-463; 17 (1933): 52-107.

1519 Shepard, Grace F. "Education at Wheaton College." NEW ENGLAND QUARTERLY 6 (1933): 803-24.

1520 _____. "Emerson as an Educator." HARVARD EDUCATIONAL REVIEW 3 (1933): 188-97.

1521 Shepard, William. "Buckingham Female Collegiate Institute." WILLIAM AND MARY COLLEGE QUARTERLY HISTORICAL MAGAZINE 20 (1940): 167-93.

1522 Sherzer, Jane. "The Higher Education of Women in the Ohio Valley Previous to 1840." OHIO ARCHAEOLOGICAL AND HISTORICAL QUARTERLY 25 (1916): 1-22.

1523 Shoemaker, F.L. "Samuel Galloway: An Educational Statesman of First Rank." HISTORY OF EDUCATION JOURNAL 5 (1954): 105-17.

1524 Shryock, Richard H. "The Psychiatry of Benjamin Rush." AMERICAN JOURNAL OF PSYCHIATRY 101 (1945): 429-32.

1525 Shumway, Daniel B. "Gottingen's American Students." AMERICAN-GERMAN REVIEW 3 (1937): 21-24.

   About American students at Gottingen University in Germany since 1782.

1526 Silcox, Harry C. "Delay and Neglect: Negro Public Education in Antebellum Philadelphia, 1800-1860." THE PENNSYLVANIA MAGAZINE OF HISTORY AND BIOGRAPHY 97 (1973): 444-64.

1527 Silverman, Robert, and Beach, Mark. "A National University for Upstate New York." AMERICAN QUARTERLY 22 (1970): 701-13.

1528 Simpson, Lewis P. "The Intercommunity of the Learned: Boston and Cambridge in 1800." NEW ENGLAND QUARTERLY 33 (1950): 491-503.

1529 "Sketch of a Plan for Endowment and Establishment of a State University in Virginia." WILLIAM AND MARY COLLEGE QUARTERLY HISTORICAL MAGAZINE 4 (1924): 266-76.

1530 Slappye, George H. "Early Foundations of Georgia's System of Common School Education." GEORGIA HISTORICAL QUARTERLY 14 (1930): 139-49.

1531 Smith, James M. "The Separate but Equal Doctrine: An Abolitionist Discusses Racial Segregation and Educational Policy During the Civil War: A Document." JOURNAL OF NEGRO HISTORY 41 (1956): 138-47.

   Refers to Andrew D. White.

1532 Smith, Joseph B. "A Frontier Experiment with Higher Education: Dickinson College." PENNSYLVANIA HISTORY 16 (1949): 1-19.

1533 Smith, Payson. "The Unique Contribution of the Common School to American Life." SCHOOL AND SOCIETY 48 (1938): 541-45.

1534 Smith, Timothy. "Protestant Schooling and American Nationality." JOURNAL OF AMERICAN HISTORY 53 (1966-67): 679-97.

1535 Soderbergh, Peter A. "Old School Days on the Middle Border, 1849-

1859: The Mary Payne Beard Letters." HISTORY OF EDUCATION QUARTERLY 8 (1968): 497-504.

> Before her death in 1921, Charles Austin Beard asked his mother to write him about her remembrances of her schooling. They begin with her recollections of the old log school house in 1849.

1536 "Some Historical Documents Bearing upon Common School Education in Virginia and South Carolina Previous to the Civil War." In UNITED STATES BUREAU OF EDUCATION, REPORT OF THE COMMISSIONER, 1899-1900. Vol. 1, pp. 431-41. Washington, D.C.: Government Printing Office, 1901.

1537 Spill, William A. "University of Michigan Beginnings." MICHIGAN HISTORY 12 (1928): 635-661; 13 (1929): 41-54, 227-44.

1538 Stephens, Roswell P. "Science in Georgia, 1800-1830." GEORGIA HISTORICAL QUARTERLY 9 (1925): 55-66.

1539 Stone, Mason S. "The First Normal School in America." TEACHERS COLLEGE RECORD 24 (1923): 263-71.

> About a school established at Concord, Vermont, in 1823.

1540 Story, Ronald. "Harvard Students, the Boston Elite, and the New England Preparatory System, 1800-1870." HISTORY OF EDUCATION QUARTERLY 15 (1975): 281-98.

1541 Swan, William O. "The Northwest Ordinances, So-Called and Confusion." HISTORY OF EDUCATION QUARTERLY 5 (1965): 235-40.

1542 Taylor, Isaac. SCENES IN AMERICA, FOR THE AMUSEMENT AND INSTRUCTION OF LITTLE TARRY-AT-HOME TRAVELLERS. 1821. Reprint. New York: Johnson Reprint, 1968. 122 p.

> Originally published in 1821 (Harris and Son). Designed for children, and covers American history from Columbus to Washington's entrance into Philadelphia. Includes many unusual engravings.

1543 Taylor, James M. "College Education for Girls in America." EDUCATIONAL REVIEW 44 (1912): 217-33, 325-47.

> Examines movements for the higher education for women prior to the opening of Vassar College for Women in 1865.

1544 Taylor, William R. "Toward a Definition of Orthodoxy: The Patrician South and the Common Schools." HARVARD EDUCATIONAL REVIEW 36 (1966): 412-26.

1545 "Teaching of Natural History at William and Mary College." WILLIAM AND MARY COLLEGE QUARTERLY HISTORICAL MAGAZINE 3 (1923): 239-40.

1546 Tewksbury, Donald G. THE FOUNDING OF AMERICAN COLLEGES AND UNIVERSITIES BEFORE THE CIVIL WAR, WITH PARTICULAR REFERENCE TO THE RELIGIOUS INFLUENCES BEARING UPON THE COLLEGE MOVEMENT. Hamden, Conn.: Archon Books, 1965. 254 p.

> Generally regarded as a classic on the subject since it first appeared in 1932. Contains excellent bibliography: pp. 221-54.

1547 Thomas, J.H. "The Academies of Indiana." INDIANA MAGAZINE OF HISTORY 10 (1914): 331-58; 11 (1915): 8-39.

1548 Thornton, Harrison J. "Locating the State University of Iowa." IOWA JOURNAL OF HISTORY 47 (1949): 50-62.

1549 Todd, Edgeley W. "Philosophical Ideas at Harvard College, 1817-1837." NEW ENGLAND QUARTERLY 16 (1943): 63-90.

1550 Townsend, John W. "Horace Holley, L.L.D., Third President of Old Transylvania." PROCEEDINGS, MISSISSIPPI VALLEY HISTORICAL ASSOCIATION 8 (1914-15): 123-34.

1551 Travers, Paul D. "John Orville Taylor: A Forgotten Educator." HISTORY OF EDUCATION QUARTERLY 9 (1969): 57-63.

1552 Turnbull, L. Minerva. "Private Schools in Norfolk, 1800-1860." WILLIAM AND MARY COLLEGE QUARTERLY HISTORICAL MAGAZINE 11 (1931): 277-303.

1553 _____. "Early Public Schools in Norfolk and Its Vicinity." WILLIAM AND MARY COLLEGE QUARTERLY HISTORICAL MAGAZINE 12 (1932): 4-9.

1554 _____. "The Southern Educational Revolt." WILLIAM AND MARY COLLEGE QUARTERLY HISTORICAL MAGAZINE 14 (1934): 60-76.

1555 Tyack, David. "Forming the National Character: Paradox in the Educational Thought of the Revolutionary Generation." HARVARD EDUCATIONAL REVIEW 36 (1966): 29-41.

1556 "The University of Virginia, a Reprint from the RICHMOND ENQUIRER of the Nineteenth Century." WILLIAM AND MARY COLLEGE QUARTERLY HISTORICAL MAGAZINE 3 (1923): 58-64.

1557 Urofsky, Melvin I. "Reforms and Response: The Yale Report of 1828." HISTORY OF EDUCATION QUARTERLY 5 (1965): 53-67.

1558 Vance, Joseph C. "Freedmen's Schools in Albemarle County During Reconstruction." VIRGINIA MAGAZINE OF HISTORY AND BIOGRAPHY 61 (1953): 430-38.

1559 Van Deusen, Glyndon G. "Seward and the School Question Reconsidered." JOURNAL OF AMERICAN HISTORY 52 (1965): 313-19.

1560 Varga, Nicholas. "Ninety-Five Pioneers: The First Students Enrolled at Loyola College, 1852-1853." MARYLAND HISTORICAL MAGAZINE 66 (1971): 181-93.

1561 Vinovskis, Maris A. "Trends in Massachusetts Education, 1826-1860." HISTORY OF EDUCATION QUARTERLY 12 (1972): 501-28.

1562 Waite, Frederick C. "The Professional Education of Pioneer Ohio Physicians." NORTHWEST OHIO QUARTERLY 48 (1939): 189-97.

1563 _____. "Manual Labor: An Experiment in American Colleges of the Early Nineteenth Century." BULLETIN, ASSOCIATION OF AMERICAN COLLEGES 36 (1950): 391-400.

1564 Warren, Charles. "Student Politics in Anti-Federalist Days." HARVARD GRADUATES MAGAZINE 24 (1916): 485-90.

    Relates specifically to two incidents at Harvard in 1790 and in 1811 where politics intruded into college affairs.

1565 Watson, Joseph S. [to David Watson]. "Letters from William and Mary College, 1798-1801." VIRGINIA MAGAZINE OF HISTORY AND BIOGRAPHY 29 (1921): 129-79.

1566 Watson, Thomas S. "William and Mary Letters from 1795 to 1799." VIRGINIA MAGAZINE OF HISTORY AND BIOGRAPHY 30 (1922): 223-49.

1567 Weathersby, William H. A HISTORY OF EDUCATIONAL LEGISLATION IN MISSISSIPPI FROM 1798 TO 1860. Chicago: University of Chicago Press, 1921. 204 p.

1568 Weeks, Stephen B. "The Beginnings of the Common School System in the South: Or Calvin Henderson Wiley and the Organization of Common Schools in North Carolina." In UNITED STATES BUREAU OF EDUCATION, REPORT OF THE COMMISSIONER, 1896-1897. Vol. 2, pp. 1379-474. Washington, D.C.: Government Printing Office, 1898.

1569 Wells, Herman G. "The Early History of Indiana University as Reflected in the Administration of Andrew Wylie, 1829-1851." FILSON CLUB 36 (1962): 113-27.

1570 Wesley, Edgar B. "Forty Acres and a Mule and a Speller." HISTORY OF EDUCATION JOURNAL 10 (1959): 56-70.

1571 West, Earle H. "The Peabody Education Fund and Negro Education, 1867-1880." HISTORY OF EDUCATION QUARTERLY 6 (1966): 3-21.

1572 Whitaker, A.P. "The Public School System of Tennessee, 1834-1860." TENNESSEE HISTORICAL QUARTERLY 2 (1916): 1-30.

1573 White, James C. "An Undergraduate's Diary, 1849-1851." HARVARD GRADUATES MAGAZINE 21 (1913): 423-30, 636-51.

1574 White, Ruth W. "James Marsh, Educational Pioneer." EDUCATIONAL FORUM 29 (1965): 217-24.

   Marsh was president of the University of Vermont in the 1820s.

1575 Whittenburg, Clarice. "The Frontier Schoolma'am on Ranch and Homestead." EDUCATIONAL FORUM 13 (1948): 79-89.

1576 "William and Mary College, 1802-1804." WILLIAM AND MARY COLLEGE QUARTERLY HISTORICAL MAGAZINE 5 (1925): 120-24.

1577 "William and Mary College, 1806." WILLIAM AND MARY COLLEGE QUARTERLY HISTORICAL MAGAZINE 3 (1923): 201-08.

1578 "William and Mary College in 1858." WILLIAM AND MARY COLLEGE QUARTERLY HISTORICAL MAGAZINE 10 (1902): 251-57.

1579 Williams, Henry S. "The Development of the Negro Public School System in Missouri." JOURNAL OF NEGRO HISTORY 5 (1920): 137-65.

1580 Wills, Elbert V. "Political Economy in the Early American College." SOUTH ATLANTIC QUARTERLY 24 (1925): 131-53.

1581 Wilson, John B. "Bronson Alcott: Platonist or Pestalozzian?" SCHOOL AND SOCIETY 81 (1955): 49-54.

1582 Wilson, Lawrence. "Thoreau of Education." HISTORY OF EDUCATION QUARTERLY 2 (1962): 19-29.

1583 Wolcott, John D. "The Southern Educational Convention of 1863." SOUTH ATLANTIC QUARTERLY 8 (1909): 354-60.

1584 Woodson, Carter G. THE EDUCATION OF THE NEGRO PRIOR TO 1861. New York and London: G.P. Putnam's Sons, 1915. 454 p.

   Traces the education of Negroes from the advent of slavery to the Civil War.

1585 Woolverton, John F. "Philip Lindsley and the Cause of Education in the Old Southwest." TENNESSEE HISTORICAL QUARTERLY 19 (1960): 3-22.

1586 Young, Homer H. "The National University of the Early National Period." EDUCATIONAL FORUM 15 (1951): 343-52.

Chapter 8

THE EXPANSION OF AMERICAN EDUCATION: 1865-1900

1587 Adams, Francis. THE FREE SCHOOL SYSTEM OF THE UNITED STATES. London: Chapman and Hall, 1875. 309 p.

1588 Allen, W.F. "The University of Wisconsin Soon After the Civil War." MID-AMERICA 9 (1926): 20-29.

1589 Alvord, John W. SEMI-ANNUAL REPORTS ON SCHOOLS AND FINANCES FOR FREEDMEN, 1866-1870. Washington, D.C.: Government Printing Office, 1866-70.

A series of ten reports constituting an invaluable repository.

1590 Ambrose, Stephen E. "Public Education in the Post-War South." EDUCATIONAL FORUM 26 (1962): 353-62.

1591 Anderson, William T. "The Freedmen's Bureau and Negro Education in Virginia." NORTH CAROLINA HISTORICAL REVIEW 29 (1952): 64-90.

1592 Andrews, Benjamin F. "First Quarter Century of Teachers College and the Professional Education of Teachers." AMERICAN EDUCATION 17 (1914): 524-26.

1593 _____. THE LAND GRANT OF 1862 AND THE LAND GRANT COLLEGES. U.S. Bureau of Education Bulletin No. 13, 1918. Washington, D.C.: Government Printing Office, 1918. 63 p.

1594 Armstrong, Warren B. "Union Chaplains and the Education of Freedmen." JOURNAL OF NEGRO HISTORY 52 (1967): 104-15.

1595 Badger, William V. "Some Ideas of Mr. Justice Holmes Regarding Education." PEABODY JOURNAL OF EDUCATION 28 (1950): 2-8.

1596 Balyeat, Frank A. "Education of White Children in the Indian Territory." CHRONICLES OF OKLAHOMA 15 (1937): 191-97.

Deals with the period: 1870-1920.

1597 _____. "Segregation in the Public Schools of Oklahoma Territory." CHRONICLES OF OKLAHOMA 36 (1961): 180-92.

1598 Barlow, Melvin L. "Development of the Concept of Industrial Education as a Public School Responsibility in California." HISTORY OF EDUCATION JOURNAL 5 (1953): 3-6.

Covers the period from the formation of the Mechanics Institute in 1854 to the Smith-Hughes Act of 1917.

1599 Barnes, Sherman B. "The Entry of Science and History in the College Curriculum, 1865-1914." HISTORY OF EDUCATION QUARTERLY 4 (1964): 44-58.

1600 Black, Marian W. "Private Aid to Public Schools: The Peabody Fund in Florida, 1867-1880." HISTORY OF EDUCATION QUARTERLY 1 (1961): 38-41.

As administered by Barnas Sears to encourage interest and participation on the county, as well as on the state levels.

1601 Blinderman, Abraham. AMERICAN WRITERS ON EDUCATION AFTER 1865. Boston: G.K. Hall, 1976. 279 p.

1602 Bond, Horace M. "Negro Education: A Debate in the Alabama Constitutional Convention of 1901." JOURNAL OF NEGRO EDUCATION 1 (1932): 49-59.

1603 Borrowman, Merle. "The False Dawn of the State University." HISTORY OF EDUCATION QUARTERLY 1 (1961): 6-21.

Deals in part with its evolution out of American higher education as a whole.

1604 Brown, Abner R. "Colorado's First Schools: A Story of Early Days in the West, Where the Children of Miners Learned Both Lessons and Discipline." JOURNAL OF AMERICAN HISTORY 15 (1921): 72-76, 147-49, 247-50.

1605 Burrell, B. Jeanette, and Eckelberry, R.H. "The Free Public High School in the Post-Civil War Period." SCHOOL REVIEW 42 (1934): 606-14, 667-75.

1606 _____. "The High School Controversy in the Post-Civil War Period: Times, Places and Participants." SCHOOL REVIEW 42 (1934): 333-45.

1607 _____. "The High School Question Before the Courts in the Post-Civil War Period." SCHOOL REVIEW 42 (1934): 255-65.

1608 Butler, Nicholas M. "The Reform of Secondary Education in the United States." In UNITED STATES BUREAU OF EDUCATION, REPORT OF THE COMMISSIONER, 1892-1893. Vol. 2, pp. 1448-56. Washington, D.C.: Government Printing Office, 1895.

1609 Butter, Josiah. "Pioneer School Teaching at the Comanche-Kiowa Agency School (1870-1873)." CHRONICLES OF OKLAHOMA 6 (1928): 483-528.

1610 Button, Henry W. "Committee of Fifteen." HISTORY OF EDUCATION QUARTERLY 5 (1965): 253-63.

1611 Campbell, Jack K. COLONEL FRANCIS W. PARKER: THE CHILDREN'S CRUSADER. New York: Teachers College, Columbia University Press, 1967. 283 p.

    A thorough, well-documented biography with some emphasis on pervading influences on educators in the latter parts of the nineteenth century in America.

1612 Carmichael, Oliver C. "The Roots of Higher Education in Minnesota." MINNESOTA HISTORY 34 (1954): 90-105.

1613 Chitty, Arthur B. RECONSTRUCTION AT SEWANEE. Sewanee, Tenn.: University Press, 1954. 206 p.

    Deals with the founding of Sewanee University and its first administration, 1857-72.

1614 Churchill, Alfred V. "The Founding of Oberlin." NORTHWEST OHIO QUARTERLY 23 (1951): 107-32.

1615 _____. "Oberlin Students, Sinners and Adolescents in the 1870's and 1880's." NORTHWEST OHIO QUARTERLY, 1952-53, pp. 41-71.

1616 Clark, Thomas D. INDIANA UNIVERSITY: MIDWESTERN PIONEER. VOLUME ONE: THE EARLY YEARS. Bloomington: Indiana State University Press, 1970. 371 p.

    A survey of the history of the university from its founding to the resignation of President Joseph Swain in 1902. Intended as a series.

1617 Coats, A.W. "Henry Carter Adams: A Case Study in the Emergence of the Social Sciences in the United States, 1850-1900." JOURNAL OF AMERICAN STUDIES 2 (1968): 177-97.

1618 Coon, Charles L. "The Beginnings of North Carolina City Schools, 1867-1887." SOUTH ATLANTIC QUARTERLY 12 (1913): 235-47.

1619 _____. "School Support and Our North Carolina Courts, 1868-1926." NORTH CAROLINA HISTORICAL REVIEW 3 (1926): 399-438.

1620 Cordasco, Francesco. THE SHAPING OF AMERICAN GRADUATE EDU-CATION: DANIEL COIT GILMAN AND THE PROTEAN PH.D. Totowa, N.J.: Rowman and Littlefield, 1973. 163 p.

Focuses on Gilman's career and his presidency of the Johns Hopkins University, 1875-1902. Deals with onset of the Ph.D. at Yale as then developed at the Johns Hopkins University under Gilman. Extensive bibliography also included.

1621 Davidson, Elizabeth H. "The Child-Labor Problem in North Carolina, 1883-1903." NORTH CAROLINA HISTORICAL REVIEW 13 (1936): 105-21.

1622 _____. "Early Development of Public Opinion Against Southern Child Labor." NORTH CAROLINA HISTORICAL REVIEW 14 (1937): 230-50.

1623 Davis, Caroline. "Education of the Chickasaws, 1856-1907." CHRONI-CLES OF OKLAHOMA 15 (1937): 415-48.

1624 Debo, Angie. "Education in the Choctaw Country After the Civil War." CHRONICLES OF OKLAHOMA 10 (1932): 383-91.

1625 Downes, Randolph C. "The People's Schools: Popular Foundations to Toledo's Public School System." NORTHWEST OHIO QUARTERLY 29 (1957-1957): 9-26; 19 (1957): 108-16.

1626 Dubois, W.E.B. "The Freedman's Bureau." ATLANTIC MONTHLY 87 (1901): 354-65.

1627 Dudley, Richard E. "Nebraska Public School Education, 1890-1910." NEBRASKA HISTORY 54 (1973): 65-90.

1628 Dye, Charles M. CALVIN MILTON WOODWARD AND AMERICAN UR-BAN EDUCATION: BIOGRAPHY OF A REFORMER. Akron, Ohio: University of Akron Press, Phi Delta Kappa, 1976. 260 p.

Essentially a doctoral dissertation by Dye, Washington University, St. Louis, 1975, about a major figure in the manual training movement. Also see the two major works by Woodward: THE MANUAL TRAINING SCHOOL (1887) and MANUAL TRAINING IN EDUCATION (1890), both regarded as classics in the manual training area.

1629 Eliot, Charles W. A TURNING POINT IN HIGHER EDUCATION: THE INAUGURAL ADDRESS OF CHARLES WILLIAM ELIOT AS PRESIDENT OF HARVARD COLLEGE, OCTOBER 19, 1869. Cambridge, Mass.: Harvard University Press, 1969. 30 p.

A centennial reprint of the 1869 inaugural address with an introduction by 1969 President Nathan M. Pusey. The address is regarded as a classic statement on higher education in America.

1630 Evans, John W. "Catholics and the Blair Education Bill." CATHOLIC HISTORY REVIEW 46 (1960): 273-98.

Examines Catholic reaction to Sen. Henry Blair's efforts in the 1880s to obtain federal aid for public schools.

1631 FEDERAL LAWS AND RULINGS RELATING TO MORRILL AND SUPPLE-MENTARY MORRILL FUNDS FOR LAND-GRANT COLLEGES AND UNI-VERSITIES. U.S. Office of Education Pamphlet No. 91, 1940. Washington, D.C.: Government Printing Office, 1940. 16 p.

Covers the texts of laws and related rulings thereon from 1862 through 1940 on land-grant institutions.

1632 Fenton, Charles A. "The Founding of the National Institute of Arts and Letters in 1898." NEW ENGLAND QUARTERLY 32 (1959): 435-44.

1633 Ferguson, James S. "An Era of Educational Change." NORTH CARO-LINA HISTORICAL REVIEW 46 (1969): 130-41.

Deals with the fusion of the populists and the Republicans between 1895 and 1899.

1634 Foreman, Carolyn T. "New Hope Seminary, 1844-1897." CHRONICLES OF OKLAHOMA 22 (1944): 271-99.

New Hope was a Choctaw school for girls.

1635 Frankfort, Roberta. COLLEGIATE WOMEN: DOMESTICITY AND CAREER IN TURN-OF-THE-CENTURY AMERICA. New York: New York University Press, 1977. 124 p.

1636 Garland, Hamlin. "Going to School in Iowa in 1871." EDUCATIONAL REVIEW 54 (1917): 495-99

Drawn from Garland's: A SON OF THE MIDDLE BORDER.
New York: Macmillan, 1917.

1637 Gates, Paul W. "Western Opposition to the Agricultural College Act."
INDIANA MAGAZINE OF HISTORY 37 (1941): 103-36.

1638 "General Conditions of Education Among the Indians." In UNITED
STATES BUREAU OF EDUCATION, REPORT OF THE COMMISSIONER,
1870, pp. 339-54. Washington, D.C.: Government Printing Office,
1870.

1639 Gerhard, Dietrich. "Development and Structure of Continental European
and American Universities--A Comparison." JAHRBUCH FUR AMERIKA-
STUDIEN 12 (1967): 19-35.

1640 Gershenberg, Irving. "Southern Values and Public Education: A Revision." HISTORY OF EDUCATION QUARTERLY 10 (1970): 413-22.

    Suggests the southern educational under-development stemmed
    from a lack of commitment to public education by the politi-
    cal establishment. Uses multiple correlation regression analy-
    sis as the base of the thesis offered here.

1641 Gersman, Elinor M. "Progressive Reform of the St. Louis School Board,
1897." HISTORY OF EDUCATION QUARTERLY 10 (1970): 3-21.

1642 Glover, Wilbur H. "The Agricultural College Crisis of 1885." WIS-
CONSIN MAGAZINE OF HISTORY 32 (1948): 17-25.

1643 Gordon, Sarah H. "Smith College Students: The First Ten Classes, 1879-
1888." HISTORY OF EDUCATION QUARTERLY 15 (1975): 147-67.

    Examines how they came from farms, small New England towns,
    and large cities.

1644 Gould, Joseph E. THE CHAUTAUQUA MOVEMENT: AN EPISODE IN
THE CONTINUING AMERICAN REVOLUTION. New York: New York
University Press, 1970. 108 p.

    Originally appeared in 1961 and was reprinted without changes.
    Describes the birth and impact of the Chautauqua movement on
    American education.

1645 Graham, Patricia A. COMMUNITY AND CLASS IN AMERICAN EDU-
CATION, 1865-1918. New York: Wiley, 1975. 256 p.

1646 Hanus, Paul H. "High School Pioneering: Denver High School, District
No. 2: 1886-1890." SCHOOL REVIEW 45 (1937): 417-28.

1647 Hardy, Carrie A. "The Evolution of the American High School." WEST-
ERN JOURNAL OF EDUCATION 4 (1911): 169-75, 222-29, 265-74.

1648 Harris, William T. "Educational Values." In UNITED STATES BUREAU
OF EDUCATION, REPORT OF THE COMMISSIONER, 1893-1894. Vol.
1, pp. 617-37. Washington, D.C.: Government Printing Office, 1896.

1649 ____. "The Old Psychology v. the New." In UNITED STATES BUREAU
OF EDUCATION, REPORT OF THE COMMISSIONER, 1893-1894. Vol.
1, pp. 433-36. Washington, D.C.: Government Printing Office, 1896.

1650 Hatch, Richard A., ed. AN EARLY VIEW OF THE LAND-GRANT COL-
LEGES. Urbana: University of Illinois Press, 1967. 147 p.

A record of the proceedings of a "Convention of Friends of
Agricultural Education," held in Chicago in 1871.

1651 Hawkins, Hugh. "The University-Builders Observe the Colleges." HIS-
TORY OF EDUCATION QUARTERLY 11 (1971): 353-62.

1652 ____. BETWEEN HARVARD AND AMERICA: THE EDUCATIONAL
LEADERSHIP OF CHARLES W. ELIOT. New York: Oxford University
Press, 1972. 404 p.

Focuses on Eliot's developing social thought and his role as
mediator between the university and society. Extensive bibliography also included.

1653 Hinsdale, B.A. "The History of Popular Education on the Western Reserve." OHIO HISTORICAL QUARTERLY 6 (1898): 35-59.

1654 Hinsdale, Mary C. "A Legislative History of the Public School System
of the State of Ohio." In UNITED STATES BUREAU OF EDUCATION,
REPORT OF THE COMMISSIONER, 1900-1901. Vol. 1, pp. 129-60.
Washington, D.C.: Government Printing Office, 1902.

1655 Hobby, Selma Ann Plowman. THE LITTLE ROCK PUBLIC SCHOOLS DUR-
ING RECONSTRUCTION, 1865-1874. Fayetteville: University of Arkansas Thesis Microfilms, 1967. n.p.

Available on microfilm from: Ann Arbor, Mich.: Xerox University Microfilms International, 1967.

1656 Hogeland, Ronald W. "Coeducation of the Sexes at Oberlin College:
A Study of Social Ideas in Mid-Nineteenth Century America." JOURNAL
OF SOCIAL HISTORY 6 (1972-73): 160-76.

1657 Hollingsworth, R.R. "Education and Reconstruction in Georgia." GEOR-
GIA HISTORICAL QUARTERLY 19 (1935): 112-33, 229-50.

1658 Hornsby, Alton, Jr. "The Freedmen's Bureau Schools in Texas." SOUTH-
WESTERN HISTORICAL QUARTERLY 76 (1973): 397-417.

1659 Hotze, W.H. "Pioneer School Days in Southwest Nebraska." NEBRASKA
HISTORY MAGAZINE 33 (1952): 41-43.

1660 Issel, William H. "Modernization in Philadelphia School Reform, 1882-
1905." PENNSYLVANIA MAGAZINE OF HISTORY AND BIOGRAPHY
94 (1970): 358-83.

1661 Jackson, L.P. "The Educational Efforts of the Freedmen's Bureau and
Freedmen's Aid Societies in South Carolina, 1862-1872." JOURNAL OF
NEGRO HISTORY 8 (1923): 1-40.

1662 Jefferson, Floyd W. "Education and Educators in Kentucky at the Turn
of the Century." FILSON CLUB (Kentucky) 30 (1956): 3-18.

1663 Jorgenson, Lloyd P. "The Origins of Public Education in Wisconsin."
MID-AMERICA 33 (1949): 15-27.

1664 Katz, Michael B. "The New Departure in Quincy, 1873-1881: The
Nature of Nineteenth Century Educational Reform." NEW ENGLAND
QUARTERLY 40 (1967): 3-30.

1665 _____. "The Emergence of Bureaucracy in Urban Education: The Boston
Case, 1850-1884." HISTORY OF EDUCATION QUARTERLY 8 (1968):
155-88, 319-57.

How grammar-oriented schoolmasters defended the professionally
directed hierarchical bureaucracy against lay reformers.

1666 King, Emma. "Some Aspects of the Work of the Society of Friends for
Negro Education in North Carolina." NORTH CAROLINA HISTORICAL
REVIEW 1 (1924): 403-11.

1667 Knight, Edgar W. "Some Fallacies Concerning the History of Public
Education in the South." SOUTH ATLANTIC QUARTERLY 13 (1914):
371-81.

1668 _____. "The Peabody Fund and Its Early Operation in North Carolina."
SOUTH ATLANTIC QUARTERLY 14 (1915): 168-80.

1669 _____. THE INFLUENCE OF RECONSTRUCTION ON EDUCATION IN
THE SOUTH. New York: Arno Press, New York Times, 1969. 100 p.

Examines who made the major contributions to public education in the Carolinas between 1868 and 1876. Originally appeared in 1913 published by Teachers College, Columbia University Press.

1670 Knight, George W. "History and Management of Land Grants for Education in the Northwest Territory." PAPERS, AMERICAN HISTORICAL ASSOCIATION 1 (1885): 79-247.

1671 Krug, Mark. THE MELTING OF THE ETHNICS: EDUCATION OF THE IMMIGRANTS, 1880-1914. Bloomington, Ind.: Phi Delta Kappa, 1976. 123 p.

1672 Lazerson, Marvin. "F.A.P. Barnard and Columbia College: Prologue to a University." HISTORY OF EDUCATION QUARTERLY 6 (1966): 49-64.

1673 Lee, Gordon C. THE STRUGGLE FOR FEDERAL AID, FIRST PHASE: A HISTORY OF THE ATTEMPTS TO OBTAIN FEDERAL AID FOR THE COMMON SCHOOLS, 1870-1890. New York: Bureau of Publications, Teachers College, Columbia University, 1949.

1674 Lindley, Harlow. "Rutherford B. Hayes and the Ohio State University." NORTHWEST OHIO QUARTERLY 55 (1946): 295-96.

1675 McAlpina, William. "The Origin of Public Education in Ohio." NORTHWEST OHIO QUARTERLY 38 (1929): 409-47.

1676 McDonald, Sister Grace. "A Finishing School of the 1880's: St. Benedict's Academy." MINNESOTA HISTORY 27 (1946): 122-24.

1677 _____. "Pioneer Teachers: The Benedictine Sisters at St. Cloud." MINNESOTA HISTORY 35 (1957): 263-71.

1678 McRae, Donald G. "Education and Sociology in America: 1865-1900: A Paradox of Creativity." EDUCATIONAL FORUM 33 (1969): 143-51.

1679 Marsh, C.S. "General Lee and a School of Commerce." JOURNAL OF POLITICAL ECONOMY 34 (1926): 657-59.

In January 1869, Lee, as president of Washington College outlined a plan for the establishment of a collegiate school of commerce.

1680 Mayo, Amory D. INDUSTRIAL EDUCATION IN THE SOUTH. U.S. Bureau of Education Information Circular No. 5, 1888. Washington, D.C.: Government Printing Office, 1888. 86 p.

1681 _____. SOUTHERN WOMEN .N THE RECENT EDUCATIONAL MOVE-MENT IN THE SOUTH. U.S. Bureau of Education Information Circular No. 1, 1892. Washington, D.C.: Government Printing Office, 1892. 300 p.

1682 _____. "Original Establishment of State School Funds." In UNITED STATES BUREAU OF EDUCATION, REPORT OF THE COMMISSIONER, 1894-1895. Vol. 2, pp. 1505-11. Washington, D.C.: Government Printing Office, 1896.

1683 _____. "The Work of Certain Northern Churches in the Education of the Freedmen, 1861-1900." In UNITED STATES BUREAU OF EDUCATION, REPORT OF THE COMMISSIONER, 1902. Vol. 1, pp. 285-314. Washington, D.C.: Government Printing Office, 1903.

1684 _____. "The Final Establishment of the American Common School System in West Virginia, Maryland, Virginia and Delaware, 1863-1900." In UNITED STATES BUREAU OF EDUCATION, REPORT OF THE COMMISSIONER, 1903. Pp. 391-462. Washington, D.C.: Government Printing Office, 1905.

1685 _____. "The Final Establishment of the American Common School System in North Carolina, South Carolina, and Georgia, 1863-1900." In UNITED STATES BUREAU OF EDUCATION, REPORT OF THE COMMISSIONER, 1904. Vol. 1, pp. 999-1090. Washington, D.C.: Government Printing Office, 1906.

1686 Meier, August, and Rudwick, Elliott M. "Early Boycotts of Segregated Schools: The Alton Illinois Case, 1897-1908." JOURNAL OF NEGRO EDUCATION 36 (1967): 394-402.

1687 _____. "Early Boycotts of Segregated Schools: The East Orange, New Jersey, Experience, 1899-1906." HISTORY OF EDUCATION QUARTERLY 7 (1967): 22-35.

1688 Miller, Edward A. "The History of Educational Legislation in Ohio." NORTHWEST OHIO QUARTERLY 27 (1918): 1-27.

1689 Miller, Kelly. "Forty Years of Negro Education." EDUCATIONAL REVIEW 36 (1908): 484-98.

1690 Mitchell, Frederic, and Skelton, James W. "The Church-State Conflict in Early Indian Education." HISTORY OF EDUCATION QUARTERLY 6 (1966): 41-51.

The problem had to do with the use of tax funds for the support of religious schools.

1691 Myers, John B. "The Education of the Alabama Freedmen During Presidential Reconstruction, 1865-1867." THE JOURNAL OF NEGRO EDUCATION 40 (1971): 163-71.

1692 Neville, Charles E. "Origin and Development of the Public High School in Philadelphia." SCHOOL REVIEW 35 (1927): 363-75.

1693 Nevins, Archie P. "The Kalamazoo Case." MICHIGAN HISTORY 44 (1960): 91-100.

1694 Pawa, Jay M. "Workingmen and Free Schools in the Nineteenth Century: A Comment on the Labor-Education Thesis." HISTORY OF EDUCATION QUARTERLY 11 (1971): 287-302.

   Cites role of urban society in the creation of free schools
   with special emphasis on the role of the middle class.

1695 Payne, John W. "Poor Man's Pedagogy: Teachers Institutes in Arkansas." ARKANSAS HISTORICAL QUARTERLY 14 (1955): 195-206.

1696 Peabody, Francis G. EDUCATION FOR LIFE: THE STORY OF HAMPTON INSTITUTE. Garden City, N.Y.: Doubleday, Page and Co., 1918. 393 p.

   Also includes a number of chapters on the Negro in the Civil
   War and in the period, 1865-1868.

1697 Pearce, Larry W. "The American Missionary Association and the Freedmen's Bureau in Arkansas, 1866-1868." ARKANSAS HISTORICAL QUARTERLY 30 (1971): 242-59.

1698 Peterson, George E. THE NEW ENGLAND COLLEGE IN THE AGE OF THE UNIVERSITY. Amherst, Mass.: Amherst College Press, 1964. 260 p.

   Examines a cluster of New England schools that resisted the
   university movement and formulated liberal arts programs pre-
   sumably suited to the twentieth century.

1699 Potts, David B. "American Colleges in the Nineteenth Century: From Localism to Denominationalism." HISTORY OF EDUCATION QUARTERLY 11 (1971): 363-80.

   Suggests a restructuring of late nineteenth-century higher education on the basis of data about the majority of students and
   colleges.

1700 Powell, J.P. "Some Nineteenth Century Views on the University Curriculum." HISTORY OF EDUCATION QUARTERLY 5 (1965): 97-109.

Suggests modern disputes in higher education are really rooted in the nineteenth century and not really in the twentieth, although this point is often overlooked.

1701 Pratt, Richard H. BATTLEFIELD AND CLASSROOM: FOUR DECADES WITH THE AMERICAN INDIAN, 1867-1904. Edited and introduced by Robert M. Utley. New Haven, Conn.: Yale University Press, 1964. 358 p.

1702 Richards, Eva L. "Alvey--Schoolgirl of the Indian Frontier." MINNE-SOTA HISTORY 33 (1952): 105-11.

1703 Ross, Earle D. "The Manual Labor Experiment in the Land Grant College." MISSISSIPPI VALLEY HISTORICAL REVIEW 21 (1935): 513-28.

1704 _____. "History in the Land-Grant College." MISSISSIPPI VALLEY HISTORICAL REVIEW 32 (1945-46): 577-81.

1705 Rudwick, Elliott M., and Meier, August. "Early Boycotts of Segregated Schools: The East Orange, New Jersey Experience, 1899-1906." HISTORY OF EDUCATION QUARTERLY 7 (1967): 22-35.

In 1905 the black citizens of the city boycotted the public schools and established a counterpart then of the modern so-called "freedom schools."

1706 Savage, W. Sherman. "Legal Provisions for Negro Schools in Missouri, 1865-1890." JOURNAL OF NEGRO HISTORY 16 (1931): 309-21.

1707 Schafer, Joseph. "Genesis of Wisconsin's Free High School System." WISCONSIN MAGAZINE OF HISTORY 10 (1920): 123-49.

1708 Shannon, James P. "Catholic Boarding Schools on the Western Frontier." MINNESOTA HISTORY 35 (1956): 133-39.

1709 Simon, John Y. "The Politics of the Morrill Act." AGRICULTURAL HISTORY 37 (1963): 103-11.

1710 Sisk, Glenn. "Negro Education in the Alabama Black Belt, 1875-1900." JOURNAL OF NEGRO EDUCATION 22 (1953): 126-35.

1711 Sizer, Theodore R. SECONDARY SCHOOLS AT THE TURN OF THE CENTURY. New Haven, Conn.: Yale University Press, 1964. 304 p.

Predicated upon the 1893 report of the "Committee of Ten," as it has come to be known, which is reprinted in its entirety. Sets its authors against the background of the period as well.

1712 Smith, Timothy L. "Progressivism in American Education, 1880-1900." HARVARD EDUCATIONAL REVIEW 31 (1961): 168-93.

1713 Smythe, Donald. "John J. Pershing at the University of Nebraska, 1891-1895." NEBRASKA HISTORY MAGAZINE 43 (1962): 169-96.

1714 Stowe, Harriet Beecher. "The Education of the Freedmen." NORTH AMERICAN REVIEW 128 (1879): 605-15.

1715 Strickland, Charles E. "The Child, the Community, and Clio: The Uses of Cultural History in Elementary School Experiments of the Eighteen-Nineties." HISTORY OF EDUCATION QUARTERLY 7 (1967): 474-92.

1716 Stuart, George. "The Raison d'Etre of the Public High School." In UNITED STATES BUREAU OF EDUCATION, REPORT OF THE COMMISSIONER, 1886-1887, pp. 1017-22. Washington, D.C.: Government Printing Office, 1888.

1717 Suarez, Raleigh A. "Chronicle of Failure: Public Education in Antebellum Louisiana." LOUISIANA HISTORY 12 (1971): 109-22.

1718 Swint, Henry Lee. THE NORTHERN TEACHER IN THE SOUTH, 1862-1870. New York: Octagon Press, 1967. 221 p.

> First appeared in 1941 (Vanderbilt Press). A brief history of why Northerners went South to teach and why the Southerners tended to react so violently against them.

1719 Taylor, Howard C. THE EDUCATIONAL SIGNIFICANCE OF THE EARLY FEDERAL LAND ORDINANCES. New York: Teachers College, Columbia University Press, 1922. 138 p.

> Traces how the earlier ordinances influenced the later acts, especially in matters of education and the development of the public school systems in the United States.

1720 Taylor, Hoy. AN INTERPRETATION OF THE EARLY ADMINISTRATION OF THE PEABODY EDUCATION FUND. Nashville: George Peabody College for Teachers, 1933. 166 p.

1721 Townsend, Sara B. "The Admission of Women to the University of Georgia." GEORGIA HISTORICAL QUARTERLY 43 (1959): 225-47.

1722 Tyack, David B. "Education and Social Unrest, 1873-1878." HARVARD EDUCATIONAL REVIEW 31 (1961): 194-212.

1723 _____. "Bureaucracy and the Common School: The Example of Portland, Oregon, 1851-1913." AMERICAN QUARTERLY 19 (1967): 475-98.

1724 Vaughn, William P. SCHOOLS FOR ALL: THE BLACKS AND PUBLIC EDUCATION IN THE SOUTH, 1865-1877. Lexington: University of Kentucky Press, 1974. 257 p.

1725 Walker, W.G. "The Development of the Free Public High School in Illinois During the Nineteenth Century." HISTORY OF EDUCATION QUARTERLY 4 (1964): 264-79.

1726 Warren, Donald R. TO ENFORCE EDUCATION: A HISTORY OF THE FOUNDING YEARS OF THE UNITED STATES OFFICE OF EDUCATION. Detroit: Wayne State University Press, 1974. 239 p.

1727 Weber, Evelyn. THE KINDERGARTEN: ITS ENCOUNTER WITH EDU-CATIONAL THOUGHT IN AMERICA. New York: Teachers College Press, 1969. 282 p.

   Deals with what came to be known as the primary issues in elementary education.

1728 Wein, Roberta. "Women's Colleges and Domesticity, 1875-1918." HIS-TORY OF EDUCATION QUARTERLY 14 (1974): 31-48.

1729 West, Earle H. "The Peabody Education Fund and Negro Education, 1867-1880." HISTORY OF EDUCATION QUARTERLY 6 (1966): 3-21.

   The Peabody Fund supported public school systems that were publicly supported and publicly controlled in the South. The result was a compromise that apparently poorly served Negro education in that era.

1730 White, Bruce. "ABC's for the American Enlisted Man: The Army Post School System, 1866-1898." HISTORY OF EDUCATION QUARTERLY 8 (1968): 479-96.

1731 White, Dana F. "Education in the Turn-of-the-Century School." URBAN EDUCATION 1 (1969): 169-82.

1732 Wirth, Arthur G. "John Dewey's Design for American Education: An Analysis of Aspects of His Work at the University of Chicago, 1894-1904." HISTORY OF EDUCATION QUARTERLY 4 (1964): 83-105.

   An appraisal of Dewey's ideas: 1894-1904.

1733 _____. JOHN DEWEY AS EDUCATOR: HIS DESIGN FOR WORK IN EDUCATION, 1894-1904. New York: Wiley, 1966. 322 p.

   Deals with Dewey's laboratory school as well as his theories in philosophy, psychology, curriculum, and methodology in that school.

1734 Woody, Thomas. "Country Schoolmaster of Long Ago." HISTORY OF EDUCATION JOURNAL 5 (1954): 41-53.

> One Mr. Dormier describes his experiences as a teacher in the Pennsylvania Dutch country in Pennsylvania in 1888.

Chapter 9

AMERICAN EDUCATION IN THE TWENTIETH CENTURY

1735 Abram, Morris. "Reflections on the University in the New Revolution." DAEDALUS 99 (1970): 122-40.

1736 Abramson, Joan. THE INVISIBLE WOMAN: DISCRIMINATION IN THE ACADEMIC PROFESSION. San Francisco: Jossey-Bass, 1975. 248 p.

Documents discrimination by use of a personal case history illustrating the point being made.

1737 Adams, Frank C., and Stephens, Clarence W. COLLEGE AND UNIVERSITY STUDENT WORK PROGRAMS: IMPLICATIONS AND IMPLEMENTATIONS. Carbondale: University of Southern Illinois Press, 1970. 272 p.

Suggests a philosophy for student work programs to relate them to vocational planning, self-help, and financial aid. Also gives some historical background.

1738 Allen, Van S. "An Analysis of Textbooks Relative to the Treatment of Black Americans." JOURNAL OF NEGRO EDUCATION 40 (1971): 140-45.

1739 Altbach, Philip. STUDENT POLITICS IN AMERICA: AN HISTORICAL ANALYSIS. New York: McGraw-Hill, 1974. 249 p.

1740 Altschuler, Alan A. COMMUNITY CONTROL: THE BLACK DEMAND FOR PARTICIPATION IN LARGE AMERICAN CITIES. New York: Pegasus, 1970. 238 p.

A general introduction to the theory, motivation, and general issues undergirding community control.

1741 Anderson, Stuart. "The Economic Status of the Teacher Personnel: Historical Development of the Economic Status of High School Teachers in the United States." JOURNAL OF EDUCATIONAL RESEARCH 43 (1950): 607-712.

1742 Armor, David J. "The Evidence on Busing." PUBLIC INTEREST 28 (1972): 90-126.

1743 Armor, David J., et al. "Professors' Attitudes Toward the Vietnam War." PUBLIC OPINION QUARTERLY 31 (1967): 159-75.

1744 Arnold, Walter K., and Britton, Russel K. "Fifty Years of Progress in Trade and Industrial Education." AMERICAN VOCATIONAL JOURNAL 31 (1956): 83-90.

Essentially a review of some of the resource materials extant in this area.

1745 Aron, Raymond. "The Education of the Citizen in Industrial Society." DAEDALUS 91 (1962): 249-63.

1746 Astin, Alexander W. "Open Admissions and Programs for the Disadvantaged." JOURNAL OF HIGHER EDUCATION 42 (1971): 629-47.

1747 Astin, Alexander W., et al. THE POWER OF PROTEST: A NATIONAL STUDY OF STUDENT AND FACULTY DISRUPTIONS WITH IMPLICATIONS FOR THE FUTURE. San Francisco: Jossey-Bass, 1975. 208 p.

An extensive examination of the reports and research on student activism and related issues. Sponsored by the American Council on Education. Covers late 1960s and early 1970s.

1748 Atzmon, Ezri. "The Educational Programs for Immigrants in the United States." HISTORY OF EDUCATION JOURNAL 9 (1950): 75-80.

1749 Axtell, James. "The Death of the Liberal Arts College." HISTORY OF EDUCATION QUARTERLY 11 (1971): 339-52.

Suggests that Whig historians have obscured the nature of the original differences between universities and their collegiate predecessors to the disadvantage of the latter.

1750 Baxton, Paul E. "Human Resources, the Changing Labor Market and Undergraduate Education." LIBERAL EDUCATION 61 (1975): 275-84.

1751 Bayer, Alan E., and Dutton, Jeffrey E. "Trends in Attitudes on Political, Social, and Collegiate Issues Among College Students: Mid-1960s to Mid-1970s." THE JOURNAL OF HIGHER EDUCATION 18 (1976): 159-71.

Takes exception to the allegation that the students of the mid-1970s are more apathetic and conservative than their counterparts in the mid-1960s had been.

1752 Bayles, Ernest E. EXPERIMENTS WITH REFLECTIVE TEACHING. No. 3, vol. 6, Kansas Studies in Education. Lawrence: University of Kansas Press, 1956. 32 p.

1753 _____. DEMOCRATIC EDUCATIONAL THEORY. New York: Harper, 1960. 266 p.

One of the works in the Harper series on teaching.

1754 Beam, Lura. HE CALLED THEM BY THE LIGHTENING: A TEACHER'S ODYSSEY IN THE NEGRO SOUTH, 1908-1919. Indianapolis: Bobbs-Merrill, 1967. 230 p.

A memoir and a sociological observation of a personal teaching experience in the South. She taught children of all ages. Includes pleasant as well as unpleasant experiences there.

1755 Beck, John M. "The Public Schools and the Chicago Newspapers, 1890-1920." SCHOOL REVIEW 62 (1954): 288-95.

1756 Beck, Robert H. "Progressive Education and American Progressivism." TEACHERS COLLEGE RECORD 60 (1958-59): 77-89, 129-37, 198-208.

1757 Bellinger, Luther G. "Education of the Black Minority and Its Effect on the National Economy." LIBERAL EDUCATION 60 (1974--Supplement): 124-30.

1758 Ben-David, Joseph. CENTERS OF LEARNING. New York: McGraw-Hill, 1977. 208 p.

An essay on centers of higher education in Britain, France, Germany, and the United States, prepared for the Carnegie Commission on Higher Education.

1759 Bender, William A. "Desegregation in the Public Schools of Mississippi." JOURNAL OF NEGRO EDUCATION 24 (1955): 287-92.

1760 Bennett, Robert L. CAREERS THROUGH COOPERATIVE WORK EXPERIENCE. New York: Wiley, 1977. 172 p.

1761 Berrol, Selma C. "The Schools of New York in Transition, 1898-1914." URBAN REVIEW 1 (1966): 15-20.

1762 _____. "William Henry Maxwell and a New Educational New York." HISTORY OF EDUCATION QUARTERLY 8 (1968): 215-28.

1763 _____. "Immigrants at School: New York City, 1900-1910." URBAN EDUCATION 4 (1969): 220-30.

1764 Besse, Ralph M. "The Case for Pluralism and Diversity in Higher Education." LIBERAL EDUCATION 60 (1974): 167-76.

1765 Billington, Monroe. "Public School Integration in Missouri, 1954-1965." JOURNAL OF NEGRO EDUCATION 35 (1966): 252-62.

1766 Bledstein, Burton J. THE CULTURE OF PROFESSIONALISM. New York: Norton, 1976. 354 p.

Essentially an educational sociology and a history detailed the role of the middle class in the development of higher education in America.

1767 Bowers, C.A. "The Ideologues of Progressive Education." HISTORY OF EDUCATION QUARTERLY 7 (1967): 452-73.

Seeks to identify the values of the progressive reform movement as being representative of the larger movement that found expression in the ideas of Louis Brandeis and Woodrow Wilson.

1768 Bowers, C.A. THE PROGRESSIVE EDUCATOR AND THE DEPRESSION: THE RADICAL YEARS. New York: Random House, 1969. 270 p.

Examines how liberal educators in the 1930s became radicalized and attempted to turn teachers into agents of social change.

1769 _____. "Social Reconstructionism: Views from the Left and the Right, 1932-1942." HISTORY OF EDUCATION QUARTERLY 10 (1970): 22-52.

How the radical Left had to contend with the social reconstructionists as a direct challenge to orthodox Marxism, and how the radical Right saw them as un-American.

1770 Boyd, William M. DESEGREGATING AMERICA'S COLLEGES: A NATIONWIDE SURVEY OF BLACK STUDENTS, 1972-1973. New York: Praeger, 1974. 110 p.

Concludes that they are a diversified group with some satisfied and some not with their experiences on white campuses, but generally looking ahead to graduate education.

1771 Boydston, Jo Ann. "John Dewey and the Journals." HISTORY OF EDUCATION QUARTERLY 10 (1970): 72-77.

Dewey appeared in: THE LADIES HOME JOURNAL, THE ROTARIAN and the DELINEATOR, as well as in professional journals.

1772 Brickman, William W., ed. AUTOMATION, EDUCATION, AND HUMAN VALUES. New York: School and Society Books, 1966. 419 p.

Collects conference papers by specialists in the fields of industry, labor, education, sociology, religion, and psychology.
Extensive bibliography also included.

1773 Brickman, William W., and Lehrer, Stanley, eds. THE COUNTDOWN
ON SEGREGATED EDUCATION. New York: Society for the Advancement of Education, 1960. 175 p.

1774 _____, eds. RELIGION, GOVERNMENT, AND EDUCATION. New
York: Society for the Advancement of Education, 1961. 292 p.

Includes: Constitutional and legal aspects of the church-state-
school problem, religious celebrations in the schools, and the
debate over public aid to religious schools.

1775 _____, eds. CONFLICT AND CHANGE ON THE CAMPUS: THE RE-
SPONSE TO STUDENT HYPERACTIVISM. New York: School and Society Books, 1970. 528 p.

On student movements and political activity on campus.

1776 _____, eds. EDUCATION AND THE MANY FACES OF THE DISAD-
VANTAGED: CULTURAL AND HISTORICAL PERSPECTIVES. New York:
Wiley, 1972. 435 p.

Ranges widely over the many aspects of the economically and
culturally deprived minorities in America.

1777 Briggs, L.D. "Support from the Top: Major Areas of Responsibility for
Professional Development in Vocational Education." AMERICAN VOCA-
TIONAL JOURNAL 46 (1971): 42-44.

A review of federal legislation on vocational education in the
United States.

1778 Briggs, Thomas H. "Secondary Education in Our Times." TEACHERS
COLLEGE RECORD 46 (1944): 177-85.

1779 Brown, Frank, and Madelon, D.S. MINORITIES IN U.S. INSTITUTIONS
OF HIGHER EDUCATION. New York and London: Praeger Publishers,
1977. 178 p.

Through use of data from the Office of Civil Rights, Census
Bureau, and the National Center for Education statistics, seeks
to show that minorities are badly under represented in institutions of higher education.

1780 Brownell, Samuel M. "Desireable Characteristics of Decentralized School
Systems." PHI DELTA KAPPAN 54 (1971): 286-88.
Emphasizes the need to maintain integrated schools and sub-
districts.

1781 Brunner, Edmund DeS., et al. "Migration and Education." TEACHERS COLLEGE RECORD 49 (1947): 98-107.

1782 Bullock, Henry A. "The Black College and the New Black Americans." DAEDALUS 100 (1971): 573-606.

1783 Burger, Henry G. "ETHNO-PEDAGOGY": A MANUAL IN CULTURAL SENSITIVITY WITH TECHNIQUES FOR IMPROVING CROSS-CULTURAL TEACHING BY FITTING ETHNIC PATTERNS. Albuquerque, N.M.: Southwestern Cooperative Educational Laboratory, 1971. 193 p.

Suggests that the school should be a major cultural institution, and that an applied anthropology approach is needed.

1784 Burns, Richard W., and Klingstedt, Joe Lars. COMPETENCY-BASED EDUCATION: AN INTRODUCTION. Englewood Cliffs, N.J.: Educational Technology Publications, 1973. 169 p.

1785 Burrin, Frank K. EDWARD CHARLES ELLIOT, EDUCATOR. Lafayette, Ind.: Purdue University Press, 1970. 187 p.

Essentially a biography of Elliot and a history of his career, (1922-1945) at Purdue University. Includes a bibliography of Elliot's writings.

1786 Butler, Fred C. COMMUNITY AMERICANIZATION. U.S. Bureau of Education Bulletin No. 76, 1919. Washington, D.C.: Government Printing Office, 1920.

1787 ____. STATE AMERICANIZATION: THE PART OF THE STATE IN THE EDUCATION AND ASSIMILATION OF THE IMMIGRANT. U.S. Bureau of Education Bulletin No. 77, 1919. Washington, D.C.: Government Printing Office, 1920. 26 p.

1788 Calhoun, David. "The City As Teacher." HISTORY OF EDUCATION QUARTERLY 9 (1969): 312-25.

Suggests that the urban setting itself is very educative and may exert stronger effects than do specific schools.

1789 Caliver, Ambrose. PROJECT IN VOCATIONAL EDUCATION AND GUIDANCE OF NEGROES. U.S. Bureau of Education Bulletin No. 38, 1937. Washington, D.C.: Government Printing Office, 1938.

1790 ____. "Certain Significant Developments in the Education of Negroes During the Last Generation." JOURNAL OF NEGRO HISTORY 35 (1950): 111-34.

1791 Campbell, Robert. THE CHASM: LIFE AND DEATH OF A GREAT EX-
PERIMENT IN GHETTO EDUCATION. Boston: Houghton Mifflin, 1974.
185 p.

   With introduction by James Baldwin.

1792 Campbell, Ronald F., and Ramspeyer, John A. THE DYNAMICS OF
SCHOOL-COMMUNITY RELATIONSHIPS. New York: Allyn and Bacon,
1955. 205 p.

1793 Carlson, Robert A. "Americanization as an Early Twentieth-Century Adult
Education Movement." HISTORY OF EDUCATION QUARTERLY 10 (1970):
440-64.

1794 "C.C.C. Camp Educational Activities." In UNITED STATES BUREAU OF
EDUCATION, REPORT OF THE COMMISSIONER, 1940, pp. 73-85.
Washington, D.C.: Government Printing Office, 1940.

1795 Chance, Norman A. MODERNIZATION AND EDUCATIONAL REFORM
IN NATIVE ALASKA. Minneapolis: Training Center for Community
Programs, University of Minnesota, 1971. 28 p.

1796 Chapman, James C., and Counts, George S. PRINCIPLES OF EDUCA-
TION. Boston and New York: Houghton Mifflin, 1924. 645 p.

1797 Cheyney, Arnold B. TEACHING CHILDREN OF DIFFERENT CULTURES
IN THE CLASSROOM: A LANGUAGE APPROACH. Columbus, Ohio:
Merrill, 1976. 189 p.

1798 Church, Robert L. "Educational Psychology and Social Reform in the
Progressive Era." HISTORY OF EDUCATION QUARTERLY 11 (1971):
390-405.

   How leading educational psychologists have rejected the expanding view of the progressive educators, and thus may have
   contributed to its demise.

1799 Clapp, Margaret A. THE MODERN UNIVERSITY. Ithaca, N.Y.: Cornell University Press, 1950. 115 p.

1800 Clift, Virgil, et al., eds. NEGRO EDUCATION IN AMERICA: ITS
ADEQUACY PROBLEMS AND NEEDS. New York: Harper, 1962. 315 p.

1801 Cohen, Andrew D. SOCIOLINGUISTIC APPROACH TO BILINGUAL
EDUCATION: EXPERIMENTS IN THE AMERICAN SOUTHWEST. Rowley,
Mass.: Newbury House, 1975. 352 p.

1802 Cohen, Arthur A., ed. HUMANISTIC EDUCATION AND WESTERN CIVILIZATION: ESSAYS FOR ROBERT M. HUTCHINS. New York: Rinehart and Winston, 1964. 250 p.

> Essays in honor of Hutchins's sixty-fifth birthday by leading American educators.

1803 Cohen, Arthur M. COLLEGE RESPONSES TO COMMUNITY DEMANDS. San Francisco: Jossey-Bass, 1975. 190 p.

1804 Cohen, Arthur M., et al. A CONSTANT VARIABLE, NEW PERSPECTIVES ON THE COMMUNITY COLLEGE. San Francisco: Jossey-Bass, 1971. 238 p.

1805 Cohen, David K. "Education and Race." HISTORY OF EDUCATION QUARTERLY 9 (1969): 281-86.

> A discussion on the segregation deficiencies of the schools versus the individual deficiencies of the children due to poverty controversy.

1806 Cohen, David R. "Jurists and Educators on Urban Schools: The Wright Decision and the Passow Report." TEACHERS COLLEGE RECORD 70 (1968): 233-45.

> Relative to Negro education in the District of Columbia.

1807 Cohen, Helen L. "Americanization by Classroom Practice." TEACHERS COLLEGE RECORD 20 (1919): 238-49.

1808 Cohen, Joseph W., ed. THE SUPERIOR STUDENT IN AMERICAN HIGHER EDUCATION: AN ANALYSIS OF HONORS PROGRAMS. New York: McGraw-Hill, 1966. 299 p.

> Essays comprehensively surveying college honors programs: 1957-65.

1809 Cohen, Michael A., et al. THE POLITICAL LIMITS TO SCHOOL FINANCE REFORM. Washington, D.C.: Urban Institute, 1973. 66 p.

1810 Cohen, Sol. "The Industrial Education Movement, 1906-1917." AMERICAN QUARTERLY 20 (1968): 95-110.

> Suggests it was an effort to block the social progress of immigrant children.

1811 _____. "Urban School Reform." HISTORY OF EDUCATION QUARTERLY 9 (1969): 298-311.

Suggests that educational historians should reconcentrate on power and its exercise in the urban context as regards education.

1812 Cohen, Wilbur J. U.S. DEPARTMENT OF HEALTH, EDUCATION AND WELFARE: ACCOMPLISHMENTS, 1963-1968. Washington, D.C.: Government Printing Office, 1968. 136 p.

A report by the then secretary to President Lyndon B. Johnson. Includes a look to the future as well.

1813 Coleman, James S. "Equal Schools or Equal Students?" THE PUBLIC INTEREST 4 (1966): 70-75.

1814 _____, et al. EQUALITY OF EDUCATIONAL OPPORTUNITY. Washington, D.C.: U.S. Department of Health, Education and Welfare, 1966. Part 1, 737 p., Part 2, 548 p.

Known as the famous Coleman Report on the effects of segregation on racial and ethnic groups. With expensive statistical data in support of the basic antisegregationist thesis predicated upon a survey of about six hundred thousand students nationally in grades one, three, six, nine, and twelve. A decade later Coleman retreated somewhat from these conclusions.

1815 Colson, Edna M. AN ANALYSIS OF THE SPECIFIC REFERENCES TO NEGROES IN SELECTED CURRICULA FOR THE EDUCATION OF TEACHERS. New York: Teachers College, Columbia University Press, 1940. 178 p.

1816 Commission on Educational Governance. PUBLIC TESTIMONY ON PUBLIC SCHOOLS/ NATIONAL COMMITTEE FOR CITIZENS IN EDUCATION. Berkeley, Calif.: McCutchan, 1975. 289 p.

1817 Conant, James B. THE REVOLUTIONARY TRANSFORMATION OF THE AMERICAN HIGH SCHOOL, 1905-1945. Cambridge, Mass.: Harvard University Press, 1959. 39 p.

Originally presented as the 1959 annual Inglis lecture.

1818 Conway, James A., and Milstein, Mike M. UNDERSTANDING COMMUNITIES. Englewood Cliffs, N.J.: Prentice-Hall, 1974. 253 p.

Deals with the community and the school, school publicity, community organization, and educational planning.

1819 Cordasco, Francesco. "Educational Pelagianism: The Schools and the Poor." TEACHERS COLLEGE RECORD 69 (1968): 705-09.

1820 _____. "Puerto Rican Pupils and American Education." SCHOOL AND SOCIETY 95 (1967): 116-19.

1821 _____. "Teachers for Disadvantaged Youth: The City University of New York Program." PEABODY JOURNAL OF EDUCATION 47 (1969): 160-63.

1822 _____. "Historical Perspectives and Contemporary Realities of Catholic Education." SCHOOL AND SOCIETY 99 (1971): 149-52, and also in: URBAN EDUCATION 4 (1971): 119-29.

   Deals with Irish immigrant children and parish schools as an analogue to the Black and Hispanic poor.

1823 _____. "The New Bedford Project for Non-English Speaking Children." JOURNAL OF HUMAN RELATIONS 20 (1972): 326-34.

   About the Portuguese community in New Bedford, Mass.

1824 _____. "Puerto Ricans on the Mainland: The Educational Experience." JOURNAL OF HUMAN RELATIONS 20 (1972): 344-78.

1825 _____. "America and the Quest for Educational Opportunity: A Prolegomenon and Overview." BRITISH JOURNAL OF EDUCATIONAL STUDIES 21 (1973): 50-63.

1826 _____. "The Children of Immigrants in Schools: Historical Analogues of Educational Deprivation." JOURNAL OF NEGRO EDUCATION 42 (1973): 3-12.

1827 _____. "Teaching the Puerto Rican Experience." In TEACHING ETHNIC STUDIES: CONCEPTS AND STRATEGIES, edited by James W. Banks, pp. 226-53. Washington, D.C.: Council for the Social Studies, 1973.

1828 _____. BILINGUAL SCHOOLING IN THE UNITED STATES: A SOURCEBOOK FOR EDUCATIONAL PERSONNEL. New York: McGraw-Hill, 1976. 387 p.

   A comprehensive text on the history, typology and definitions, linguistic perspectives, programs, and so forth, and an overview of court decisions and legislation affecting bilingual education, as well as with program and project descriptions and a selective bibliography.

1829 _____. "The Urban Demos and the Schoolmen." EDUCATIONAL FORUM 40 (1976): 179-84.

1830 Cordasco, Francesco, and Alloway, David N., eds. "Poverty in America: Economic Inequality, New Ideologies and the Search for Educational Opportunity." JOURNAL OF HUMAN RELATIONS 20 (1972): 234-396. Special issue.

1831 Cordasco, Francesco, et al. THE SCHOOL IN THE SOCIAL ORDER: A SOCIOLOGICAL INTRODUCTION TO EDUCATIONAL UNDERSTANDING. Scranton, Pa.: International Textbook, 1970. 425 p.

> Includes the text of the Mayor's Advisory Council report in Decentralization of the New York City school system.

1832 Council of State Governments. HIGHER EDUCATION IN THE FORTY-EIGHT STATES. Chicago: Governors' Conference, 1952. 317 p.

> On the organization and financing of state programs of higher education at that time.

1833 Counts, George S. SCHOOL AND SOCIETY IN CHICAGO. New York: Harcourt, Brace, 1928. 367 p.

> A history of the Chicago school situation and the McAndrew-Thompson controversy over vocational education.

1834 _____. SECONDARY EDUCATION AND INDUSTRIALISM. Cambridge, Mass.: Harvard University Press, 1929. 70 p.

> The 1929 Inglis lecture.

1835 _____. THE AMERICAN ROAD TO CULTURE: A SOCIAL INTERPRETATION OF EDUCATION IN THE UNITED STATES. New York: John Day, 1930. 194 p.

1836 _____. THE SOCIAL FOUNDATIONS OF EDUCATION. New York: Charles Scribner's Sons, 1934. 579 p.

> The report of the Commission on the Social Studies of the American Historical Association.

1837 _____. AMERICAN EDUCATION THROUGH THE SOVIET LOOKING GLASS. New York: Bureau of Publications, Teachers College, Columbia University, 1951. 48 p.

> An analysis of an article by N.K. Goncharov on "The School and Pedagogy in the United States in the Service of Reaction."

1838 _____. EDUCATION AND AMERICAN CIVILIZATION. New York: Bureau of Publications, Teachers College, Columbia University, 1952. 491 p.

1839 _____ . DARE THE SCHOOL BUILD A NEW SOCIAL ORDER? 1932. Reprint. New York: Arno Press, 1969. 56 p.

1840 _____ . THE SELECTIVE CHARACTER OF AMERICAN SECONDARY EDUCATION. 1922. Reprint. New York: Arno Press, 1969. 162 p.

> Classical sociological survey of social class in America then and how it relates to secondary education with added proposals for the equalization of educational opportunity.

1841 _____ . THE SOCIAL COMPOSITION OF BOARDS OF EDUCATION. New York: Arno Press, 1969. 100 p.

> An examination of the social control of public education in the United States.

1842 Covello, Leonard. "A High School and Its Immigrant Community." JOURNAL OF EDUCATIONAL SOCIOLOGY 9 (1936): 333-46.

> About Benjamin Franklin High School in East Harlem, New York City.

1843 Covello, Leonard, and D'Agostino, Guido. THE TEACHER IN THE URBAN COMMUNITY: A HALF CENTURY IN CITY SCHOOLS. Totowa, N.J.: Littlefield, Adams, 1970. 275 p.

> Originally appeared as: THE HEART IS THE TEACHER, New York: McGraw-Hill, 1958. An autobiography of an educational optimist with much insight into educational problems in New York City in the first half of the present century.

1844 Crain, Robert L. THE POLITICS OF SCHOOL DESEGREGATION. Chicago: Aldine Publishing Co., 1968. 390 p.

> A comparative case study on community structure and policymaking. Also appears as: National Opinion Research Center Social Research Monograph, no. 14.

1845 Cremin, Lawrence A. "Toward a More Common School." TEACHERS COLLEGE RECORD 51 (1950): 308-19.

> Examines the attacks on the idea that education alone will eventually provide freedom and equality for all.

1846 _____ . "The Progressive Movement in American Education: A Perspective." HARVARD EDUCATIONAL REVIEW 27 (1957): 251-70.

> On the need for educational reform as seen by the progressive educational movement in the United States.

1847 _____. "John Dewey and the Progressive-Education Movement, 1915-1952." THE SCHOOL REVIEW 67 (1959): 160-73.

Points out how Dewey was a spokesman for the Progressive movement, but did not direct it as he has been charged with doing.

1848 _____. "What Happened to Progressive Education?" TEACHERS COLLEGE RECORD 61 (1959): 23-29.

Suggests four reasons why it declined and then ultimately collapsed.

1849 _____. "The Origins of Progressive Education." THE EDUCATIONAL FORUM 24 (1960): 134-40.

Suggests the origins of the Progressive education movement can be found in the pre-World War I reform movement.

1850 Cremin, Lawrence A., and Borrowman, Merle. PUBLIC SCHOOLS IN OUR DEMOCRACY. New York: Macmillan, 1956. 226 p.

1851 Cubberley, Ellwood P. CHANGING CONCEPTIONS OF EDUCATION. Boston and New York: Houghton Mifflin, 1909. 69 p.

1852 _____. THE IMPROVEMENT OF RURAL SCHOOLS. Boston and New York: Houghton Mifflin, 1912. 75 p.

1853 _____. THE PORTLAND SURVEY: A TEXTBOOK ON CITY SCHOOL ADMINISTRATION BASED ON A CONCRETE STUDY. Yonkers-on-Hudson, N.Y.: World Book, 1915. 441 p.

1854 _____. RURAL LIFE AND EDUCATION: A STUDY OF THE RURAL SCHOOL PROBLEM AS A PHASE OF THE RURAL LIFE PROBLEM. Boston and New York: Houghton Mifflin, 1922. 377 p.

1855 _____. THE PRINCIPAL AND HIS SCHOOL: THE ORGANIZATION, ADMINISTRATION, AND SUPERVISION OF INSTRUCTION IN AN ELEMENTARY SCHOOL. Boston: Houghton Mifflin, 1923. 571 p.

1856 _____. PUBLIC SCHOOL ADMINISTRATION; A STATEMENT OF THE FUNDAMENTAL PRINCIPLES UNDERLYING THE ORGANIZATION AND ADMINISTRATION OF PUBLIC EDUCATION. Boston and New York: Houghton Mifflin, 1929. 710 p.

A revised and enlarged edition of a Riverside textbook in education that first appeared in 1916 and was revised in 1922.

1857 Davis, Arthur. RACIAL CRISIS IN PUBLIC EDUCATION. New York: Vantage Press, 1975. 250 p.

Seeks to suggest a form of social order.

1858 Davis, Howard V. FRANK PARSONS: PROPHET, INNOVATOR, COUNSELOR. Carbondale: University of Southern Illinois Press, 1969. 163 p.

1859 Dewing, Rolland. "The American Federation of Teachers and Desegregation." JOURNAL OF NEGRO EDUCATION 42 (1973): 79-92.

1860 Dexter, Beverly L. SPECIAL EDUCATION AND THE CLASSROOM TEACHER: CONCEPTS, PERSPECTIVES AND STRATEGIES. Springfield, Ill.: C.C. Thomas, 1977. 256 p.

1861 Drake, William E. "Some Implications of the Institutionalization of American Education." HISTORY OF EDUCATION QUARTERLY 1 (1961): 41-47.

Suggests the public school is the main agency for transmission of the cultural heritage and for the maintenance of the social order, as well as for the development of individual opportunities.

1862 Drost, Walter H. "Clarence Kingsley--The New York Years." HISTORY OF EDUCATION QUARTERLY 6 (1966): 18-34.

On social efficiency and Kingsley's chairmanship of the committee that produced the "Cardinal Principles Record" proposal.

1863 _____. DAVID SNEDDEN AND EDUCATION FOR SOCIAL EFFICIENCY. Madison: University of Wisconsin Press, 1968. 242 p.

A biography of the man and a description of the nature and success of the movement.

1864 Duberman, Martin. BLACK MOUNTAIN: AN EXPLORATION IN COMMUNITY. New York: E.P. Dutton, 1972. 527 p.

On how to make history "relevant" and the Black Mountain College (1933-56) effort as a counter culture institution directed at the arts.

1865 Duffus, Robert L. DEMOCRACY ENTERS COLLEGE; A STUDY OF THE RISE AND DECLINE OF THE ACADEMIC LOCKSTEP. New York: Charles Scribner's Sons, 1936. 244 p.

On the unit system method of determining college admission.

1866 Educational Policies Commission. RESEARCH MEMORANDUM ON EDU-
CATION IN THE DEPRESSION. Social Studies Council Research Bulletin No. 28, 1937. New York: Social Sciences Research Council, 1937.
144 p.

1867 Ellsworth, Frank L., and Burns, Martha A. STUDENT ACTIVISM IN
AMERICAN HIGHER EDUCATION. Washington, D.C.: American College Personnel Association, 1970. 64 p.

1868 Esmond, Irwin. PUBLIC EDUCATION IN NEW YORK STATE: A BRIEF
OUTLINE OF THE HISTORY, DEVELOPMENT AND ORGANIZATION OF
THE STATE PUBLIC SCHOOL SYSTEM AND A DIGEST OF THE LAWS
UNDER WHICH IT OPERATES. Albany: New York State Teachers Asso-
ciation, 1937. 61 p.

1869 Fantini, Mario D. THE PEOPLE AND THEIR SCHOOLS: COMMUNITY
PARTICIPATION. Bloomington, Ind.: Phi Delta Kappa Educational
Foundation, 1975. 37 p.

1870 Fantini, Mario D., et al. COMMUNITY CONTROL AND THE URBAN
SCHOOL. New York: Praeger Publishers, 1970. 268 p.

> Focuses on community control in New York City and seeks to
> explain and support the concepts upon which it is predicated.
> Introduction by Kenneth B. Clark.

1871 Fein, Leonard J. THE ECOLOGY OF THE PUBLIC SCHOOLS. New
York: Pegasus, 1971. 170 p.

> An inquiry into community control. Part of the Pegasus series
> on decentralization and the urban crisis.

1872 Feinberg, Walter, et al., eds. WORK, TECHNOLOGY, AND EDUCA-
TION: DISSENTING ESSAYS IN THE INTELLECTUAL FOUNDATIONS
OF AMERICAN EDUCATION. Urbana: University of Illinois Press, 1975.
222 p.

> Essays on education in the United States and how education
> has been affected by the development of technology.

1873 Filler, Louis. "Main Currents in Progressivist American Education." HIS-
TORY OF EDUCATION JOURNAL 8 (1956): 33-57.

1874 Fishman, Joshua. BILINGUAL EDUCATION. Rowley, Mass.: Newbury
House, 1976. 208 p.

> From an international sociological perspective with an appen-
> dix by E. Glyn Lewis.

1875 Friedman, Marjorie. "Public School: Melting Pot or What?" TEACHERS COLLEGE RECORD 70 (1969): 347-51.

> On pluralism in the schools being predicated on the idea that minority cultures are valid educational material.

1876 Friedrichs, Robert W. "Moral Man and Immoral Academy?: Leaves from the Notebook of a Tamed Cynic." JOURNAL OF HIGHER EDUCATION 45 (1974): 285-95.

1877 Fund for the Advancement of Education. TEACHING BY TELEVISION. New York: The Fund, 1961. 87 p.

> A joint report by the Fund and the Ford Foundation.

1878 Garcia, Ricardo L. "Affirmative Action Hiring: Some Perceptions." JOURNAL OF HIGHER EDUCATION 45 (1974): 268-72.

1879 Gaubard, Allen. FREE THE CHILDREN: RADICAL REFORM AND THE FREE SCHOOL MOVEMENT. New York: Random House, 1972. 306 p.

> A survey of the "free school" movement in the United States with notices of the work of John Holt, Paul Goodman, Charles Silberman, and others.

1880 Gauerke, Warren E. "Organized Labor and Federal Aid to Education." HISTORY OF EDUCATION JOURNAL 4 (1953): 81-92.

> An exposition of the positions of organized labor on the matter of the use of federal funds to aid education between World War I and 1952.

1881 Gerard, Harold B., and Miller, Norman. SCHOOL DESEGREGATION. New York: Plenum Press, 1975. 315 p.

> A comprehensive (1966-71) study of the effects of school de- segregation for a program that bussed black children into pre- dominately white Riverside, California, schools.

1882 Gettelman, Marvin E. "John H. Finley at CCNY--1903-1913." HIS- TORY OF EDUCATION QUARTERLY 10 (1970): 423-39.

1883 Glazer, Nathan. "Who Wants Higher Education, Even When It's Free?" PUBLIC INTEREST 39 (1975): 130-35.

1884 Goodlad, John I. SCHOOL CURRICULUM REFORM IN THE UNITED STATES. New York: Fund for the Advancement of Education, 1964. 45 p.

1885 _____. SCHOOL CURRICULUM AND THE INDIVIDUAL. Waltham, Mass.: Blaisdell Publishing, 1966. 259 p.

1886 _____. THE DYNAMICS OF EDUCATIONAL CHANGE: TOWARD RESPONSIVE SCHOOLS. New York: McGraw-Hill, 1975. 267 p.

   A Charles F. Kettering Foundation program on school management, organization, and innovations. Introduction by Samuel G. Sava. Extensive bibliography included.

1887 _____. THE USES OF ALTERNATIVE THEORIES OF EDUCATIONAL CHANGE: A MONOGRAPH. Bloomington, Ind.: Phi Delta Kappa International, 1976. 35 p.

1888 _____. EDUCATION AND SOCIAL ACTION: COMMUNITY SERVICE AND THE CURRICULUM IN HIGHER EDUCATION. London: Allen and Unwin, 1975. 203 p.

1889 Goodlad, John I., and Anderson, Robert H. THE NONGRADED ELEMENTARY SCHOOL. Rev. ed. New York: Harcourt, Brace and World, 1963. 248 p.

1890 Goodlad, John I., et al. THE CHANGING SCHOOL CURRICULUM. New York: Fund for the Advancement of Education, 1966. 122 p.

   An overview of the changes since the early 1950s. Includes an annotated bibliography.

1891 _____. COMPUTERS AND INFORMATION SYSTEMS IN EDUCATION. New York: Harcourt, Brace and World, 1966. 152 p.

   On electronic data processing systems.

1892 _____. EARLY SCHOOLING IN THE UNITED STATES. New York: McGraw-Hill, 1973. 240 p.

   A report by the Institute for the Development of Educational Activities in the Early Schooling Series. Forward by Samuel G. Sava.

1893 _____. THE CONVENTIONAL AND THE ALTERNATIVE IN EDUCATION. Berkeley, Calif.: McCutchan, 1975. 276 p.

1894 Goodlad, John I., and Shane, Harold G., eds. THE ELEMENTARY SCHOOL IN THE UNITED STATES. Chicago: University of Chicago Press, 1973. 418 p.

   The 1972 yearbook of the National Society for the Study of Education as prepared by the N.S.S.E. committee on the elementary school.

1895 Gower, Calvin W. "The Civilian Conservation Corps and American Education: Threat to Local Control." HISTORY OF EDUCATION QUARTERLY 7 (1967): 58-70.

1896 Graham, Patricia A. PROGRESSIVE EDUCATION: FROM ARCADY TO ACADEME: A HISTORY OF THE PROGRESSIVE EDUCATION ASSOCIATION, 1919-1955. New York: Teachers College, Columbia University Press, 1967. 193 p.

　　　Traces its rise and fall, as well as all facets about the P.E.A. Extensive bibliography included.

1897 Grant, Gerald, and Riesman, David. "An Ecology of Academic Reform." DAEDALUS 104 (1975): 166-91.

　　　Volume 2 of the Proceedings of the American Academy of Arts and Sciences--American Education: Toward an Uncertain Future.

1898 Greene, Maxine. THE PUBLIC SCHOOL AND THE PRIVATE VISION. New York: Random House, 1965. 185 p.

　　　Connects the vision of education to the historical paradox in which the ideal of creative striving is pitted against the dream of equalitarian populism.

1899 Gribble, Stephen C. TEACHER QUALIFICATIONS AND SCHOOL ATTENDANCE IN NEW MEXICO, 1918-1948. Albuquerque: University of New Mexico Press, 1948. 39 p.

1900 Gross, Barry E., ed. REVERSE DISCRIMINATION. Buffalo, N.Y.: Prometheus Books, 1977. 397 p.

　　　A collection of dissenting views on affirmative action in higher education.

1901 Gulik, Luther H., and Modley, Rudolf. THE NEW YORK PRIMER. New York: Regents Inquiry, 1939. 46 p.

　　　An inquiry by the New York State Board of Regents on the character and cost of public education in that state.

1902 Gumbert, Edgar B., and Spring, Joel H. THE SUPERSCHOOL AND THE SUPERSTATE, AMERICAN EDUCATION IN THE TWENTIETH CENTURY, 1918-1970. New York: Wiley, 1974. 214 p.

1903 Hamilton, Andrew, and Jackson, John B. UCLA ON THE MOVE DURING FIFTY GOLDEN YEARS, 1919-1969. Los Angeles: Ward Ritchie, 1969. 230 p.

Essentially biographical vignettes of founders, administrators, noted faculty members, students, and athletes. Well illustrated.

1904 Hansen, Carl F. DANGER IN WASHINGTON: THE STORY OF MY TWENTY YEARS IN THE PUBLIC SCHOOLS IN THE NATION'S CAPITOL. West Nyack, N.Y.: Parker Publishing, 1968. 237 p.

A case study by a major administrator in the Washington system for twenty years. On changes, policies, and problems.

1905 Harris, Michael R. FIVE COUNTERREVOLUTIONISTS IN HIGHER EDUCATION: IRVING BABBITT, ALBERT JAY NOCK, ABRAHAM FLEXNER, ROBERT MAYNARD HUTCHINS, ALEXANDER MEIKELJOHN. Corvallis: Orgeon State University Press, 1970. 224 p.

On the role for higher education as advanced by each of the five. A philosophy of education monograph.

1906 Hassenger, Robert, ed. THE SHAPE OF CATHOLIC HIGHER EDUCATION. Chicago: University of Chicago Press, 1967. 373 p.

A survey of an area that had remained generally ignored till recently.

1907 Havighurst, Robert J. "The Impact of Population Change and Working Force Change on American Education." EDUCATIONAL RECORD 41 (1960): 346-58.

1908 Hechinger, Fred. "Students of the Sixties: Salvaging the Youth Movement." CHANGE 5 (1973): 31-35.

By the education editor of the NEW YORK TIMES. Essentially a journalistic essay and account.

1909 Heerman, Barry. COOPERATIVE EDUCATION IN COMMUNITY COLLEGES. San Francisco: Jossey-Bass, 1973. 219 p.

A sourcebook devoted to the growing cooperative education movement in community colleges and other two-year schools.

1910 Henry, David D. CHALLENGES PAST, CHALLENGES PRESENT: AN ANALYSIS OF AMERICAN HIGHER EDUCATION SINCE 1930. San Francisco: Jossey-Bass, 1975. 173 p.

Generally regarded as a perceptive survey of the most recent half century in American higher education.

1911 Herbst, Jurgen, "High School and Youth in America." JOURNAL OF CONTEMPORARY HISTORY 2 (1967): 165-82.

Also included as a part of: Laqueur, Walter, and Mosse, George L., EDUCATION AND SOCIAL STRUCTURE IN THE TWENTIETH CENTURY, 1968.

1912 Hills, P.J. THE SELF-TEACHING PROCESS IN HIGHER EDUCATION. New York: Wiley, 1976. 144 p.

1913 Hillson, Maurie, comp. EDUCATION AND THE URBAN COMMUNITY. New York: American Book Co., 1969. 506 p.

A series of essays and lectures by Hillson, Francesco Cordasco, and Francis P. Purcell. Bibliographical footnotes included.

1914 Institute for the Study of Educational Policy. EQUAL EDUCATIONAL OPPORTUNITY FOR BLACKS IN U.S. HIGHER EDUCATION: AN AS-SESSMENT. Washington, D.C.: Howard University Press, 1976. 330 p.

Seeks to ascertain the degree to which equal access to gradu-ate and undergraduate education has been achieved as of 1973-74.

1915 Iwamoto, David. SMALL HIGH SCHOOLS, 1960-1961. Washington, D.C.: National Education Association, 1963. 119 p.

1916 Jackson, Reid E. "The Development and Character of Permissive and Partly Segregated Schools." JOURNAL OF NEGRO EDUCATION 16 (1947): 301-10.

1917 Jencks, Christopher, et al. INEQUALITY: A REASSESSMENT OF THE EFFECT OF FAMILY AND SCHOOLING IN AMERICA. New York: Basic Books, 1972. 399 p.

A generally controversial, socialistic reworking of the Cole-man Report with extensive appendexes, footnotes, and refer-ences filling half the work.

1918 Jennings, Robert E., and Milstein, Mike M. "Citizens' Attitudes in School Tax Voting." EDUCATION AND URBAN SOCIETY 5 (1973): 299-320.

1919 Johnson, Carrol F., and Usdan, Michael D., eds. EQUALITY OF EDU-CATIONAL OPPORTUNITY IN THE LARGE CITIES OF AMERICA. New York: Teachers College, Columbia University Press, 1968. 197 p.

Explores the relationship between decentralization of schools and racial integration. A report sponsored by the department of educational administration of the Teachers College of Colum-bia University, 10-12 July 1968.

1920 Jones, Harold E., et al. ADOLESCENCE. Bloomington, Ind.: National Council of Social Studies Education, 1944.

Issued as part one of the 43d yearbook of the council.

1921 Jones, Lewis W. "Desegregation of Public Education in Alabama." JOURNAL OF NEGRO EDUCATION 24 (1955): 165-71.

1922 _____. "Two Years of Desegregation in Alabama." JOURNAL OF NEGRO EDUCATION 25 (1956): 205-11.

1923 Jones, Thomas J. RECENT PROGRESS IN NEGRO EDUCATION. U.S. Bureau of Education Bulletin No. 27, 1919. Washington, D.C.: Government Printing Office, 1919. 16 p.

1924 Judd, Charles H. "Changing Conceptions of Secondary and Higher Education in America." SCHOOL REVIEW 45 (1937): 93-104.

1925 Kandel, Isaac L. THE IMPACT OF THE WAR UPON AMERICAN EDUCATION, 1939-1947. Chapel Hill: University of North Carolina Press, 1948. 285 p.

1926 Keil, Thomas J. "Environmental Differentiation and Policy Output: The Sociology of Local Public Education." EDUCATION AND URBAN SOCIETY 5 (1973): 277-98.

1927 Keppel, Francis. THE NECESSARY REVOLUTION IN AMERICAN EDUCATION. New York: Harper and Row, 1966. 201 p.

A strong statement on the need for developing policy in education along with an assessment of the growing partnership between state, local, and federal governments by the former U.S. commissioner of education (1962-66).

1928 Kizer, George A. "Federal Aid to Education: 1945-1963." HISTORY OF EDUCATION QUARTERLY 10 (1970): 84-102.

Basically about the religious issue involved, in addition to the segregation problem.

1929 Kilpatrick, William H. THE MONTESSORI SYSTEM EXAMINED. Boston: Houghton Mifflin, 1914. 71 p. Reprint. New York: Arno Press, 1910.

A Riverside educational monograph originally.

1930 _____. FOUNDATIONS OF METHOD: INFORMAL TALKS ON TEACHING. New York: Macmillan, 1926. 383 p.

Recently reprinted by the Arno Press.

1931 _____. OUR EDUCATIONAL TASK, AS ILLUSTRATED IN THE CHANG-
ING SOUTH. Chapel Hill: University of North Carolina Press, 1930.
123 p.

1932 _____. A RECONSTRUCTED THEORY OF THE EDUCATIVE PROCESS.
New York: Teachers College, Columbia University Press, 1935. 30 p.

1933 _____. EDUCATION FOR A CHANGING CIVILIZATION. New York:
Macmillan, 1937. 143 p.

Three lectures in the Laflin Kellogg Foundation series at Rutgers University, 1926.

1934 _____. PHILOSOPHY OF EDUCATION. New York: Macmillan, 1951.
465 p.

1935 Kilpatrick, William H., ed. THE EDUCATIONAL FRONTIER. New York
and London: Century, 1933. 325 p. Reprint. Arno Press, 1970.

Includes materials by Boyd H. Bode, John Dewey, John L.
Childs, R.B. Raup, H. Gordon Hullfish, and V.T. Thayer.

1936 Koch, Raymond, and Koch, Charlotte. EDUCATIONAL COMMUNE: THE
STORY OF COMMONWEALTH COLLEGE. Boston: Schocken, 1972.
211 p.

About a small Arkansas school that devoted itself to training
radical union activists and other "change agents."

1937 Kozol, Jonathan. "Halls of Darkness: In the Ghetto Schools." HAR-
VARD EDUCATIONAL REVIEW 37 (1967): 379-407.

About the author's experiences in ghetto schools in a major
city including traits and attitudes of teachers, administrators,
and students, supposedly representative of them generally.

1938 Krug, Edward A. THE SHAPING OF THE AMERICAN HIGH SCHOOL.
New York: Harper, 1964. 486 p.

1939 Ladd, Everett C., Jr., and Lipset, Seymour M. THE DIVIDED ACADE-
MY: PROFESSORS AND POLITICS. New York: McGraw-Hill, 1975.
407 p.

Generally on political activism within the American university.

1940 LaNoue, George R., and Smith, Bruce L.R. THE POLITICS OF SCHOOL
DECENTRALIZATION. Lexington, Mass.: Lexington Books, 1973. 358 p.

On issues, conflicts, and confrontations in school decentralization. Deals with the politics thereof in five major cities.

1941 Lazerson, Marvin, and Olneck, Michael R. "The School Achievement of Immigrant Children, 1900-1930." HISTORY OF EDUCATION QUARTERLY 14 (1974): 453-82.

Compares them to similar achievements by native, white Americans and with variations between various different nationality groups.

1942 Lee, Gordon C. "Government Pressures on the Schools During World War II." HISTORY OF EDUCATION JOURNAL 3 (1951): 65-74.

1943 Lentz, Donald W. "History and Development of the Junior High School." TEACHERS COLLEGE RECORD 58 (1956): 522-30.

1944 Levin, Henry M., ed. COMMUNITY CONTROL OF SCHOOLS: BROOKINGS CONFERENCE ON THE COMMUNITY SCHOOL, 1968. Washington, D.C.: Brookings Institution, 1970. 318 p.

Essays on community control: historic and philosophic rationale, black nationalism, the Ocean Hill-Brownsville experiment, and others.

1945 Levine, Daniel U. "The Integration-Compensatory Education Controversy." EDUCATIONAL FORUM 32 (1968): 323-32.

1946 Lincoln, C. Eric. "The Negro Colleges and Cultural Change." DAEDALUS 100 (1971): 603-29.

1947 Lipset, Seymour M. REBELLION IN THE UNIVERSITY. Chicago: University of Chicago Press, 1976. 319 p.

1948 Lipset, Seymour M., and Riesman, David. EDUCATION AND POLITICS AT HARVARD. New York: McGraw-Hill, 1975. 440 p.

Two essays prepared initially for the Carnegie Commission on Higher Education.

1949 Lipset, Seymour M., and Wolin, Sheldon S. THE BERKELEY STUDENT REVOLT: FACTS AND INTERPRETATIONS. Garden City, N.Y.: Anchor Books, 1965. 585 p.

1950 Long, Larry H. "Does Migration Interfere with Children's Progress in School?" SOCIOLOGY OF EDUCATION 48 (1975): 369-81.

1951 McBride, Paul W. "The Co-Op Industrial Education Experiment, 1900-1917." HISTORY OF EDUCATION QUARTERLY 14 (1974): 209-21.

A survey and an analysis of its usefulness and effectiveness.

1952 McGaughy, J.R. "The Extension of the Frontier in Elementary Education Since 1900." TEACHERS COLLEGE RECORD 34 (1933): 580-86.

1953 McKeefrey, William J. PARAMETERS OF LEARNING: PERSPECTIVES IN HIGHER EDUCATION TODAY. Carbondale: Southern Illinois University Press, 1970. 169 p.

1954 McPhail, James H., ed. A HISTORY OF DESEGREGATION DEVELOPMENTS IN CERTAIN MISSISSIPPI SCHOOL DISTRICTS. Hattiesburg: University of Southern Mississippi Press, 1971. 140 p.

   A survey done for the Mississippi School Study Council.

1955 Mahoney, John J. AMERICANIZATION IN THE UNITED STATES. U.S. Bureau of Education Bulletin No. 31, 1923. Washington, D.C.: Government Printing Office, 1923. 42 p.

1956 Manier, Edward, and Houck, John, eds. ACADEMIC FREEDOM IN THE CATHOLIC UNIVERSITY. Notre Dame, Ind.: Fides Press, 1967. 225 p.

1957 Marty, Martin E. "Feeling Saved and Feeling Good." NEW YORK UNIVERSITY EDUCATION QUARTERLY 9 (1978): 2-8.

   Suggests that education and religion do not have to be at war with each other. Traces the intellectual history of the West from Aquinas and Maimonides to recent times.

1958 Mays, Arthur B. "Fifty Years of Progress in Vocational and Practical Arts Education." AMERICAN VOCATIONAL JOURNAL 31 (1956): 29-38.

1959 Meyer, Peter. AWARDING COLLEGE CREDIT FOR NON-COLLEGE LEARNING. San Francisco: Jossey-Bass, 1975. 195 p.

   Procedural guide to the granting of college credit for experiential learning obtained outside the classroom, on the job, or through life experience.

1960 Miller, Carroll L. "Trends in Negro Education from 1930 to 1939 and Prospects for the 1940's." JOURNAL OF NEGRO EDUCATION 10 (1941): 280-93.

1961 Morison, Samuel E. THE SCHOLAR IN AMERICA: PAST, PRESENT AND FUTURE. New York: Oxford University Press, 1961. 32 p.

1962 Mosteller, Frederick, and Moynihan, Daniel P., eds. ON EQUALITY OF EDUCATIONAL OPPORTUNITY. New York: Random House, 1972. 546 p.

A series of papers by Christopher Jencks, James Coleman, Edmund Gordon, Henry Dyer, and others on the Coleman Report (1966) at a Harvard University faculty seminar on the report.

1963 Mowsesian, Richard. REPORT OF THE FIRST NATIONAL CONGRESS OF BLACK PROFESSIONALS IN HIGHER EDUCATION. Austin: Hogg Foundation for Mental Health, 1973. 97 p.

1964 Murphy, Judith, and Gross, Ronald. LEARNING BY TELEVISION. New York: Fund for the Advancement of Education, 1966. 95 p.

1965 Norton, John K. "The Civilian Conservation Corps, the National Youth Administration, and the Public Schools." TEACHERS COLLEGE RECORD 43 (1941): 174-82.

1966 Olneck, Michael R., and Lazerson, Marvin. "The School Achievement of Immigrant Children, 1900-1930." HISTORY OF EDUCATION QUARTERLY 14 (1974): 453-82.

Compares especially southern Italian and Russian Jewish immigrant children with white, native born on measurements of school attendance and continuance.

1967 Painter, Nell. "Jim Crow at Harvard: 1923." THE NEW ENGLAND QUARTERLY 44 (1971): 627-34.

1968 Perdew, Phillip W. "The Secondary School Program in World War II." HISTORY OF EDUCATION JOURNAL 3 (1952): 43-48

On how the schools were used to prepare young men for their forthcoming military service in that era.

1969 Perry, Glen. "Communication Between the Academician and the Businessman." BUSINESS HISTORY REVIEW 36 (1962): 87-97.

1970 Peterson, Patti M. "Colonialism and Education: The Case of the Afro-American." COMPARATIVE EDUCATION REVIEW 15 (1971): 146-57.

1971 Peterson, Paul E. "Politics of Educational Reform in England and the United States." COMPARATIVE EDUCATION REVIEW 17 (1973): 160-79.

1972 Peterson, Richard E. "The Student Left in American Higher Education." DAEDALUS 97 (1968): 293-317.

1973 Pettigrew, Thomas F. "The Role of Whites in the Black Colleges of the Future." DAEDALUS 100 (1971): 813-32.

1974 Pfnister, Allan O. "The Role of Faculty in University Governance." JOURNAL OF HIGHER EDUCATION 41 (1970): 430-49.

1975 Phenix, Philip H. "Religion in Public Education: Principles and Issues." JOURNAL OF CHURCH AND STATE 14 (1972): 415-30.

1976 Phillips, J.O.C. "The Education of Jane Addams." HISTORY OF EDUCATION QUARTERLY 14 (1974): 49-68.

1977 Phillips, Myrtle R. "Origin, Development, and Present Status of Public Secondary Education for Negroes in Kentucky." JOURNAL OF NEGRO EDUCATION 1 (1932): 414-23.

1978 Picott, J. Rupert. "The Negro Public College in Virginia." JOURNAL OF NEGRO EDUCATION 31 (1962): 275-83.

1979 Piedmont, Eugene B. "Changing Racial Attitudes at a Southern University: 1947-1964." JOURNAL OF NEGRO EDUCATION 36 (1967): 32-41.

1980 Pitkin, Royce S. PUBLIC SCHOOL SUPPORT IN THE UNITED STATES DURING PERIODS OF ECONOMIC DEPRESSION. Brattleboro, Vt.: Stephen Daye Press, 1933. 143 p.

1981 Polishook, Sheila S. "Collective Bargaining and the City University of New York." JOURNAL OF HIGHER EDUCATION 41 (1970): 377-86.

1982 Porter, Gilbert L. "Negro Publicly-Supported Higher Institutions in Florida." JOURNAL OF NEGRO EDUCATION 31 (1962): 293-98.

1983 Pusey, Nathan M. AMERICAN HIGHER EDUCATION, 1945-1970. Cambridge, Mass.: Harvard University Press, 1978. 204 p.

   An overview of the major developments that changed higher education during the postwar years in the form of a personal report by a former president of Harvard University.

1984 Redefer, Frederick L. "What Has Happened to Progressive Education?" SCHOOL AND SOCIETY 67 (1948): 345-49.

1985 A Report of the Carnegie Council on Policy Studies in Higher Education. MAKING AFFIRMATIVE ACTION WORK IN HIGHER EDUCATION: AN ANALYSIS OF INSTITUTIONAL AND FEDERAL POLICIES WITH RECOMMENDATIONS. San Francisco: Jossey-Bass, 1975. 272 p.

1986 Richey, Herman G. "Educational Status of Important Population Groups Between the First and Second World Wars." SCHOOL REVIEW 57 (1949): 16-27, 89-100.

Comparison of the twenty-five to twenty-nine and the forty to forty-four age groups in 1940.

1987 Rippa, S. Alexander. "The Textbook Controversy and the Free Enterprise Campaign, 1940-1941." HISTORY OF EDUCATION JOURNAL 9 (1958): 49-58.

1988 _____. "Retrenchment in a Period of Defensive Opposition to the New Deal: The Business Community and the Public Schools, 1932-1934." HISTORY OF EDUCATION QUARTERLY 2 (1962): 76-82.

1989 _____. "The Business Community and the Public Schools on the Eve of the Great Depression." HISTORY OF EDUCATION QUARTERLY 4 (1964): 33-43.

On the demand for a more functional educational curriculum as universal education was extended, and which slackened off during the Great Depression (1929-33).

1990 Rist, Ray C. THE INVISIBLE CHILDREN: SCHOOL INTEGRATION IN AMERICAN SOCIETY. Cambridge, Mass.: Harvard University Press, 1978. 289 p.

Discusses integration from four perspectives: as racial assimilation, as racial pluralism, as class assimilation, and as class pluralism.

1991 Robertson, Florence K. "The Historical Development of Evening Schools." SCHOOL AND SOCIETY 32 (1930): 297-99.

1992 Robinson, Donald W. "What Happened to Our Schools?" SOCIAL EDUCATION 23 (1958): 18-22.

On problems and changes in the schools since adoption of the compulsory school attendance laws in 1890.

1993 Romanofsky, Peter. "The Public is Aroused: The Missouri Children's Code Commission, 1915-1919." MISSOURI HISTORICAL REVIEW 68 (1974): 204-22.

1994 Rosenstein, David. "Contributions of Education to Ethnic Fusion in America." SCHOOL AND SOCIETY 13 (1921): 673-82.

1995 Rothman, Esther P. THE AGE INSIDE WENT SOUR. New York: David McKay, 1971. 333 p.

On the author's decade as principal at Livingston School in New York City. An autobiographical account. Harshly anecdotal.

American Education in 20th Century

1996 Rotzel, Grace. THE SCHOOL IN ROSE VALLEY: A PARENT VENTURE IN EDUCATION. Baltimore: Johns Hopkins University Press, 1971. 147 p.

>About the Rose Valley, Pennsylvania, school and its emphasis on self-development and firsthand experiences. A history of the school over a forty-year period.

1997 Rourke, Francis E., and Brooks, Glenn E. THE MANAGERIAL REVOLU-TION IN HIGHER EDUCATION. Baltimore: Johns Hopkins University Press, 1966. 184 p.

>An analysis of questionnaires about college administrative practices in use now.

1998 Rudwick, Elliot, and Meier, August. "Early Boycotts of Segregated Schools: The Case of Springfield, Ohio, 1922-1923." AMERICAN QUAR-TERLY 20 (1968): 744-58.

1999 Rudy, Willis. SCHOOLS IN AN AGE OF MASS CULTURE: AN EX-PLORATION OF SELECTED THEMES IN THE HISTORY OF TWENTIETH CENTURY AMERICAN EDUCATION. Englewood Cliffs, N.J.: Prentice-Hall, 1965. 374 p.

>A series of essays on educational matters of interest to the author, but without any central or integrating theme to them.

2000 Russell, William F. "Liberty and Learning: A Discussion of Education and the New Deal." TEACHERS COLLEGE RECORD 35 (1933): 89-103.

2001 Salisbury, Robert H. "Schools and Politics in the Big City." HARVARD EDUCATIONAL REVIEW 37 (1967): 408-24.

>Suggests that education would be better served if it were more closely tied to the political structure, and also suggests how this might be done.

2002 Sanchez, Ramon. "John Dewey's THE SCHOOL AND SOCIETY-- Perspec-tives, 1969." HISTORY OF EDUCATION QUARTERLY 10 (1970): 78-83.

>Defends Dewey's idea that the school should be brought into step with the changes the Industrial Revolution has wrought on our society.

2003 Sanders, Shirley. "Analysis of Junior College Growth, 1928-1948." JUNIOR COLLEGE JOURNAL 18 (1948): 307-13.

2004 Schnell, Rudolph L. NATIONAL ACTIVIST STUDENT ORGANIZATIONS IN AMERICAN HIGHER EDUCATION, 1905-1944. Ann Arbor: Univer-sity of Michigan School of Education Press, 1976. 258 p.

2005 Schudson, Michael S. "Organizing the 'Meritocracy': A History of the College Entrance Examination Board." HARVARD EDUCATIONAL REVIEW 42 (1972): 54-69.

2006 Seguel, Mary L. THE CURRICULUM FIELD: ITS FORMATIVE YEARS. New York: Teachers College, Columbia University Press, 1966. 203 p.

   Covers period 1895-1937 and the ideas of seven major thinkers in the field about this matter.

2007 Siebert, Wilbert H. "The Ohio State University in the World War." NORTHWEST OHIO QUARTERLY 31 (1922): 141-71.

2008 Silberman, Charles E. CRISIS IN THE CLASSROOM: THE REMAKING OF AMERICAN EDUCATION. New York: Random House, 1970. 553 p.

   Advances the thesis that schools tend to make children become docile and proposes the use of British informal education experimental techniques as the necessary corrective for this.

2009 Silver, Catherine B. BLACK TEACHERS IN URBAN SCHOOLS: THE CASE OF WASHINGTON, D.C. New York: Praeger, 1973. 222 p.

   Based upon a 1967 survey questionnaire of the district elementary school teachers.

2010 Sisk, Glenn. "Educational Awakening in Alabama and Its Effects upon the Black Belt, 1900-1917." JOURNAL OF NEGRO EDUCATION 25 (1956): 191-96.

2011 Smith, G. Kerry, ed. TWENTY-FIVE YEARS: 1945 TO 1970. San Francisco: Jossey-Bass, 1970. 330 p.

   Suggests current problems had been foreseen by earlier thinkers. Cites examples.

2012 Smith, Timothy L. "Immigrant Social Aspirations and American Education, 1880-1930." AMERICAN QUARTERLY 21 (1969): 523-43.

2013 Smith, W.R., et al. THE VALUE OF PROFESSIONAL TRAINING IN EDUCATION. Lawrence: University of Kansas Press, 1933. 15 p.

   A critique of the A.A.U.P. Bulletin on required courses in education.

2014 Spivack, Robert G. "Growth of an American Youth Movement, 1905-1941." AMERICAN SCHOLAR 10 (1941): 352-61.

2015 Spring, Joel. "Education and Progressivism." HISTORY OF EDUCATION
QUARTERLY 10 (1970): 53-71.

Suggests that the Progressive educators of the 1920s offered
both a meaningful as well as a radical alternative to education.

2016 Stambler, Moses. "The Effect of Compulsory Education and Child Labor
Laws on High School Attendance in New York City, 1898-1917." HIS-
TORY OF EDUCATION QUARTERLY 8 (1968): 189-214.

2017 Stevens, Edward W., Jr. "Social Centers, Politics, and Social Efficiency
in the Progressive Era." HISTORY OF EDUCATION QUARTERLY 12 (1972):
16-33.

Sees the schools as such centers and as agencies of adjustment
to changing social values. Also discusses the major literature
on this subject (1913-21).

2018 Studolsky, Susan S., and Lesser, Gerald. "Learning Patterns in the Disadvantaged." HARVARD EDUCATIONAL REVIEW 37 (1967): 546-89.

Takes exception to James S. Coleman's definition of "equal
educational opportunity," and suggests an alternative to it.

2019 Summerscales, William. AFFIRMATION AND DISSENT: COLUMBIA'S
RESPONSE TO THE CRISIS OF WORLD WAR I. New York: Teachers
College, Columbia University Press, 1970. 159 p.

On the matter of administrative rigidity under Nicholas Murray
Butler and its problems and consequences.

2020 Super, Donald E., and Wright, Robert D. "From School to Work in the
Depression Years." SCHOOL REVIEW 49 (1941): 123-30.

2021 Teitelbaum, Herbert, and Hiller, Richard L. "Bilingual Education: The
Legal Mandate." HARVARD EDUCATIONAL REVIEW 47 (1977): 138-70.

A review of the "Nichols" decision, as well as a discussion of
options available to end discrimination based upon language
without violation of constraints on segregation at the same time.

2022 Thelin, John R. "Life and Learning in Southern California: Private
Colleges in the Popular Culture." HISTORY OF EDUCATION QUARTER-
LY 15 (1975): 111-17.

2023 Thomas, Alan M., Jr. "American Education and the Immigrant."
TEACHERS COLLEGE RECORD 55 (1954): 253-67.

2024 Thut, I.N., and Adams, Don. EDUCATIONAL PATTERNS IN CON-
TEMPORARY SOCIETIES. New York: McGraw-Hill, 1964. 494 p.

Part of the McGraw-Hill series in education. Done in the sociohistorical methodology.

2025 Toppin, Edgar A. "Walter White and the Atlanta NAACP's Fight for Equal Schools." HISTORY OF EDUCATION QUARTERLY 7 (1967): 3-21.

2026 Touraine, Alain. THE ACADEMIC SYSTEM IN AMERICAN SOCIETY. New York: McGraw-Hill, 1974. 319 p.

Suggests education has been used by the ruling class to perpetuate the present system.

2027 Trattner, Walter I. CRUSADE FOR CHILDREN: A HISTORY OF THE NATIONAL CHILD LABOR COMMITTEE AND CHILD LABOR REFORM IN AMERICA. Chicago: Quadrangle, 1970.

A sociopolitical history of the effort to abolish child labor. Reviewed in some depth by: Joseph F. Kett, HISTORY OF EDUCATION QUARTERLY 13 (1973): 191-94.

2028 Tyack, David B. "Growing Up Black: Perspectives on the History of Education in Northern Ghettos." HISTORY OF EDUCATION QUARTERLY 9 (1969): 287-97.

Suggests investigative approaches in examining same.

2029 Unger, Irwin. THE MOVEMENT: A HISTORY OF THE AMERICAN NEW LEFT, 1959-1972. New York: Dodd, Mead, 1974. 217 p.

On radical political activity on the college campuses in that era.

2030 United States Commission on Civil Rights. SCHOOL DESEGREGATION IN TEN COMMUNITIES. Washington, D.C.: Government Printing Office, 1973. 235 p.

2031 United States Congress. Senate. Select Committee on Equal Educational Opportunity. TOWARD EQUAL EDUCATIONAL OPPORTUNITY. 1972. Reprint. New York: AMS Press, 1974. 459 p.

Originally published by the Government Printing Office in 1972. Reprinted, with editing by Francesco Cordasco in 1974. A compendium of materials covering all aspects of educational opportunity in the United States.

2032 United States Immigration Commission, 1907-1910. THE CHILDREN OF IMMIGRANTS IN SCHOOLS. 1911. Reprint. Metuchen, N.J.: Scarecrow Press, 1970. 5 vols.

A mass of data covering two million children, forty-nine thousand teachers, and thirty-two thousand eight hundred college students in thirty-seven cities. Includes introduction by Francesco Cordasco.

2033 Urban, Wayne. "Organized Teachers and Educational Reform During the Progressive Era: 1890-1920." HISTORY OF EDUCATION QUARTERLY 16 (1976): 35-52.

2034 Valentine, Marian G. "William H. Maxwell and Progressive Education." SCHOOL AND SOCIETY 75 (1952): 353-56.

2035 Veysey, Laurence. "Experiments in Higher Education." HARVARD EDUCATIONAL REVIEW 43 (1973): 258-68.

2036 Violas, Paul C. THE TRAINING OF THE URBAN WORKING CLASS: A HISTORY OF TWENTIETH CENTURY AMERICAN EDUCATION. Chicago: Rand McNally, 1978. 245 p.

A study of the transformation of American public education between 1890-1930.

2037 Wayland, Sloan R., and Brunner, Edmund. THE EDUCATIONAL CHARACTERISTICS OF THE AMERICAN PEOPLE. New York: Bureau of Applied Social Research, Columbia University, 1958. 258 p.

Compares levels of education with the indexes, occupations, and characteristics of American teachers as revealed in the 1950 census.

2038 Weinberg, Meyer. A CHANCE TO LEARN: THE HISTORY OF RACE AND EDUCATION IN THE UNITED STATES. Cambridge, Mass.: Cambridge University Press, 1977. 471 p.

2039 Weinrich, R.C., et al. "Vocational, Technical, and Practical Arts Education: History of Vocational Education." REVIEW OF EDUCATIONAL RESEARCH 32 (1962): 370 p.

Traces developments since World War I including some materials on federal roles in the period.

2040 Wendt, Erhard F. "Brief History of Industrial Arts and Vocational Education." INDUSTRIAL ARTS AND VOCATIONAL EDUCATION 35 (1946): 151-54.

Outlines its history and identifies its leading figures.

2041 Whittemore, Richard. "Nicholas Murray Butler and Public Education, 1862-1911." Ph.D. dissertation, Columbia University, 1962.

Outlines Butler's philosophy, educational thought, political
involvements, and role for the Carnegie Endowment for International Peace.

2042 Widen, Irwin. "Public Support for Parochial Schools: Why the Issue Has
Re-emerged." HISTORY OF EDUCATION JOURNAL 4 (1952): 58-72.

Author suggests six bases for the re-emergence of the question.

2043 Williamson, E.G. "Historical Perspectives of the Vocational Guidance
Movement." PERSONAL AND GUIDANCE JOURNAL 42 (1964): 854-59.

An outline of the history of vocational guidance in America.

2044 Winsor, Charlotte, ed. EXPERIMENTAL SCHOOLS REVISITED. New
York: Agathon Press, 1973. 340 p.

A reprinting of the 1917-24 bulletins of the Bureau of Educa-
tional Experiments (later the Bank Street College of Education).
Reviewed in some depth in: Jonathan Messerli, TEACHERS
COLLEGE RECORD 75 (1974): 566-68.

2045 Wirth, Arthur G. JOHN DEWEY AS EDUCATOR. New York: Wiley,
1966. 322 p.

Essentially a review of the philosophical side of Dewey and
how he regarded education as the most significant area where
such might be applied.

2046 _____. EDUCATION IN THE TECHNOLOGICAL SOCIETY: THE
VOCATIONAL-LIBERAL STUDIES CONTROVERSY IN THE EARLY TWEN-
TIETH CENTURY. Scranton, Pa.: Intext, 1972. 275 p.

Covers all sides and aspects of the issues as they have been
raised in the past three-quarters of a century.

2047 Wynn, Dale R., et al. AMERICAN EDUCATION. New York: McGraw-
Hill, 1977. 441 p.

2048 Zanden, James W.V. "Accommodation to Undesired Change: The Case
of the South." JOURNAL OF NEGRO EDUCATION 31 (1962): 30-35.

2049 Zimet, Melvin. DECENTRALIZATION AND SCHOOL EFFECTIVENESS.
New York: Teachers College, Columbia University Press, 1973. 186 p.

Deals with the events and forces leading to the 1969 decentralization law in New York City, and especially to the early
developments in this respect in district seven.

Chapter 10

TEACHERS, TEACHING, TEXTBOOKS, AND CURRICULUM

2050 Adams, Bess. ABOUT BOOKS AND CHILDREN: A HISTORICAL SURVEY
OF CHILDREN'S LITERATURE. New York: Holt, Rinehart and Winston,
1953. 456 p.

2051 Alilunos, Leo J. "The Image of Public Schools in Roman Catholic American History Textbooks." HISTORY OF EDUCATION QUARTERLY 3 (1963):
159-65.

2052 Almack, John C. "History of Oregon Normal Schools." OREGON HIS-
TORICAL SOCIETY QUARTERLY 21 (1920): 95-169.

2053 [American Library Association]. Children's Services Division. NOTABLE
CHILDREN'S BOOKS, 1940-1970. Chicago: American Library Association, 1973. 340 p.

   Updated by the issuance of regular annual supplements.

2054 Arbuthnot, May H., and Sutherland, Zena. CHILDREN AND BOOKS.
4th ed. Glenview, Ill.: Scott, Foresman, 1972. 460 p.

   A comprehensive recent text with detailed bibliographies.
   Also see Adams, Bess (entry 2050).

2055 Arnold, Arnold. PICTURES AND STORIES FROM FORGOTTEN CHILD-
REN'S BOOKS. New York: Dover, 1969. 330 p.

   A facsimile reprint of original title pages with carefully selected passages and excerpts from rare and unusual texts.

2056 Baldwin, Ruth M. 100 NINETEENTH-CENTURY RHYMING ALPHABETS
IN ENGLISH. Carbondale: Southern Illinois University Press, 1972.
170 p.

2057 Bardeen, Charles W. CATALOGUE OF RARE BOOKS ON PEDAGOGY.
Syracuse, N.Y.: Bardeen, 1894. 240 p.
   Includes extensive references from the period.

2058 Barnard, Henry. "American Textbooks." AMERICAN JOURNAL OF
EDUCATION 13 (1863): 202-22, 401-08, 626-40; 14 (1864): 751-57;
15 (1865): 639-75.

> Mostly bibliographical checklists. See: Francesco Cordasco,
> "Henry Barnard's AMERICAN JOURNAL OF EDUCATION."
> HISTORY OF EDUCATION QUARTERLY 11 (1971): 328-32.

2059 Betts, John R. "P.T. Barnum and the Popularization of Natural History."
JOURNAL OF THE HISTORY OF IDEAS 20 (1959): 353-68.

2060 Bigelow, Karl W. "The Passing of the Teachers College." TEACHERS
COLLEGE RECORD 58 (1957): 409-17.

2061 Black, Marian W. "The Battle Over Uniformity of Textbooks in Florida,
1868-1963." HISTORY OF EDUCATION QUARTERLY 4 (1964): 106-18.

> An act in 1883 required countywide textbook uniformity.
> Another in 1911 extended this to elementary texts, and in
> 1917 this was further extended to secondary texts.

2062 Blenner-Hassett, Roland. "A Brief History of Celtic Studies in North
America." PUBLICATIONS, MODERN LANGUAGE ASSOCIATION 69
(1954): 3-21.

2063 Briggs, Thomas H. "The Secondary School Curriculum: Yesterday, Today, and Tomorrow." TEACHERS COLLEGE RECORD 52 (1951): 399-
448.

2064 Brink, William G., et al. ADAPTING THE SECONDARY SCHOOL
PROGRAM TO THE NEEDS OF YOUTH. 52d Yearbook. Chicago:
National Social Studies Education Association, 1953. Part 1, 540 p.

2065 Brown, Ralph. "The American Geographies of Jedediah Morse." AN-
NALS, ASSOCIATION OF AMERICAN GEOGRAPHIES 31 (1941): 145-
217.

2066 Bryson, Gladys. "The Comparable Interests of the Old Moral Philosophy
and the Modern Social Sciences." SOCIAL FORCES 11 (1932): 19-27.

2067 _____. "The Emergence of the Social Sciences from Moral Philosophy."
INTERNATIONAL JOURNAL OF ETHICS 42 (1932): 304-23.

2068 _____. "Sociology Considered as Moral Philosophy." AMERICAN SO-
CIOLOGICAL REVIEW 24 (1932): 26-36.

2069 Buchner, Edward F. EDUCATIONAL SURVEYS. United States Bureau of Education Bulletin No. 45, 1918. Washington, D.C.: Government Printing Office, 1919. 56 p.

2070 CARDINAL PRINCIPLES OF SECONDARY EDUCATION: A REPORT OF THE COMMISSION ON THE REORGANIZATION OF SECONDARY EDUCATION, APPOINTED BY THE NATIONAL EDUCATION ASSOCIATION. United States Bureau of Education Bulletin No. 35, 1918. Washington, D.C.: Government Printing Office, 1918. 32 p.

2071 Carmichael, Leonard. "Scientific Psychology and the Schools of Psychology." AMERICAN JOURNAL OF PSYCHIATRY 88 (1932): 955-68.

2072 Carpenter, Charles. HISTORY OF AMERICAN SCHOOLBOOKS. Philadelphia: University of Pennsylvania Press, 1963. 240 p.

  A general survey of the field that includes a sketch of the pioneer day school system in terms of textbook production and usages. Annotated bibliography included.

2073 Coleman, Charles H. "The Normal School Comes to Charleston." JOURNAL OF THE ILLINOIS STATE HISTORICAL SOCIETY 41 (1948): 117-33.

2074 Commager, Henry S. "Noah Webster, 1758-1958." SATURDAY REVIEW 41 (1958): 12ff.

2074a Cordasco, Francesco. TEACHER EDUCATION IN THE UNITED STATES: A GUIDE FOR FOREIGN STUDENTS. New York: Institute for International Education, 1971. xii, 74 p.

2075 Cremin, Lawrence A. "The Revolution in American Secondary Education, 1893-1918." TEACHERS COLLEGE RECORD 56 (1955): 295-308.

2076 Dale, Edward E. "Teaching on the Prairie Plains, 1890-1900." MISSISSIPPI VALLEY HISTORICAL REVIEW 33 (1946-1947): 293-307.

2077 Dewey, John, et al. THE RELATION OF THEORY TO PRACTICE IN THE EDUCATION OF TEACHERS. 3d Yearbook. NATIONAL SOCIAL STUDIES EDUCATION ASSOCIATION. Bloomington, Ind.: 1904. Part 1, 260 p.

2078 Donnally, Williams. "The Haymarket Riot in Secondary School Textbooks." HARVARD EDUCATIONAL REVIEW 8 (1938): 105-216.

2079 Dougherty, Mary L. "History of the Teaching of Handwriting in America." ELEMENTARY SCHOOL JOURNAL 18 (1917): 280-86.

2080 Dunfee, Maxine, ed. ELIMINATING ETHNIC BIAS IN INSTRUCTIONAL MATERIAL: COMMENT AND BIBLIOGRAPHY. Washington, D.C.: Association for Supervision and Curriculum Development, 1974. 53 p.

Discussion and analyses on pluralism, ethnic bias, efforts at change, and educational resources on racism and sexism. Bibliographies included.

2081 Earle, Alice M. CHILD LIFE IN COLONIAL DAYS. 1899. Reprint. Norwood, Pa.: Norwood Editions, 1974. 403 p.

Includes sections on hornbooks, primers, schoolbooks, diaries, commonplace books, and story and picture books.

2082 Edelfelt, Roy A., ed. "A Symposium on James Bryant Conant's: THE EDUCATION OF AMERICAN TEACHERS." JOURNAL OF TEACHER EDUCATION 15 (1964): 5-49.

2083 Eliot, Charles W. "Contributions to the History of American Teaching." EDUCATIONAL REVIEW 42 (1911): 346-66.

2084 Eliot, Charles W., and Nelson, Ernesto. NEEDED CHANGES IN SECONDARY EDUCATION. United States Bureau of Education Bulletin No. 10, 1916. Washington, D.C.: U.S. Government Printing Office, 1916. 32 p.

2085 Ellis, Alec. HOW TO FIND OUT ABOUT CHILDREN'S LITERATURE. 3d ed. New York: Pergamon, 1973. 240 p.

An analytical guide and general history of the development of children's literature with included examples.

2086 Elson, Ruth M. "American Schoolbooks and 'Culture' in the Nineteenth Century." MISSISSIPPI VALLEY HISTORICAL REVIEW 46 (1959-60): 411-35.

2087 _____ . GUARDIANS OF TRADITION: AMERICAN SCHOOLBOOKS OF THE NINETEENTH CENTURY. Lincoln: University of Nebraska Press, 1964. 437 p.

A compendium of nineteenth-century textbooks as repositories of approved ideas of the period. Includes a bibliography of textbooks commonly used: 1776-1900.

2088 England, J. Merton. "The Democratic Faith in American Schoolbooks of the Republic, 1783-1861." AMERICAN QUARTERLY 15 (1963): 191-99.

For another aspect, also see England's similar essay in UNIVERSITY OF BIRMINGHAM HISTORICAL JOURNAL 9 (1963): 92-111.

2089 Fell, Marie L. THE FOUNDATIONS OF NATIVISM IN AMERICAN TEXT-BOOKS, 1783-1860. Washington, D.C.: Catholic University of America Press, 1941. 270 p.

> An examination of anti-Catholicism and xenophobic attitudes in school texts that may have derived from the 1830s nativist, and the 1850s Know-Nothing movements.

2090 Ford, Paul L., ed. THE NEW ENGLAND PRIMER: A HISTORY OF ITS ORIGIN AND DEVELOPMENT WITH A REPRINT OF THE UNIQUE COPY OF THE EARLIEST KNOWN EDITION AND MANY FACSIMILE ILLUSTRA-TIONS AND REPRODUCTIONS. New York: Dodd, Mead, 1897. Reprint. 78 p. Teachers College, Columbia University Press, 1962.

> With a new introduction by Lawrence A. Cremin. Refers to the 1687-88 original primer.

2091 Garfinkle, Norton. "Conservatism in American Textbooks, 1800-1860." NEW YORK HISTORY 35 (1954): 49-63.

2092 George, Anne E. "The Montessori Movement in America." In UNITED STATES BUREAU OF EDUCATION, REPORT OF THE COMMISSIONER, 1914. Vol. 1, pp. 355-62. Washington, D.C.: Government Printing Office, 1915.

2093 Gordy, J.P. RISE AND GROWTH OF THE NORMAL SCHOOL IDEA IN THE UNITED STATES. U.S. Bureau of Education Information Circular No. 8, 1891. Washington, D.C.: Government Printing Office, 1891. 145 p.

2094 Gore, Joseph. "The Economy of Time Movement in Elementary Education: The Impact of Social Forces upon Curriculum Organization in the United States." PAEDAGOGICA HISTORICA 7 (1967): 489-518.

2095 Greenwood, James M., and Artemas, Martin. "Notes on the History of American Textbooks on Arithmetic." In UNITED STATES BUREAU OF EDUCATION, REPORT OF THE COMMISSIONER, 1897-1898. Vol. 1, pp. 789-868. Washington, D.C.: Government Printing Office, 1899.

> Describes the texts used in the eighteenth and nineteenth centuries with accompanying biographical sketches of their authors.

2096 Hall, G. "Psychological Education." AMERICAN JOURNAL OF PSY-CHIATRY 53 (1896): 228-41.

2097 Hamilton, Sinclair. EARLY AMERICAN BOOK ILLUSTRATORS AND WOOD ENGRAVERS. Princeton: Princeton University Library, 1958. 240 p.

Essentially a "catalogue raisonne" on the early schoolbooks
with special emphasis on the work of Alexander Anderson,
probably the major illustrator of the period.

2098 Handschin, Charles H. THE TEACHING OF MODERN LANGUAGES IN
THE UNITED STATES. U.S. Bureau of Education Bulletin No. 3, 1913.
Washington, D.C.: Government Printing Office, 1913. 154 p.

2099 Haney, John L. "The First High School Diplomas." SCHOOL REVIEW
38 (1930): 544-47.

2100 Harris, William T. "The Curriculum for Secondary Schools." In UNITED
STATES BUREAU OF EDUCATION, REPORT OF THE COMMISSIONER,
1892-1893. Vol. 2, pp. 1452-64. Washington, D.C.: U.S. Government Printing Office, 1895.

2101 _____. "The Growth of the Public High-School System in the Southern
States and a Study of Its Influence." EDUCATIONAL REVIEW 37 (1904):
259-69.

2102 Harris, Wilmer C. "The Use, the Abuse, and the Writing of Textbooks
in American History." MISSISSIPPI VALLEY HISTORICAL REVIEW extra
issue (1921): 299-303.

2103 Haviland, Virginia. CHILDREN'S LITERATURE: A GUIDE TO REFERENCE
SOURCES. Washington, D.C.: Library of Congress, 1966. 341 p.

Includes history and criticism, authorship, illustration, and
international studies principally. Supplemented in 1972.

2104 Heartman, Charles F. AMERICAN PRIMERS, INDIAN PRIMERS, ROYAL
PRIMERS. Highland Park, N.J.: Weiss, 1935. 205 p.

Essentially a listing of same with some facsimile pages of pre-
1830 works.

2105 Herbst, Jurgen. "Social Darwinism and the History of American Geography." PROCEEDINGS, AMERICAN PHILOSOPHICAL SOCIETY 105
(1961): 538-44.

2106 Hervery, Walter L. "Historical Sketch of Teachers College from Its
Foundation to 1897." TEACHERS COLLEGE RECORD 1 (1900): 12-35.

2107 Issel, William H. "Teachers and Educational Reform During the Progressive
Era: A Case Study of the Pittsburgh Teachers Association." HISTORY OF
EDUCATION QUARTERLY 7 (1967): 220-33.

2108 Jackson, Clara O., and Quimby, Harriet B. "Building a Children's Literature Collection: A Suggested Basic Reference Collection for Academic Libraries." CHOICE (Association of College and Research Libraries) 11 (1974): 1261-74.

>   A compendium of texts, histories, authors, illustrators, anthologies, selection aids, and reviewing journals with added references. A bibliographical overview of the subject.

2109 Jenkins, Ralph C. "Henry Barnard: Educator of Teachers." EDUCATIONAL FORUM 4 (1939): 25-34.

2110 Jewett, James P. "The Fight Against Corporal Punishment in American Schools." HISTORY OF EDUCATION JOURNAL 4 (1952): 1-10.

2111 Johnson, Clifton. OLD TIME SCHOOLS AND SCHOOLBOOKS. New York: Dover, 1963. 381 p.

>   Includes copious extracts and illustrations from texts prior to 1850. Also see: Clifton Johnson, THE COUNTRY SCHOOL. New York: Appleton, 1893.

2112 Judd, Charles H. "The Historical Development of Secondary Education in America." SCHOOL REVIEW 43 (1935): 173-83.

2113 Katz, Michael B. "American History Textbooks and Social Reform in the 1930s." PAEDAGOGICA HISTORICA 6 (1966): 143-60.

2114 Kersey, Harry A. "Michigan Teachers' Institutes in the Mid-Nineteenth Century: A Representative Document." HISTORY OF EDUCATION QUARTERLY 5 (1965): 40-52.

2115 Kiefer, Monica. AMERICAN CHILDREN THROUGH THEIR BOOKS, 1700-1835. Philadelphia: University of Pennsylvania Press, 1970. 248 p.

>   A sociological analysis with bibliographical materials.

2116 Knight, Edgar W. "A Century of Teacher Education." EDUCATIONAL FORUM 9 (1945): 149-61.

2117 La Bue, Anthony C. "Teacher Certification in the United States: A Brief History." JOURNAL OF TEACHER EDUCATION 11 (1960): 147-72.

2118 Lindberg, Stanley W., ed. THE ANNOTATED McGUFFEY: SELECTIONS FROM THE McGUFFEY ECLECTIC READERS, 1836-1920. New York: Van Nostrand, Reinhold, 1976. 358 p.

Selections from various of same which sold an estimated 122 million copies between 1836 and 1920. Includes the values espoused in the readers.

2119 Linton, Clarence, and Katsuranis, Joseph J. "Study of Alumni of Teachers College Receiving Degrees from 1928 to 1935." TEACHERS COLLEGE RECORD 39 (1938): 407-22, 734-46; 40 (1938): 159-59.

2120 Littlefield, George E. EARLY SCHOOLS AND SCHOOLBOOKS OF NEW ENGLAND. Boston: Club of Odd Volumes, 1904. 240 p.

Collection of plate facsimiles and illustrations. Also see: George E. Littlefield, EARLY BOSTON BOOKSELLERS, 1642-1711. Boston: Club of Odd Volumes, 1900.

2121 Livengood, W.W., comp. AMERICANA AS TAUGHT TO THE TUNE OF A HICKORY STICK. [N.p.]: Women's National Book Association, 1954. 180 p.

A collection of facsimile pages, extracts, and so forth, from nineteenth-century elementary books.

2122 Lyman, Rollo L. ENGLISH GRAMMAR IN AMERICAN SCHOOLS BEFORE 1850. United States Bureau of Education Bulletin No. 12, 1921. Washington, D.C.: Government Printing Office, 1922. 170 p.

2123 Lyte, Eliphalet O. "The State Normal Schools of the United States." In UNITED STATES BUREAU OF EDUCATION, REPORT OF THE COMMISSIONER, 1903. Vol. 1, pp. 1103-36. Washington, D.C.: Government Printing Office, 1905.

2124 Martin, Helen. NATIONALISM IN CHILDREN'S LITERATURE. Chicago: American Library Association, 1936. 260 p.

2125 Meigs, Cornelia, et al. A CRITICAL HISTORY OF CHILDREN'S LITERATURE. Rev. ed. New York: Macmillan, 1969. 624 p.

Covers from the early period to 1967 rather comprehensively.

2126 Meyer, Karl W. "Post-World War II Conversion of the Teachers College." JOURNAL OF TEACHER EDUCATION 11 (1960): 335-39.

2127 Meyers, Ira B. "A History of the Teaching of Nature in the Elementary and Secondary Schools of the United States." ELEMENTARY SCHOOL TEACHERS 6 (1906): 258-64.

2128 _____. "The Evolution of Aims and Methods in the Teaching of Nature-Study in the Common Schools of the United States." ELEMENTARY SCHOOL TEACHER 11 (1910): 205-13, 237-48.

2129 Minnich, Harvey C. WILLIAM HOLMES McGUFFEY AND HIS READERS. New York: American Book, 1936. 260 p.

> A critical biographical study of McGuffey (1800-73); a complete list of all the readers under that rubric and an extended bibliography on both.

2130 _____, ed. OLD FAVORITES FROM THE McGUFFEY READERS. New York: Macmillan, 1936. 482 p.

> Reissued in 1969 by the Singing Tree Press (Detroit: Gale Research Co.). Originally an anniversary (Centennial) commemorative issue of the appearance of the first McGuffey in 1836. A collection of 150 selections from same.

2131 Mosier, Richard D. MAKING THE AMERICAN MIND: SOCIAL AND MORAL IDEAS IN THE McGUFFEY READERS. Rev. ed. New York: Kings Crown Press, 1965. 207 p.

> Deals mainly with their influence. Also see: Alice McGuffey Ruggles, THE STORY OF THE McGUFFEYS, New York: n.p., 1930.

2132 Muir, Percival H. ENGLISH CHILDREN'S BOOKS, 1600-1900. New York: Praeger, 1969. 280 p.

> On English influences on American books with an included series of bibliographies.

2133 Newell, M.A. "Contributions to the History of Normal Schools in the United States." In UNITED STATES BUREAU OF EDUCATION, REPORT OF THE COMMISSIONER, 1898-1899. Vol. 2, pp. 2263-90. Washington, D.C.: Government Printing Office, 1900.

2134 Nietz, John A. "Evolution of American School Textbooks, 1762-1900." EDUCATIONAL FORUM 24 (1960): 295-305.

2135 _____. OLD TEXTBOOKS: SPELLING, GRAMMAR, READING, ARITHMETIC, GEOGRAPHY, AMERICAN HISTORY, CIVIL GOVERNMENT, PHYSIOLOGY, PENMANSHIP, ART, MUSIC--AS TAUGHT IN THE COMMON SCHOOLS FROM COLONIAL DAYS TO 1900. Pittsburgh: University of Pittsburgh Press, 1961. 364 p.

2136 _____. "Why the Longevity of the McGuffey Readers." HISTORY OF EDUCATION QUARTERLY 4 (1964): 119-25.

2137 _____. THE EVOLUTION OF AMERICAN SECONDARY SCHOOL TEXTBOOKS. Rutland, Vt.: Tuttle, 1966. 265 p.

> A in-depth survey of the books used in the Latin and the grammar schools from the colonial period to 1900.

2138 O'Donnell, W.F. "Five Decades of Teacher Education in Kentucky."
FILSON CLUB 30 (1956): 115-24.

2139 Osgood, Edith W. "The Development of Historical Study in the Secondary Schools of the United States." SCHOOL REVIEW 32 (1914): 444-
54, 511-26.

2140 Packer, Katherine H. EARLY AMERICAN SCHOOL BOOKS: A BIB-
LIOGRAPHY BASED ON THE BOSTON BOOKSELLERS' CATALOGUE OF
1804. Ann Arbor: University of Michigan Press, 1964. 260 p.

Partially annotated, alphabetized, and index listing of books
used prior to 1804.

2141 Parker, Francis W. "An Account of the Work of the Cook County and
Chicago Normal School from 1883 to 1899." ELEMENTARY SCHOOL
TEACHER 2 (1901-1902): 752-80.

2142 Peltier, Gary L. "Teacher Participation in Curriculum Revision: An
Historical Case Study." HISTORY OF EDUCATION QUARTERLY 7 (1967):
209-19.

2143 Phillips, Richard C. "The Historical Development of the Term, Experience
Curriculum." HISTORY OF EDUCATION QUARTERLY 5 (1965): 121-30.

2144 Reavis, G.H. "The Development of Teacher Training as a Profession."
TEACHERS COLLEGE RECORD 24 (1923): 208-12.

2145 Rickard, Garrett E. "Establishment of Graded Schools in American Cities."
ELEMENTARY SCHOOL JOURNAL 47 (1947): 575-85; 18 (1948): 326-35.

2146 Rivlin, Herry N., et al. MENTAL HEALTH IN MODERN EDUCATION.
54th Yearbook. National Social Studies Education Association. Part 2.
Chicago: 1955. 380 p.

2147 Rosenbach, A.S.W. EARLY AMERICAN CHILDREN'S BOOKS. Portland,
Maine: Southworth Press, 1933. 190 p. Reprint. New York: Dover
Publications, 1970. 245 p.

Essentially a bibliographical descriptive study of rare schoolbooks.

2148 Rowman and Littlefield. CHILDREN'S BOOKS OF THE RARE BOOK DI-
VISION OF THE LIBRARY OF CONGRESS. AUTHOR/TITLE AND
CHRONOLOGICAL CATALOGUES. 2 vols. Totowa, N.J.: 1975.

Encompasses fifteen thousand children's books published between
1721 and 1975.

2149 Rudy, Willis. "America's First Normal School: The Formative Years."
JOURNAL OF TEACHER EDUCATION 5 (1954): 263-70.

About the one established at Lexington, Massachusetts, in 1839.

2150 Rugg, Harold. "After Three Decades of Scientific Method in Education."
TEACHERS COLLEGE RECORD 36 (1934): 111-22.

2151 _____, et al. THE FOUNDATION AND TECHNIQUE OF CURRICULUM-
MAKING, PAST AND PRESENT. 26th Yearbook, Part 1. Bloomington,
Ind.: National Social Studies Education Association, 1926. 340 p.

2152 Sahli, John R. "The Slavery Issue in Early Geography Textbooks." HIS-
TORY OF EDUCATION QUARTERLY 3 (1963): 153-58.

2153 Shankland, Rebecca H. "The McGuffey Readers and Moral Education."
HARVARD EDUCATIONAL REVIEW 31 (1961): 60-72.

2154 Sherman, Jay J. "History of the Office of County Superintendent of
Schools in Iowa." IOWA JOURNAL OF HISTORY 21 (1923): 3-93.

2155 Shoemaker, Ervin C. NOAH WEBSTER: PIONEER OF LEARNING. New
York: Columbia University Press, 1936. 347 p.

Also see: Emily Ellsworth, et al. A BIBLIOGRAPHY OF THE
WRITINGS OF NOAH WEBSTER, 1958; Horace E. Scudder,
NOAH WEBSTER, 1881; and Emily E.F. Ford, NOTES ON THE
LIFE OF NOAH WEBSTER, 2 vols., 1912.

2156 Smith, Elva. THE HISTORY OF CHILDREN'S LITERATURE. Chicago:
American Library Association, 1937. 280 p.

Essentially a detailed outline and a descriptive bibliography.

2157 Smith, Henry L., et al. ONE HUNDRED FIFTY YEARS OF ARITHMETIC
BOOKS. Bloomington: Bureau of Cooperative Research and Field Service,
Indiana University, 1945. 380 p.

Includes many extracts and facsimile pages from American
school textbooks since the Revolution.

2158 _____. ONE HUNDRED FIFTY YEARS OF GRAMMAR TEXTBOOKS.
Bloomington: Bureau of Cooperative Research and Field Service, Indiana
University, 1946. 240 p.

2159 Snedden, David. "Cardinal Principles of Secondary Education." SCHOOL
AND SOCIETY 9 (1919): 517-27.

2160 Spieseke, Alice W. THE FIRST TEXTBOOKS IN AMERICAN HISTORY AND THEIR COMPILER, JOHN McCULLOCH. New York: Teachers College, Columbia University Press, 1938. 230 p.

> Regarding John McCulloch (1754?-1824).

2161 Stone, Mason S. "The First Normal School in America." TEACHERS COLLEGE RECORD 24 (1923): 263-71.

2162 Strayer, George D. "The Education of the Superintendent of Schools." TEACHERS COLLEGE RECORD 46 (1944): 169-76.

2163 Sunderman, Lloyd F. "History of Public School Music in the United States, 1830 to 1890." EDUCATIONAL RECORD 22 (1941): 205-11.

2164 Thwaite, Mary F. FROM PRIMER TO PLEASURE READING. Boston: Horn Book, 1973. 180 p.

2165 Tuer, Andrew W. PAGES AND PICTURES FROM FORGOTTEN CHILDREN'S BOOKS. Reprint. Detroit: Gale Research Co., 1969. 278 p.

> Also see: A.W. Tuer, HISTORY OF THE HORNBOOK. London: Leadenhall Press, 1897.

2166 Tyler, Louis L. "Psychoanalysis and Curriculum Theory." SCHOOL REVIEW 66 (1958): 446-60.

2167 Vail, Henry H. HISTORY OF THE McGUFFEY READERS. Rev. ed. Cleveland: Privately printed, 1911. 190 p.

> Essentially three portraits, and a brief history with included bibliographical data.

2168 Voorhees, Margaretta W. "Social Studies in the Beaver County Day School." PROGRESSIVE EDUCATION 2 (1925): 241-46.

2169 Wall, James H. "Psychiatric Disorders in Fifty School Teachers." AMERICAN JOURNAL OF PSYCHIATRY 96 (1939): 137-45.

2170 Warfel, Harry R. NOAH WEBSTER: SCHOOLMASTER TO AMERICA. New York: Macmillan, 1936. 460 p.

> A very full biography with an extensive section on sources and bibliography.

2171 [Webster, Noah]. NOAH WEBSTER'S AMERICAN SPELLING BOOK. 1831. Reprint. New York: Bureau of Publications, Teachers College, Columbia University, 1962. 180 p.

Revision of Webster's "blue-backed speller" that first appeared
in 1783 and eventually sold over 15 million copies by 1837.

2172 Weiss, Harry B. PRINTERS AND PUBLISHERS OF CHILDREN'S BOOKS
IN NEW YORK CITY, 1698-1830. New York: New York Public Library,
1948. 240 p.

Essentially a bibliographical list with historical notes included.

2173 Welch, d'Alte. A BIBLIOGRAPHY OF CHILDREN'S BOOKS PRINTED
PRIOR TO 1821. Charlottesville: University of Virginia Press, 1974.
360 p.

A list of 1,478 titles and all known editions thereof. Done
in conjunction with the American Antiquarian Society.

2174 Wells, Guy F. "The First School Survey." EDUCATIONAL REVIEW 50
(1915): 166-74.

Done in Rhode Island in 1845.

2175 Wheat, Harry G. "Changes and Trends in Arithmetic Since 1910."
ELEMENTARY SCHOOL JOURNAL 47 (1946): 134-44.

2176 Whitford, W.G. "Brief History of Art Education in the United States."
ELEMENTARY SCHOOL JOURNAL 24 (1923): 109-15.

2177 Willcott, Paul. "The Initial American Reception of the Montessori
Method." SCHOOL REVIEW 76 (1968): 147-65.

2178 Winters, Elmer A. "Man and His Changing Society: The Textbooks of
Harold Rugg." HISTORY OF EDUCATION QUARTERLY 7 (1967): 493-
514.

2179 Wright, Frank W. "The Evolution of the Normal Schools." ELEMENTARY
SCHOOL JOURNAL 30 (1930): 363-71.

2180 Younker, Donna L. "The Moral Philosophy of William Holmes McGuffey."
EDUCATIONAL FORUM 28 (1963): 71-77.

Chapter 11

MISCELLANEOUS

2181 Abramson, David A. "Academic Studies in High School and College." TEACHERS COLLEGE RECORD 74 (1972): 171-94.

2182 Adkins, Edwin P. "The Federal Government and Higher Education." EDUCATIONAL FORUM 32 (1967): 423-27.

2183 Allport, Gordon W. "Values and Our Youth." TEACHERS COLLEGE RECORD 63 (1961): 211-19.

2184 Anderson, Lewis F. "The System of Mutual Instruction and the Beginnings of the High School." SCHOOL AND SOCIETY 8 (1918): 571-76.

2185 Anderson, Stuart A. "The Economic Status of Teachers Personnel: Historical Development of the Economic Status of High School Teachers in the United States." JOURNAL OF EDUCATIONAL RESEARCH 43 (1950): 697-712.

   Covers the period 1642 to 1947.

2186 Armytage, W.H.G. "Alcott House: An Anglo-American Educational Experience." EDUCATIONAL THEORY 8 (1958): 129-42.

2187 Arnold, Christian K. "Federal Support of Basic Research in Institutions of Higher Learning: A Critique." EDUCATIONAL RECORD 45 (1964): 199-203.

2188 Arnstein, George E. "Cubberley: The Wizard of Stanford." HISTORY OF EDUCATION JOURNAL 5 (1954): 73-81.

2189 Ashworth, Kenneth H. "Coordinating the Federal Role in Higher Education." EDUCATIONAL RECORD 49 (1968): 316-24.

2190 Atkinson, James H. "Memoirs of a University Student, 1906-1910." ARKANSAS HISTORICAL QUARTERLY 39 (1971): 213-41.

2191 Auerbach, Eugene. "Aspects of the History and Present Status of Liberal Arts Opposition to Professors of Education." EDUCATIONAL FORUM 22 (1957): 83-94.

2192 Aydelotte, Frank. "Honors Work in College." PROGRESSIVE EDUCATION 2 (1925): 135-38.

2193 Babbitt, Irving. "President Eliot and American Education." FORUM 81 (1929): 1-10.

2194 Balyeat, F.A. "Rural School Houses in Early Oklahoma." CHRONICLES OF OKLAHOMA 22 (1944): 315-23.

2195 Barr, William M. AMERICAN PUBLIC SCHOOL FINANCES, 1635-1960. New York: American Book Co., 1960. 406 p.

2196 Basset, John S. "The Round Hill School." PROCEEDINGS, AMERICAN ANTIQUARIAN SOCIETY 27 (1917): 18-62.

2197 Bates, Ralph S. SCIENTIFIC SOCIETIES IN THE UNITED STATES. 3d ed. Cambridge, Mass.: M.I.T. Press, 19-- . 326 p.

   On the history and influence of such in the United States to the present. Bibliography included.

2198 Beatty, Willard W. "The Federal Government and the Education of Indians and Eskimos." JOURNAL OF NEGRO EDUCATION 7 (1938): 267-72.

2199 Beisner, Robert L. "Brooks Adams and Charles Francis Adams, Jr., Historians of Massachusetts." NEW ENGLAND QUARTERLY 35 (1962): 48-70.

2200 Ben-David, Joseph, and Collins, Randall. "Social Factors in the Origins of a New Science: The Case of Psychology." AMERICAN SOCIOLOGICAL REVIEW 31 (1966): 451-65.

2201 Benne, Kenneth D. "The Educational Outlook of Herbert Spencer." HARVARD EDUCATIONAL REVIEW 10 (1940): 436-53.

2202 Berkson, Isaac B. "Science, Ethics, and Education in the Deweyan Experimentalist Philosophy." SCHOOL AND SOCIETY 88 (1959): 387-91.

2203 Bestor, Arthur E., Jr. "The Transformation of American Scholarship, 1875-1917." LIBRARY QUARTERLY 23 (1953): 164-79.

2204 Bigelow, Maurice A. "Thirty Years of Practical Arts in Teachers College Under the Administration of Dean James E. Russell, 1897-1927." TEACHERS COLLEGE RECORD 28 (1927): 765-75.

2205 Billington, Ray A. FREDERICK JACKSON TURNER: HISTORIAN, SCHOLAR, TEACHER. New York: Oxford University Press, 1973. 270 p.

2206 Blanshard, Brand, ed. EDUCATION IN THE AGE OF SCIENCE. New York: Basic Books, 1959. 302 p.

   A series of eight papers given at a 1958 symposia series that range widely over the subject in most all of its aspects.

2207 Blau, Joseph L. "John Dewey and American Social Thought." TEACHERS COLLEGE RECORD 61 (1959): 121-27.

2208 Bolmeier, E.C. "Court Decisions and Enrollment Trends in Public and Non-Public Schools." ELEMENTARY SCHOOL JOURNAL 50 (1950): 318-25, 396-415.

2209 Bolton, Frederick E. "High Schools in Territorial Washington." WASHINGTON HISTORICAL QUARTERLY 24 (1933): 211-20, 271-81.

2210 Boone, Richard G. SCIENCE OF EDUCATION. New York: Charles Scribner's Sons, 1904. 407 p.

2211 Bossing, Nelson L. "The History of Educational Legislation in Ohio From 1851-1925." NORTHWEST OHIO QUARTERLY 39 (1930): 78-219.

2212 Bowers, C.A. "The SOCIAL FRONTIER Journal: A Historical Sketch." HISTORY OF EDUCATION QUARTERLY 4 (1964): 167-80.

2213 _____. "The Ideologies of Progressive Education." HISTORY OF EDUCATION QUARTERLY 7 (1967): 452-73.

2214 Bragdon, Henry W. WOODROW WILSON: THE ACADEMIC YEARS. Cambridge, Mass.: Harvard University Press, 1967. 180 p.

2215 Bramfeld, Theodore B. "President Hutchins and the New Reaction." EDUCATIONAL FORUM 1 (1937): 271-82.

2216 Brickman, William W. "Essentialism Ten Years After." SCHOOL AND SOCIETY 57 (1948): 361-65.

2217 Broderick, Francis L. "The Academic Training of W.E.B. DuBois." JOURNAL OF NEGRO EDUCATION 27 (1958): 10-16.

2218 Brown, Elmer E. "The Development of Education as a University Subject." TEACHERS COLLEGE RECORD 24 (1923): 190-96.

2219 Brown, Samuel W. THE SECULARIZATION OF AMERICAN EDUCATION. New York: Teachers' College, Columbia University Press, 1912. 160 p.

On how state legislation, provisions of various constitutions, and court decisions have effectuated such secularization processes.

2220 Brown, William H. THE EDUCATION AND ECONOMIC DEVELOPMENT OF THE NEGRO IN VIRGINIA. Charlottesville, Va.: Surber-Arundale, 1923. 190 p.

2221 Bruce, Philip A. INSTITUTIONAL HISTORY OF VIRGINIA IN THE SEVENTEENTH CENTURY. 2 vols. New York: G.P. Putnam's Sons, 1910.

An inquiry into the religious, moral, educational, legal, military, and political conditions.

2222 Buffum, Hugh S. "Federal and State Aid to Education in Iowa." IOWA JOURNAL OF HISTORY 4 (1906): 554-98; 5 (1907): 3-45, 147-92, 311-25.

2223 Burks, Jesse D. "History of the Speyer School." TEACHERS COLLEGE RECORD 3 (1902): 6-12.

The Speyer School was the Teachers College Laboratory School.

2224 Butts, R. Freeman. "Our Tradition of States' Rights and Education." HISTORY OF EDUCATION JOURNAL 6 (1955): 211-28.

Suggests there are multiple answers to this question in terms of our historical traditions.

2225 _____. "States' Rights and Education." TEACHERS COLLEGE RECORD 58 (1957): 189-97.

2226 Caldwell, Otis W. THEN AND NOW IN EDUCATION, 1845-1923. Yonkers-on-Hudson, N.Y.: World Book, 1924. 400 p.

2227 Calhoun, Daniel H. THE AMERICAN CIVIL ENGINEER: ORIGINS AND CONFLICT. Cambridge, Mass.: Technology Press, 1960. 169 p.

2228 _____. PROFESSIONAL LIVES IN AMERICA: STRUCTURE AND ASPIRATION, 1750-1850. Cambridge, Mass.: Harvard University Press, 1965. 231 p.

2229 ____. THE INTELLIGENCE OF A PEOPLE. Princeton, N.J.: Princeton University Press, 1973. 408 p.

2230 Calista, Donald J. "Booker T. Washington: Another Look." JOURNAL OF NEGRO HISTORY 49 (1964): 240-55.

2231 Callahan, Raymond E. "Leonard Ayres and the Educational Balance Sheet." HISTORY OF EDUCATION QUARTERLY 1 (1961): 5-13.

2232 Calvert, Monte A. THE MECHANICAL ENGINEER IN AMERICA, 1830-1910: PROFESSIONAL CULTURE IN CONFLICT. Baltimore: Johns Hopkins University Press, 1967. 210 p.

2233 Capen, Samuel P. "The Effect of the World War 1914-18 on American Colleges and Universities." EDUCATIONAL RECORD 21 (1940): 40-48.

2234 Carbone, Peter, Jr. THE SOCIAL AND EDUCATIONAL THOUGHT OF HAROLD RUGG. Durham, N.C.: Duke University Press, 1977. 226 p.

2235 Carpenter, Hazen C. "Emerson, Eliot, and the Elective System." NEW ENGLAND QUARTERLY 24 (1951): 13-34.

2236 Cartwright, Morse A. "History of Adult Education in the United States." JOURNAL OF NEGRO EDUCATION 14 (1945): 283-92.

2237 Chambers, Gurney. "Michael John Demiashkevich and the Essentialist Committee for the Advancement of American Education." HISTORY OF EDUCATION QUARTERLY 9 (1969): 46-56.

2238 Chambliss, J.J. "William Torry Harris' Philosophy of Education." PAEDAGOGICA HISTORICA 5 (1965): 319-39.

2239 Chase, Harry W. "Hutchins' 'Higher Learning' Grounded." AMERICAN SCHOLAR 6 (1937): 236-44.

2240 Childs, John L. "Experimentalism and American Education." TEACHERS COLLEGE RECORD 44 (1943): 539-43.

2241 ____. "Boyd H. Bode and the Experimentalists." TEACHERS COLLEGE RECORD 55 (1953): 1-9.

2242 ____. "John Dewey and American Education." TEACHERS COLLEGE RECORD 61 (1959): 128-33.

2243 Church, Robert L. "Economists as Experts: The Rise of an Academic Profession in America, 1870-1917." In THE UNIVERSITY IN SOCIETY, vol. 2, edited by Lawrence Stone, pp. 571-609. Princeton, N.J.: Princeton University Press, 1974.

2244 Citron, Abraham F. "Experimentalism and the Classicism of President Hutchins." TEACHERS COLLEGE RECORD 44 (1943): 544-53.

2245 Clive, John, and Bailyn, Bernard. "England's Cultural Provinces: Scotland and America." WILLIAM AND MARY QUARTERLY 11 (1954): 200-13.

2246 Coats, A.W. "American Scholarship Comes of Age: The Louisiana Purchase Exposition of 1904." JOURNAL OF THE HISTORY OF IDEAS 22 (1961): 404-17.

2247 Collier, James M., and George, John J. "Education and the Supreme Court." JOURNAL OF HIGHER EDUCATION 21 (1950): 77-83.

2248 Congressional Quarterly. THE FEDERAL ROLE IN EDUCATION. Washington, D.C.: 1965. 170 p.

2249 Cooke, Flora J. "Colonel Francis W. Parker as Interpreted Through the Work of the Francis W. Parker School." ELEMENTARY SCHOOL TEACHER 12 (1912): 397-544.

2250 Coon, Charles L. "School Support and Our North Carolina Courts, 1868-1926." NORTH CAROLINA HISTORY REVIEW 3 (1926): 399-438.

     Traces progress of public school support as a consequence of court decisions in the period.

2251 Coriat, Isador H. "The Psycho-Analytic Approach to Education." PROGRESSIVE EDUCATION 3 (1926): 19-25.

2252 Counts, George S. "The Need for a Great Education." TEACHERS COLLEGE RECORD 53 (1951): 77-88.

2253 Cowley, W.H. "European Influences upon American Higher Education." EDUCATIONAL RECORD 20 (1939): 165-90.

2254 _____. "Three Curricular Conflicts." LIBERAL EDUCATION 46 (1960): 467-83.

     Between: special and general education, humanities and the sciences, and teaching and research.

2255 Cox, Oliver C. "The Leadership of Booker T. Washington." SOCIAL FORCES 30 (1951): 91-97.

2256 Craig, Hardin. WOODROW WILSON AT PRINCETON. Norman: University of Oklahoma Press, 1960. 175 p.

A limited biography to explain his opinions and principles in education.

2257 Crane, Theodore R. FRANCIS WAYLAND: POLITICAL ECONOMIST AS EDUCATOR. Providence, R.I.: Brown University Press, 1962. 220 p.

2258 Cremin, Lawrence A. "Toward a More Common Common School." TEACHERS COLLEGE RECORD 51 (1950): 308-19.

2259 Cremin, Lawrence A. "John Dewey and the Progressive-Education Movement, 1915-1952." SCHOOL REVIEW 67 (1959): 160-73.

2260 Cuban, Larry. URBAN SCHOOL CHIEFS UNDER FIRE. Chicago: University of Chicago Press, 1976. 223 p.

2261 Cubberley, Ellwood P. SCHOOL FUNDS AND THEIR APPORTIONMENT. New York: Teachers College, Columbia University Press, 1905. 255 p.

Suggests how a more equal apportionment might be made so as to equalize both the burdens and the advantages of education.

2262 Daniels, George H. AMERICAN SCIENCE IN THE AGE OF JACKSON. New York: Columbia University Press, 1968. 345 p.

2263 Davidson, Elizabeth H. "Child-Labor Reformers in North Carolina Since 1903." NORTH CAROLINA HISTORICAL REVIEW 14 (1937): 109-30.

2264 De Costa, Frank A. "The Relative Enrollment of Negroes in the Common Schools in the United States." JOURNAL OF NEGRO EDUCATION 22 (1953): 416-31.

2265 Denos, Raphael, et al. "A Symposium on Educational Philosophy." PHILOSOPHY AND PHENOMENOLOGICAL RESEARCH 2 (1946): 187-213.

2266 Dewey, John. "President Hutchins' Proposals to Remake Higher Education." SOCIAL FRONTIER 4 (1937): 103-66.

2267 Diener, Thomas J. "The United States Office of Education One Hundred Years of Service to Higher Education." EDUCATIONAL FORUM 33 (1969): 453-66.

2268 Doherty, R.E., and Oberer, W.E. TEACHERS, SCHOOL BOARDS, AND COLLECTIVE BARGAINING: A CHANGING OF THE GUARD. Ithaca, N.Y.: State School of Industrial and Labor Relations, Cornell University, 1967. 139 p.

2269 Doudna, Edgar G. "The Making of Our Wisconsin Schools: 1848-1948." WISCONSIN JOURNAL OF EDUCATION 80 (1948): 219-50.

2270 Dreeben, Robert. "Political and Educational Ideas in the Writing of George H. Mead." HARVARD EDUCATIONAL REVIEW 25 (1955): 157-68.

2271 Dresslar, Fletcher B. "A Brief Survey of Educational Progress During the Decade 1900 to 1910." In ANNUAL REPORT: U.S. BUREAU OF EDU-CATION, vol. 1, pp. 1-35. Washington, D.C.: Government Printing Office, 1912.

2272 Drost, Walter H. "Clarence Kingsley-'The New York Years.'" HISTORY OF EDUCATION QUARTERLY 6 (1966): 18-34.

2273 Dykhuizen, George. "John Dewey, the Vermont Years, 1859-1882." JOURNAL OF THE HISTORY OF IDEAS 29 (1959): 515-44.

2274 _____. "John Dewey at Johns Hopkins, 1882-1884." JOURNAL OF THE HISTORY OF IDEAS 22 (1961): 103-16.

2275 _____. "John Dewey and the University of Michigan, 1889-1904." JOURNAL OF THE HISTORY OF IDEAS 23 (1962): 513-44.

2276 Edwards, Newton. "Social Forces in American Education." HISTORY OF EDUCATION JOURNAL 1 (1949): 70-77.

   Suggests education is never separated from the society it serves.

2277 Eells, Walter C. ACADEMIC DEGREES: EARNED AND HONORARY DEGREES CONFERRED BY INSTITUTIONS OF HIGHER EDUCATION IN THE UNITED STATES. U.S. Office of Education Bulletin No. 28, 1960. Washington, D.C.: Government Printing Office, 1960. 240 p.

2278 _____. "First Degrees in Music." HISTORY OF EDUCATION QUAR-TERLY 1 (1961): 35-40

2279 Ellsworth, Clayton S. "The Coming of Rural Consolidated Schools to the Ohio Valley, 1892-1912." AGRICULTURAL HISTORY 30 (1970): 119-28.

2280 Ensign, Forest C. COMPULSORY SCHOOL ATTENDANCE AND CHILD LABOR. Iowa City, Iowa: Athens Press, 1921. 263 p.

On the historical development of compulsory attendance and the limitation of child labor in a selected group of states.

2281 Falk, Charles J. THE DEVELOPMENT AND ORGANIZATION OF EDUCATION IN CALIFORNIA. New York: Harcourt, Brace and World, 1968. 264 p.

A fairly concise, straightforward history of the development of education in California. Selected bibliographies included.

2282 Farnsworth, Dana L. "Psychiatry and Higher Education." AMERICAN JOURNAL OF PSYCHIATRY 109 (1952): 266-71.

2283 Farrison, W. Edward. "Booker T. Washington: A Study in Educational Leadership." SOUTH ATLANTIC QUARTERLY 41 (1942): 313-19.

2284 Feuer, Lewis S. "John Dewey's Reading at College." JOURNAL OF THE HISTORY OF IDEAS 19 (1958): 415-21.

2285 _____. "John Dewey and the Back to the People Movement in American Thought." JOURNAL OF THE HISTORY OF IDEAS 20 (1959): 545-68.

2286 Fierst, Edith U. "Constitutionality of Educational Segregation." GEORGE WASHINGTON LAW REVIEW 17 (1949): 208-25.

On segregation of Negroes and whites in tax-supported schools: 1871-1948.

2287 Fisch, Max H. "Evolution in American Philosophy." PHILOSOPHICAL REVIEW 55 (1947): 357-73.

2288 Fisher, Sara C. "The Psychological and Educational Work of Granville Stanley Hall." AMERICAN JOURNAL OF PSYCHIATRY 36 (1925): 1-52.

2289 Ford, Charles E. "Botany Texts: A Survey of Their Development in American Higher Education, 1643-1906." HISTORY OF EDUCATION QUARTERLY 4 (1964): 59-71.

2290 "Francis Wayland Parker and His Work for Education." In UNITED STATES BUREAU OF EDUCATION, REPORT OF THE COMMISSIONER, 1902. Vol. 1, pp. 231-84. Washington, D.C.: Government Printing Office, 1903.

2291 Frankel, Charles. "John Dewey's Legacy." AMERICAN SCHOLAR 29 (1960): 313-31.

2292 _____. "Appearance and Reality in Kilpatrick's Philosophy." TEACH-ERS COLLEGE RECORD 66 (1965): 352-64

2293 Funderburk, Robert S. THE HISTORY OF CONSERVATION EDUCATION IN THE UNITED STATES. Nashville: George Peabody College for Teachers, 1948. 151 p.

2294 Funke, Loretta. "The Negro in Education." JOURNAL OF NEGRO HISTORY 5 (1920): 1-21.

2295 Furner, Mary O. ADVOCACY AND OBJECTIVITY: A CRISIS IN THE PROFESSIONALIZATION OF AMERICAN SOCIAL SCIENCE, 1865-1905. Lexington: University Press of Kentucky, 1975. 180 p.

2296 Fussell, Clyde G. "The Emergence of Public Education as a Function of the State in Vermont." PROCEEDINGS, VERMONT HISTORICAL SO-CIETY 28 (1960): 179-94, 268-78; 29 (1961): 210-19.

2297 Gagliardo, Domenico. "A History of Kansas Child-Labor Legislation." KANSAS HISTORICAL QUARTERLY 1 (1932): 379-401.

2298 Galpin, Charles J. "The Development of the Science and Philosophy of American Rural Society." AGRICULTURAL HISTORY 12 (1938): 195-208.

2299 Gard, Willis. "European Influence on Early Western Education." OHIO HISTORICAL QUARTERLY 25 (1916): 23-36.

2300 Gatewood, Willard B. PREACHERS, PEDAGOGUES AND POLITICIANS: THE EVOLUTION CONTROVERSY IN NORTH CAROLINA, 1920-1927. Chapel Hill: University of North Carolina Press, 1966. 268 p.

2301 Gauerke, Warren E. "Organized Labor and Federal Aid to Education." HISTORY OF EDUCATION JOURNAL 4 (1953): 81-92.

2302 George, John J., and Collier, James M. "The Supreme Court and Ra-cial Segregation in Education, 1896-1949." SOUTH ATLANTIC QUAR-TERLY 48 (1949): 521-28.

2303 Going, Allen J. "The South and the Blair Education Bill." MISSISSIPPI VALLEY HISTORICAL REVIEW 64 (1957): 267-91.

2304 Grant, Gerald, and Riesman, David. THE PERPETUAL DREAM: REFORM
AND EXPERIMENT IN THE AMERICAN COLLEGE. Chicago: University
of Chicago Press, 1978. 474 p.

2305 Greene, Maxine. "Dewey and American Education, 1894-1920."
SCHOOL AND SOCIETY 87 (1959): 381-86.

2306 Grinder, Robert E., and Strickland, Charles E. "G. Stanley Hall and
the Social Significance of Adolescence." TEACHERS COLLEGE RECORD
64 (1963): 390-99.

2307 Gutek, Gerald L. JOSEPH NEEF: THE AMERICANIZATION OF PEST-
ALOZZIANISM. University: University of Alabama Press, 1978. 159 p.

2308 Hall, G. Stanley. "Philosophy in the United States." MIND 4 (1879):
89-105.

2309 Hamilton, J.G. deR, and Knight, E.W. "Education for Citizenship."
HISTORICAL OUTLOOK 12 (1921): 197-208.

2310 Hammond, Charles A. "New England Academies and Classical Schools."
In UNITED STATES BUREAU OF EDUCATION, REPORT OF THE COM-
MISSIONER, 1867-1868, pp. 403-29. Washington, D.C.: Government
Printing Office, 1868.

    Covers the period: 1638-1833.

2311 Hansen, James E. DEMOCRACY'S COLLEGE IN THE CENTENNIAL
STATE: A HISTORY OF COLORADO STATE UNIVERSITY. Ft. Collins:
Colorado State University Press, 1977. 494 p.

2312 Harlan, Louis R. "Booker T. Washington and the White Man's Burden."
AMERICAN HISTORICAL REVIEW 71 (1966): 441-67.

2313 _____. "Booker T. Washington in Biographical Perspective." AMERI-
CAN HISTORICAL REVIEW 75 (1970): 1581-99.

2314 Harms, Ernest. "Child Guidance Yesterday, Today, and Tomorrow."
SCHOOL AND SOCIETY 72 (1950): 129-32.

2315 Harrington, John H. "The Cinderella Schools of Los Angeles, 1855-1955."
HISTORY OF EDUCATION JOURNAL 6 (1954): 162-64.

2316 Harris, Michael R. FIVE COUNTER-REVOLUTIONISTS IN HIGHER EDU-
CATION. Corvallis: Oregon State University Press, 1970. 224 p.

Miscellaneous

2317 Harris, Seymour. THE ECONOMICS OF HARVARD. New York: McGraw-Hill, 1970. 180 p.

2318 Hawkins, Hugh. "Charles W. Eliot, University Reform, and Religious Faith in America, 1869-1909." JOURNAL OF AMERICAN HISTORY 51 (1964): 191-213.

2319 Herbst, Jurgen. "Herbert Spencer and the Genteel Tradition in American Education." EDUCATIONAL THEORY 11 (1961): 99-111.

2320 _____. THE GERMAN HISTORICAL SCHOOL IN AMERICAN SCHOLAR-SHIP: A STUDY IN THE TRANSFER OF CULTURE. Ithaca, N.Y.: Cornell University Press, 1965. 262 p.

2321 Higham, John. "The Schism in American Scholarship." AMERICAN HISTORICAL REVIEW 72 (1966): 1-21.

2322 Hislop, Codman. ELIPHALET NOTT. Middletown, Conn.: Wesleyan University Press, 1971. 680 p.

2323 Hofstadter, Richard. ANTI-INTELLECTUALISM IN AMERICAN LIFE. New York: Knopf, 1963. 240 p.

2324 Hollingworth, Leta S. "The Founding of Public School 500: Speyer School." TEACHERS COLLEGE RECORD 38 (1936): 119-28.

　　　　Refers to the Teachers College Laboratory School.

2325 Holmes, Brian. "Some Writings of William Torrey Harris." BRITISH JOURNAL OF EDUCATIONAL STUDIES 5 (1956-57): 47-66.

2326 Holmes, Pauline. A TERCENTENARY HISTORY OF THE BOSTON PUB-LIC LATIN SCHOOL, 1635-1935. Cambridge: Harvard University Press, 1935. 541 p.

　　　　A history of one of America's most venerable schools and of some of its members.

2327 Holt, W. Stull. "The Idea of Scientific History in America." JOURNAL OF THE HISTORY OF IDEAS 1 (1940): 352-62.

2328 Horton, Aimee. "The Highlander Folk School: Pioneer of Integration in the South." TEACHERS COLLEGE RECORD 68 (1966): 242-50.

2329 Howard, Charles A. "A History of High School Legislation in Oregon to 1910." OREGON HISTORICAL SOCIETY QUARTERLY 24 (1923): 201-37.

　　　　For the period: 1878-1910.

2330 Howe, Daniel W. THE UNITARIAN CONSCIENCE: HARVARD MORAL PHILOSOPHY, 1805-1861. Cambridge, Mass.: Harvard University Press, 1970. 190 p.

2331 Jackson, George L. THE DEVELOPMENT OF STATE CONTROL OF PUBLIC INSTRUCTION IN MICHIGAN. Lansing, Mich.: Historical Commission, 1926. 381 p.

2332 Jencks, Christopher, and Riesman, David. THE ACADEMIC REVOLUTION. New York: Doubleday, 1968. 580 p.

2333 Jerabek, Esther. "Antonin Jurka, A Pioneer Czechoslovakia Schoolmaster in Minnesota." MINNESOTA HISTORY 13 (1933): 142-48.

2334 Jersild, Arthur T. "Child Psychology in the United States." TEACHERS COLLEGE RECORD 50 (1948): 114-27.

2335 Johanningmeier, Erwin V. "William Chandler Bagley's Changing Views on the Relationship Between Psychology and Education." HISTORY OF EDUCATION QUARTERLY 9 (1969): 3-27.

2336 Johnson, Charles S., and Bond, Horace M. "The Investigation of Racial Differences Prior to 1910." JOURNAL OF NEGRO EDUCATION 3 (1934): 328-39.

2337 Johnson, Irmgard. "Mao Among the Classics." JOURNAL OF GENERAL EDUCATION 25 (1973): 29-37.

2338 Johnson, Walter, and Colligan, Francis J. THE FULBRIGHT PROGRAM: A HISTORY. Chicago: University of Chicago Press, 1965. 380 p.

   A comprehensive account of this famous program in educational scholarships and how it worked around the world.

2339 Johnson, William R. "Professors in Process: Doctors and Teachers in American Culture." HISTORY OF EDUCATION QUARTERLY 15 (1975): 185-99.

2340 Jones, Arthur J. THE CONTINUATION SCHOOL IN THE UNITED STATES. U.S. Bureau of Education Bulletin No. 1, 1907. Washington, D.C.: Government Printing Office, 1907. 157 p.

2341 Jones, Howard M. AMERICAN HUMANISM: ITS MEANING FOR WORLD SURVIVAL. New York: Harper and Bros., 1957. 108 p.

   A study of American humanism with special reference to its development and the historical contexts in which it is to be understood.

2342 Judd, Charles H. "A Century of Applications of Psychology to Education." TEACHERS COLLEGE RECORD 27 (1926): 771-81.

2343 Karier, Clarence J. "The Rebel and the Revolutionary: Sigmund Freud and John Dewey." TEACHERS COLLEGE RECORD 64 (1963): 605-13.

2344 Kazamias, Andres. "Meritocracy and Isocracy in American Education: Retrospect and Prospect." EDUCATIONAL FORUM 25 (1961): 345-54.

2345 Kennedy, John F. JOHN F. KENNEDY ON EDUCATION. New York: Teachers College, Columbia University Press, 1966. 305 p.

   From Kennedy's public papers. Mostly speeches, bills, the Peace Corps, and related matters.

2346 Keppel, Ann M. "The Myth of Agrarianism in Rural Educational Reform, 1890-1914." HISTORY OF EDUCATION QUARTERLY 2 (1962): 100-12.

2347 Keppel, Ann M., and Clark, James I. "James H. Stout and the Menomonie Schools." WISCONSIN MAGAZINE OF HISTORY 42 (1959): 200-10.

2348 Kilpatrick, William H. "The Philosophy of American Education." TEACHERS COLLEGE RECORD 30 (1928): 13-22.

2349 _____. "Dewey's Philosophy of Education." EDUCATIONAL FORUM 17 (1953): 143-54.

2350 Kirschner, Joseph. "Programmed Learning: An Historical Accident." EDUCATIONAL FORUM 32 (1967): 97-103.

2351 Kizer, George A. "Federal Aid to Education, 1945-1963." HISTORY OF EDUCATION QUARTERLY 10 (1970): 84-102.

2352 Knapp, Robert H. THE ORIGINS OF AMERICAN HUMANISTIC SCHOLARS. Englewood Cliffs, N.J.: Prentice-Hall, 1964. 172 p.

2353 Knight, Edgar W. "Public Education in the South: Some Inherited Ills and Some Needed Reforms." SCHOOL AND SOCIETY 11 (1920): 31-38.

2354 Knox, Ellis O. "A Historical Sketch of Secondary Education for Negroes." JOURNAL OF NEGRO EDUCATION 11 (1940): 440-53.

2355 _____. "The Origin and Development of the Negro Separate School." JOURNAL OF NEGRO EDUCATION 16 (1947): 269-79.

2356 Kohlbrenner, Richard J. "William Torrey Harris: Superintendent of Schools, St. Louis." HISTORY OF EDUCATION JOURNAL 2 (1950-51): 18-24, 54-61.

2357 Koos, Leonard V. "The Rise of the People's College." SCHOOL REVIEW 55 (1947): 138-49.

2358 Lane, David A., Jr. "The Development of the Present Relationship of the Federal Government to Negro Education." JOURNAL OF NEGRO EDUCATION 7 (1938): 273-81.

2359 Lane, Russell A. "Legal Trends Toward Increased Provisions for Negro Education in the United States Between 1920 and 1940." JOURNAL OF NEGRO EDUCATION 1 (1932): 396-99.

2360 Lee, Gordon C. "Policies for Federal Aid to Education: An Historical Interpretation." HISTORY OF EDUCATION JOURNAL 1 (1949): 46-54.

An analysis of the role of the federal government since December 1857.

2361 Lehne, Richard. THE QUEST FOR JUSTICE: THE POLITICS OF SCHOOL FINANCE REFORM. New York: Longman, 1978. 246 p.

Examines school finance reform measures in New Jersey after the New Jersey State Supreme Court declared the state's elementary and secondary schools funding programs unconstitutional. It was predicated almost entirely upon the use of the real estate tax.

2362 Leland, Waldo G. "The American Council of Learned Societies and Its Relation to Humanistic Studies." PROCEEDINGS, AMERICAN PHILOSOPHICAL SOCIETY 71 (1932): 179-89.

2363 "Letters of John Dewey to Robert V. Daniels, 1946-1950." JOURNAL OF THE HISTORY OF IDEAS 20 (1959): 569-76.

2364 Leverette, William E., Jr. "E.L. Youman's Crusade for Scientific Autonomy and Respectability." AMERICAN QUARTERLY 17 (1965): 12-32.

2365 Lewis, Hal G. "Meikeljohn and Experimentalism." TEACHERS COLLEGE RECORD 44 (1943): 563-71.

2366 Lilge, Frederic. "John Dewey in Retrospect: An American Reconsideration." BRITISH JOURNAL OF EDUCATIONAL STUDIES 8 (1960): 99-111.

2367 Limbert, Paul M. "Trends and Patterns in the Changing College Curriculum." TEACHERS COLLEGE RECORD 49 (1939): 669-84.

2368 Logan, Frenise A. "Legal Status of Public School Education for Negroes in North Carolina, 1877-1894." NORTH CAROLINA HISTORICAL REVIEW 32 (1955): 346-57.

2369 Lorge, Irving. "Thorndyke's Contribution to the Psychology of Learning of Adults." TEACHERS COLLEGE RECORD 41 (1940): 778-88.

2370 Lyons, John O. THE COLLEGE NOVEL IN AMERICA. Carbondale: Southern Illinois University Press, 1962. 210 p.

2371 McCaul, Robert L. "Dewey and the University of Chicago." SCHOOL AND SOCIETY 89 (1961): 152-57, 179-83, 202-06.

2372 _____. "Dewey in College, 1875-1879." SCHOOL REVIEW 70 (1962): 437-56.

2373 _____. "Dewey's School Days, 1867-1875." ELEMENTARY SCHOOL JOURNAL 63 (1962): 15-21.

2374 McCollum, M.G., Jr. "Robert L. Tidwell and Public Education in Alabama." PAEDAGOGICA HISTORICA 8 (1968): 81-107.

2375 McGaughy, J.R. "The Extension of the Frontier in Elementary Education Since 1900." TEACHERS COLLEGE RECORD 24 (1933): 580-86.

2376 McGaughty, Robert A. JOSIAH QUINCY, 1772-1864: THE LAST FEDERALIST. Cambridge, Mass.: Harvard University Press, 1974. 380 p.

2377 McGrath, Earl J. "Sputnik and American Education." TEACHERS COLLEGE RECORD 59 (1958): 379-95.

2378 McLachlan, James. "American Colleges and the Transmission of Culture: The Case of the Mugwumps." In THE HOFSTADTER AEGIS: A MEMORIAL, edited by Stanley Elkins and Eric McKittrick, pp. 275-301. New York: Knopf, 1974.

2379 _____. "The Choice of Hercules: American Student Societies in the Early 19th Century." In THE UNIVERSITY IN SOCIETY, vol. 2, edited by Lawrence Stone, pp. 449-94. Princeton, N.J.: Princeton University Press, 1974.

2380 McLeish, Archibald. "Professional Schools of Liberal Education." YALE REVIEW 10 (1926): 362-72

2381 McMillin, Lawrence. THE SCHOOLMAKER: SAWNEY WEBB AND THE BELL BUCKLE STORY. Chapel Hill: University of North Carolina Press, 1971. 186 p.

About the Webb School at Bell Buckle, Tennessee, in the nineteenth century, then regarded as an outstanding preparatory school in the South.

2382 McPherson, James M. "White Liberals and Black Power in Negro Education, 1865-1915." AMERICAN HISTORICAL REVIEW 75 (1970): 1357-86

2383 McPherson, James W. "The New Puritanism: Values and Goals of Freedmen's Education in America." In THE UNIVERSITY IN SOCIETY, vol. 2, edited by Lawrence Stone, pp. 611-39. Princeton, N.J.: Princeton University Press, 1974.

2384 MacVannel, John A. "The Educational Theories of Herbart and Froebel." TEACHERS COLLEGE RECORD 6 (1905): 1-114.

2385 Mangham, Ian. "Education for Autonomy: Some Comments on the Educational Thought of David Riesman." BRITISH JOURNAL OF EDUCATIONAL STUDIES 15 (1957): 40-50.

2386 Marpiner, Ernest C. THE MAN OF MAYFLOWER HILL: A BIOGRAPHY OF FRANKLIN W. JOHNSON. Waterville, Maine: Colby College Press, 1967. 137 p.

Largely about Johnson's role as a school educator, professor and college president with glimpses on college and educational life: 1870-1956.

2387 Mayo, Amory D. TALKS WITH TEACHERS. Boston: New England Publishing, 1881. 200 p.

2388 Mead, George H. "The Philosophies of Royce, James, and Dewey in Their American Setting." INTERNATIONAL JOURNAL OF ETHICS 49 (1929-30): 211-31.

2389 Mead, Margaret. "Are Marriage and College Compatible?" DARTMOUTH ALUMNI MAGAZINE 56 (1960): 18-20.

2390 Mehl, Bernard. "The Conant Report and the Committee of Ten: A Historical Appraisal." EDUCATIONAL RESEARCH BULLETIN 39 (1960): 29-38, 56.

2391 Meikeljohn, Alexander. "The Unity of the Curriculum." NEW REPUBLIC 32 (1922): 2-3.

2392 Merk, Lois B. "Boston's Historic Public School Crisis." NEW ENGLAND QUARTERLY 31 (1958): 172-200.

2393 Messerli, Jonathan. HORACE MANN: A BIOGRAPHY. New York: Knopf, 1974. 604 p.

2394 Mezvinsky, Norton. "Scientific Temperance Instruction in the Schools." HISTORY OF EDUCATION QUARTERLY 1 (1961): 48-56.

   About the women's Christian temperance movement, 1869-1920.

2395 Michael, Richard B. "The American Institute of Instruction." HISTORY OF EDUCATION JOURNAL 3 (1951): 27-32.

2396 Miller, Henry. "John Dewey on Urban Education: An Extrapolation." TEACHERS COLLEGE RECORD 69 (1968): 771-83.

2397 Miller, Richard L. "Admiral Rickover on American Education." JOURNAL OF TEACHER EDUCATION 10 (1959): 332-57.

2398 Miller, Robert W. "Resort to Corporal Punishment in Enforcing School Discipline, 1815-1949." SYRACUSE LAW REVIEW 1 (1949): 247-66.

2399 Montgomery, Winfield S. HISTORICAL SKETCH OF EDUCATION FOR THE COLORED RACE IN THE DISTRICT OF COLUMBIA, 1807-1905. Washington, D.C.: Smith Brothers Printers, 1907. 49 p.

   Part of a report to the Board of Education for the district, 1904-05.

2400 Morison, Emily M. THE JOURNAL OF A VISIT TO ST. PAUL'S SCHOOL IN CONCORD, NEW HAMPSHIRE. New York: Uphill Press, 1967. 41p.

   A diary by the mother of Samuel Eliot Morison.

2401 Mosier, Richard D. "The Educational Philosophy of William T. Harris." PEABODY JOURNAL OF EDUCATION 29 (1951): 24-33.

2402 _____. "Hegelianism in American Education." EDUCATIONAL THEORY 3 (1953): 97-103.

2403 Moulton, Gerald L. "The American Herbartian: A Portrait from His Yearbooks." HISTORY OF EDUCATION QUARTERLY 3 (1963): 134-42, 187-97.

2404 Mowrer, O. Hobart. "Learning Theory: Historical Review and Re-Interpretation." HARVARD EDUCATIONAL REVIEW 24 (1954): 37-58.

2405 Neumann, Henry. MORAL VALUES IN SECONDARY EDUCATION: A REPORT OF THE COMMISSION ON THE REORGANIZATION OF SEC-ONDARY EDUCATION APPOINTED BY THE NATIONAL EDUCATION ASSOCIATION. U.S. Bureau of Education Information Bulletin No. 51, 1917. Washington, D.C.: Government Printing Office, 1917. 37 p.

2406 Newlon, Jesse H. "John Dewey's Influence in the Schools." TEACHERS COLLEGE RECORD 31 (1929): 224-38.

2407 Newman, John H. THE IDEA OF A UNIVERSITY. New York: Oxford University Press, 1976. 684 p.

2408 Norton, John K. "The Role of Education in a Period of Mobilization." TEACHERS COLLEGE RECORD 52 (1952): 137-44.

2409 Ogbu, John U. MINORITY EDUCATION AND CASTE: THE AMERICAN SYSTEM IN CROSS-CULTURAL PERSPECTIVE. New York: Academic Press, 1978. 410 p.

  Examines schooling and racial stratification in American educa-tion with references to India, Israel, Japan, and New Zealand. Sponsored by the Carnegie Council on Children.

2410 Olson, Keith. THE G.I. BILL, THE VETERANS, AND THE COLLEGES. Lexington: University Press of Kentucky, 1974. 190 p.

2411 Parker, Franklin. "Francis Wayland Parker, 1837-1902." PAEDAGOGICA HISTORICA 1 (1961): 120-33.

2412 _____. "The Case of Harold Rugg." PAEDAGOGICA HISTORICA 2 (1962): 95-122.

2413 Parkinson, Henry J. "Rousseau's Emile: Political Theory and Education." HISTORY OF EDUCATION QUARTERLY 5 (1965): 81-96.

2414 Paterson, Donald G. "The Genesis of Modern Guidance." EDUCATION-AL RECORD 19 (1938): 36-46.

2415 Patty, Ernest N. NORTH COUNTRY CHALLENGE. New York: David McKay, 1969. 272 p.

  On teaching in Alaska from 1922 through 1968 at the Univer-sity of Alaska. An autobiographical account of his reactions to the university's cooperation with business and industry, as well as his somewhat anticonservationist stance.

2416 Paulston, Roland G. "French Influence in American Institutions of Higher Learning, 1784-1825." HISTORY OF EDUCATION QUARTERLY 8 (1968): 229-45.

2417 Perrin, John W. "Beginnings in Compulsory Education." EDUCATIONAL REVIEW 25 (1903): 240-43.

2418 _____. "Indirect Compulsory Education: The Factory Laws of Massachusetts and Connecticut." EDUCATIONAL REVIEW 31 (1906): 383-94.

2419 Pope, Arthur U. "Alexander Meikeljohn." AMERICAN SCHOLAR 34 (1965): 641-45.

2420 Powers, Alfred, and Corning, Howards, eds. HISTORY OF EDUCATION IN PORTLAND. Portland, Oreg.: W.P.A. Adult Education Project, 1937. 373 p.

2421 Preston, E. Delorus, Jr. "William Syphax, A Pioneer in Negro Education in the District of Columbia." JOURNAL OF NEGRO HISTORY 20 (1935): 448-76.

2422 Radosavljevich, Paul R. "The Oswego Movement and the New Education." EDUCATIONAL FORUM 2 (1937): 90-100.

2423 Raushenbush, Esther. THE STUDENT AND HIS STUDIES. Middletown, Conn.: Wesleyan University Press, 1964. 185 p.

2424 Ravi-Booth, Vincent. "A New College for Women." PROGRESSIVE EDUCATION 2 (1925): 138-45.

      About Bennington College, Vermont.

2425 Reavis, William C. "Federal Aid for Education, 1787-1949." AMERICAN ACADEMY OF POLITICAL SCIENCE ANNUAL 265 (1949): 56-60.

2426 Recay, Edward E. "Pioneering in Negro Education." JOURNAL OF NEGRO EDUCATION 6 (1937): 38-53.

2427 Reddick, L.D. "The Education of Negroes in States Where Separate Schools Are Not Legal." JOURNAL OF NEGRO EDUCATION 16 (1947): 290-300.

2428 Reid, Herbert O. "The Supreme Court Decision and Interposition." JOURNAL OF NEGRO EDUCATION 25 (1956): 109-17.

2429 Reid, Ira De A. "The Development of Adult Education for Negroes in the United States." JOURNAL OF NEGRO EDUCATION 14 (1945): 299-306.

2430 Reidler, A. "American Technological Schools." In UNITED STATES BUREAU OF EDUCATION, REPORT OF THE COMMISSIONER, 1892-1893. Vol. 1, pp. 657-86. Washington, D.C.: Government Printing Office, 1895.

2431 Rich, John M. INNOVATIONS IN EDUCATION: REFORMERS AND THEIR CRITICS. 2d ed. Boston: Allyn and Bacon, 1978. 402 p.

An anthology of included representational materials by leading educational reformers, with notice of the most prominent innovations.

2432 Riesman, David. CONSTRAINT AND VARIETY IN AMERICAN EDUCATION. Rev. ed. Lincoln: University of Nebraska Press, 1977. 137 p.

Regarded by some as more or less a popular classic on this subject.

2433 Riesman, David, and Stadtman, Verne, eds. ACADEMIC TRANSFORMATION: SEVENTEEN INSTITUTIONS UNDER PRESSURE. New York: McGraw-Hill, 1973. 190 p.

2434 Robarts, Jason R. "The Quest for a Science of Education in the Nineteenth Century." HISTORY OF EDUCATION QUARTERLY 8 (1968): 431-46.

2435 Robbins, Gerald. "Rossa B. Cooley and Penn School: Social Dynamo in a Negro Rural Subculture, 1901-1930." JOURNAL OF NEGRO EDUCATION 33 (1964): 43-51.

2436 Robinson, Elmo A. "One Hundred Years of Philosophy Teaching in California, 1857-1957." JOURNAL OF THE HISTORY OF IDEAS 20 (1959): 369-84.

2437 Robinson, Sylvan H. "Equal Educational Facilities Under the Equal Protection Clause of the Fourteenth Amendment." WASHINGTON UNIVERSITY LAW QUARTERLY 14 (1950): 594-616.

2438 Rock, Robert T., Jr. "Thorndike's Contribution to the Psychology of Learning." TEACHERS COLLEGE RECORD 41 (1940): 751-61.

2439 Ross, Dorothy G. STANLEY HALL: PSYCHOLOGIST AS PROPHET. Chicago: University of Chicago Press, 1972. 412 p.

2440 Rousmaniere, John P. "Cultural Hybrid in the Slums: The College Woman and the Settlement House, 1889-1894." AMERICAN QUARTERLY 32 (1970): 45-66.

2441 Rozwenc, Edwin C. "Agricultural Education and Politics in Vermont." PROCEEDINGS, VERMONT HISTORICAL SOCIETY 36 (1958): 69-106.

2442 Rudwick, Elliott M. "W.E.B. DuBois and the Atlanta University Studies on the Negro." JOURNAL OF NEGRO EDUCATION 26 (1957): 466-76.

2443 Rudy, Willis. "Josiah Royce and the Art of Teaching." EDUCATIONAL THEORY 2 (1952): 158-69.

2444 Russell, William F. "Philosophical Bases of Organization and Operation of American Schools: The Influence of the New Psychology." TEACHERS COLLEGE RECORD 50 (1949): 386-95.

2445 Sack, Saul. "Liberal Education: What Was It? What Is IT?" HISTORY OF EDUCATION QUARTERLY 3 (1962): 210-24.

2446 Schuyler, William. "The St. Louis Philosophical Movement." EDUCATIONAL REVIEW 29 (1905): 450-67.

2447 Scott, Emmett J. "Twenty Years After: An Appraisal of Booker T. Washington." JOURNAL OF NEGRO EDUCATION 5 (1936): 543-54.

2448 Sears, Jesse B., and Henderson, Adin D. CUBBERLEY OF STANFORD AND HIS CONTRIBUTIONS TO AMERICAN EDUCATION. Stanford, Calif.: Stanford University Press, 1957. 340 p.

2449 Sher, Jonathan P., ed. EDUCATION IN RURAL AMERICA: A REASSESSMENT OF CONVENTIONAL WISDOM. Boulder, Colo.: West View Press, 1977. 392 p.

    Examines the salient issues of reform in rural education both over time and through an analysis of two case studies.

2450 Sloan, Douglas. "Harmony, Chaos, and Concensus: The American College Curriculum." TEACHERS COLLEGE RECORD 73 (1971): 221-51.

2451 Smith, Wilson. "Apologia pro Alma Mater: The College as Community in Ante-Bellum America." In THE HOFSTADTER AEGIS: A MEMORIAL, edited by Stanley Elkins and Eric McKittrick, pp. 241-73. New York: Knopf, 1974.

2452 Sorensen, Theodore C. "Legislative Control of Loyalty in the Schools, 1884-1950." NEBRASKA LAW REVIEW 29 (1950): 485-505.

2453 Sperber, Robert I. "Federal Aid and Federal Control of Education, 1890-1959." TEACHERS COLLEGE RECORD 61 (1960): 331-38.

2454 Stafford, Douglas K. "Roots of the Decline of Herbartianism in Nineteenth Century America." HARVARD EDUCATIONAL REVIEW 25 (1955): 231-41.

2455 Steere, Geoffrey H. "Freudianism in Child-Rearing in the Twenties." AMERICAN QUARTERLY 20 (1968): 759-67.

2456 Stephenson, Martha. "Education in Kentucky." REGISTER OF KENTUCKY STATE HISTORICAL SOCIETY 15 (1917): 67-79.

2457 Stinnett, T.M., ed. "A Symposium: Educationists and Other Academics." JOURNAL OF TEACHER EDUCATION 10 (1959): 157-210.

2458 Stocking, George W., Jr. RACE, CULTURE, AND EVOLUTION: ESSAYS IN THE HISTORY OF ANTHROPOLOGY. New York: Free Press, 1968. 270 p.

2459 Stout, John E. THE DEVELOPMENT OF HIGH SCHOOL CURRICULA IN THE NORTH CENTRAL STATES FROM 1860 TO 1918. Chicago: University of Chicago Press, 1921 322 p.

2460 Sutton, W.S. "The Contribution of Booker T. Washington to the Education of the Negro." SCHOOL AND SOCIETY 4 (1916): 457-63.

2461 Swisher, Jacob. "A Century of School Legislation in Iowa." IOWA JOURNAL OF HISTORY 44 (1946): 174-205.

2462 Taopi, Cigala Wotamin. "Publications of an Indian School." NEBRASKA HISTORY MAGAZINE 19 (1938): 234-37.

2463 Taylor, Harold. THE WORLD AS TEACHER. New York: Doubleday, 1969. 322 p.

2464 Terrell, Mary C. "The History of the High Schools for Negroes in Washington." JOURNAL OF NEGRO HISTORY 2 (1917): 252-66.

2465 Thomas, Russell. THE SEARCH FOR A COMMON LEARNING: GENERAL EDUCATION, 1800-1960. New York: McGraw-Hill, 1962. 340 p.

2466 Thorndike, Edward L. "The Measurement of Educational Products." SCHOOL REVIEW 20 (1912): 289-99.

2467 Thursfield, Richard E. "Ellwood Patterson Cubberley." HARVARD EDU-CATIONAL REVIEW 9 (1939): 43-62.

2468 Thut, I.N. "Some Historical Factors Bearing Upon the Authority of States in Education." EDUCATIONAL THEORY 9 (1959): 193-202.

2469 Toppin, Edgar A. "Walter White and the Atlanta NAACP's Fight for Equal Schools." HISTORY OF EDUCATION QUARTERLY 7 (1967): 3-21.

2470 Tostberg, Robert E. "Colonel Parker's Quest for 'A School in Which All Good Things Come Together.'" HISTORY OF EDUCATION QUARTERLY 6 (1966): 22-42.

2471 Trowbridge, Hoyt. "Forty Years of General Education." JOURNAL OF GENERAL EDUCATION 11 (1958): 161-69.

2472 True, Alfred C. A HISTORY OF AGRICULTURAL EXTENSION WORK IN THE UNITED STATES, 1785-1923. U.S. Department of Agriculture Miscellaneous Publication No. 15, 1928. Washington, D.C.: Government Printing Office, 1928. 436 p.

2473 Tyack, David B. GEORGE TICKNOR AND THE BOSTON BRAHMINS. Cambridge, Mass.: Harvard University Press, 1967. 340 p.

2474 U.S. Library of Congress. LEGISLATIVE REFERENCE SERVICE. THE HISTORIC AND CURRENT FEDERAL ROLE IN EDUCATION. Washington, D.C.: Government Printing Office, 1961. 66 p.

    A report to the Subcommittee on Education: Committee on Labor and Public Welfare, U.S. Senate.

2475 Van Patten, James. "Search for Substance in Conant's Educational Writings." JOURNAL OF TEACHER EDUCATION 16 (1965): 193-201.

2476 Veysey, Laurence R. "The Academic Mind of Woodrow Wilson." MISSISSIPPI VALLEY HISTORICAL REVIEW 49 (1963): 613-34.

2477 Walton, John. "The Apostasy of Robert M. Hutchins." EDUCATIONAL THEORY 3 (1953): 162-65.

2478 Watson, Goodwin. "John Dewey as a Pioneer in Social Psychology." TEACHERS COLLEGE RECORD 51 (1949): 139-43.

2479 Weiss, Robert M. "He Wanted to Abolish Public Schools." TEACHERS COLLEGE RECORD 57 (1956): 222-31.

   About the journalist, Richard G. White: 1821-85.

2480 West, H.F. "Common School, Advocate--The Earliest Indiana School Journal." INDIANA MAGAZINE OF HISTORY 6 (1910): 118-26.

2481 White, Morton G. "The Revolt Against Formalism in American Social Thought of the Twentieth Century." JOURNAL OF THE HISTORY OF IDEAS 8 (1947): 131-52.

2482 Wilkins, Burleigh T. "James Dewey, and Hegelian Idealism." JOURNAL OF THE HISTORY OF IDEAS 17 (1956): 332-46.

2483 Willard, H.K. "Contributions to the History of the Hopkins Grammar School, New Haven, Conn., 1660 to 1900." In UNITED STATES BU-REAU OF EDUCATION, REPORT OF THE COMMISSIONER, 1899-1900. Vol. 2, pp. 1281-96. Washington, D.C.: Government Printing Office, 1901.

2484 Willoughby, W.W. "The History of Summer Schools in the United States." In UNITED STATES BUREAU OF EDUCATION, REPORT OF THE COMMIS-SIONER, 1891-1892. Vol. 2, pp. 893-959. Washington, D.C.: Government Printing Office, 1894.

2485 Wilson, J. Ormond. "Eighty Years of the Public Schools of Washington: 1805 to 1885." In UNITED STATES BUREAU OF EDUCATION, REPORT OF THE COMMISSIONER, 1894-1895. Vol. 2, pp. 1673-98. Washington, D.C.: Government Printing Office, 1896.

2486 Winton, Ruth M. "Negro Participation in Southern Expositions, 1881-1915." JOURNAL OF NEGRO EDUCATION 16 (1947): 34-43.

2487 Wirth, Arthur G. "The Deweyan Tradition Revisited: Any Relevance for Our Time?" TEACHERS COLLEGE RECORD 69 (1967): 265-69.

2488 Wish, Harvey. "Negro Education and the Progressive Movement." JOUR-NAL OF NEGRO HISTORY 49 (1964): 184-200.

2489 Woerdehoff, Frank J. "Dr. Charles McCarthy: Planner of the Wisconsin System of Vocational and Adult Education." WISCONSIN MAGAZINE OF HISTORY 41 (1958): 270-74.

2490 Woodrow Wilson Foundation. EDUCATION IN THE NATION'S SERVICE. New York: Praeger, 1960. 193 p.

A collection of some eighty essays on Wilsonian ideas and
ideals by numerous leading American educators.

2491 Woodson, Carter G. "Negro Life and History as Presented in the Schools."
JOURNAL OF NEGRO HISTORY 4 (1919): 273-80.

2492 _____. "Early Negro Education in West Virginia." JOURNAL OF
NEGRO HISTORY 7 (1922): 23-63.

2493 Wormeley, G. Smith. "Educators of the First Half-Century of the Public
Schools of the District of Columbia." JOURNAL OF NEGRO HISTORY 17
(1932): 124-40.

2494 Wylie, Andrew T. "A Brief History of Mental Tests." TEACHERS COL-
LEGE RECORD 23 (1922): 19-33.

2495 Yengo, Carmine A. "John Dewey and the Cult of Efficiency." HAR-
VARD EDUCATIONAL REVIEW 34 (1964): 33-53.

AUTHOR INDEX

This index includes all authors, editors, and other contributors cited in the text. It is alphabetized letter by letter, and numbers refer to entry numbers.

A

Abbott, Martin 1231
Abrahams, Harold J. 1151
Abram, Morris 1735
Abramson, David A. 2181
Abramson, Joan 1736
Adams, Bess 2050
Adams, Don 2024
Adams, Francis 1587
Adams, Frank C. 1737
Adams, Herbert B. 554-55, 801, 1232
Adams, James Truslow 1-2
Adkins, Edwin P. 2182
Ahern, Patrick H. 556
Akers, Charles N. 1233
Alcott, William A. 1234
Aldrich, F.R. 1235
Alilunos, Leo J. 2051
Allen, Van S. 1738
Allen, W.F. 1588
Allmendinger, David F., Jr. 1236-39
Alloway, David N. 1830
Allport, Gordon W. 2183
Almack, John C. 2052
Altbach, Philip G. 76, 347, 557, 1739
Altman, Robert A. 558
Altschule, Mark 570
Altschuler, Alan A. 1740

Alvord, John W. 1589
Ambrose, Stephen E. 802, 1240, 1590
American Antiquarian Society 954
American Bibliographical Center 45
American Historical Association 46, 47
American Library Association. Children's Services Division 2053
Anderson, Dice R. 955
Anderson, Lewis F. 282, 1241, 2184
Anderson, Robert H. 1889
Anderson, Stuart 1741, 2185
Anderson, William T., Jr. 1242, 1591
Andersson, Theodore 348-49
Andresen, Robert L. 81
Andress, J. Mace 1243
Andrews, Benjamin F. 1244, 1592-93
Andrews, Edward D. 1245
Andrews, Wayne 3
Angell, James B. 559
Appel, John J. 350
Aptheker, Herbert 560
Arbuthnot, May H. 2054
Archambault, Reginald D. 186
Armor, David J. 1742-43
Armstrong, Warren B. 1594
Armytage, W.H.G. 2186

Author Index

Burnham, William H. 373
Burns, J.A. 289
Burns, Martha A. 1867
Burns, Richard W. 1784
Burr, Nelson R. 53
Burrage, Henry S. 1283
Burrell, B. Jeanette 1605
Burrin, Frank K. 1785
Bush, George G. 591, 972
Butler, Fred C. 1786-87
Butler, Nicholas M. 90, 1608
Butter, Josiah 1609
Butterfield, Lymon H. 973-74
Button, Henry W. 1610
Butts, R. Freeman 158, 291-92,
   374-76, 1284, 2224-25
Byse, Clark 592

C

Cadbury, Henry J. 975
Calam, John 377
Caldwell, E.W. 593
Caldwell, Otis W. 197, 2226
Calhoun, Daniel H. 198, 2227-29
Calhoun, David 1788
Calhoun, F.P. 1285
California, University of. Department
   of Pedagogy 91
Calista, Donald J. 2230
Caliver, Ambrose 92, 594, 1789-90
Calkins, Earnest E. 1286
Callahan, Raymond E. 378, 2231
Calvert, Monte A. 2232
Camp, William L. 73
Campbell, H.G. 976
Campbell, Jack K. 1611
Campbell, Robert 1791
Campbell, Ronald F. 1792
Capen, Eliza P. 1287
Capen, Samuel P. 2233
Carbone, Peter, Jr. 2234
Carey, James C. 819
Carlson, Robert A. 1793
Carlton, Frank T. 1288
Carmichael, Leonard 2071
Carmichael, Oliver C. 595, 1612
Carnay, Martin 379
Carnegie Commission on Higher
   Education 596-600

Carnoy, Martin 380
Carpenter, Charles 2072
Carpenter, Hazen C. 2235
Carrell, William D. 93, 601-2,
   977
Carrier, Lyman 1289
Carroll, J.C. 1290
Carron, Malcolm 820
Carstensen, Vernon 821
Carter, Harvey L. 46
Cartwright, Morse A. 2236
Cartwright, William H. 381
Cary, Harold W. 822
Cassara, Ernest 49
Castaneda, Carlos E. 978
Castel, Albert 979, 1291
Cattell, Jacques 63
Chadbourne, Ava H. 199
Chambers, Gurney 2237
Chambers, Merritt M. 94, 215,
   603
Chambliss, J.J. 2238
Chance, Norman A. 1795
Chandler, Charles C. 226
Chaper, Jesse H. 382
Chapman, James C. 1796
Chase, Harry W. 2239
Chase, Wayland J. 980
Cheyney, Arnold B. 1797
Cheyney, Edward P. 823
Childs, John L. 383, 2240-42
Chinard, Gilbert 1292
Chitty, Arthur B. 1613
Church, Robert L. 293, 384-85,
   1798, 2243
Churchill, Alfred V. 604, 1293,
   1614-15
Citron, Abraham F. 2244
Clapp, Gordon R. 605
Clapp, Margaret A. 1799
Clark, Burton R. 824
Clark, Felton G. 606
Clark, James I. 2347
Clark, Kenneth B. 1870
Clark, Thomas D. 1294, 1616
Clegg, Ambrose A., Jr. 386
Clement, Rufus E. 387, 607
Clews, Elsie W. 200
Clifford, Geraldine J. 294, 388-89
Clift, Virgil 1800

Author Index

Author Index

Gartner, Lloyd P. 222
Gates, Charles M. 852
Gates, Paul W. 1637
Gatewood, Willard B. 2300
Gatke, Robert M. 1323
Gaubard, Allen 1879
Gauerke, Warren E. 1880, 2301
Gaustad, Edwin S. 46
Geiger, Louis G. 853
Genovese, Eugene D. 484
George, Anne E. 2092
George, John J. 2247, 2302
Gerard, Harold B. 1881
Gerhard, Dietrich 645, 1639
Gershenberg, Irving 1640
Gersman, Elinor M. 117-23, 1641
Gettelman, Marvin E. 854, 1882
Gideonese, Harry D. 646
Gilbert, Felix 429
Gillett, Margaret 312
Gintis, Herbert 367
Glass, Bentley 647
Glazer, Nathan 1883
Glazer, Penina 648
Gleazer, Edmund J. 649
Glenner-Hassett, Roland 2062
Glover, Wilbur H. 1642
Gobbel, Luther L. 430
Going, Allen J. 2303
Goncharov, N.K. 1837
Good, Harry G. 124, 313, 431, 1324-26
Goode, G. Brown 1327
Goodfellow, Donald M. 1328
Goodlad, John I. 1884-94
Goodman, Paul 1879
Goodsell, Willystine 223, 1329
Goodspeed, Thomas W. 855
Goodwin, Mary F. 1029
Gordon, Edmund 1962
Gordon, Mary A. 739
Gordon, Sarah H. 1643
Gordy, J.P. 2093
Gore, Joseph 2094
Gougher, Ronald L. 125
Gould, Joseph E. 1644
Gould, Julius 16
Gower, Calvin W. 1895
Grabo, Norman S. 1030

Graham, Patricia A. 1645, 1896
Grant, Gerald 1897, 2304
Grantham, Dewey W., Jr. 46
Grattan, C. Hartley 224
Graubard, Stephen R. 429, 650
Gray, James 856
Gray, Ruth A. 126
Greeley, Andrew M. 432, 651
Green, Paul G. 127
Greenbaum, Leonard 857
Greene, Evarts B. 17, 1031, 1330
Greene, Jack P. 46, 53
Greene, Maxine 433-34, 1898, 2305
Greenwood, James M. 2095
Greer, Colin 435-36
Gresham, Luveta W. 1331
Greven, Philip J., Jr. 225
Gribble, Stephen C. 1899
Griffin, Grace G. 5
Grinder, Robert E. 2306
Grob, Gerald N. 53
Gross, Barry E. 1900
Gross, Carl H. 226
Gross, Richard E. 314
Gross, Ronald 1964
Grubb, W. Norton 245
Gruber, Carol S. 652
Gulik, Luther H. 1901
Gumbert, Edgar B. 1902
Gummere, R.M. 1032
Guralnick, Stanley M. 1332
Gustad, John W. 653
Gutek, Gerald L. 315, 2307

H

Haar, Charles M. 1333
Hagan, William T. 46
Halber, Mabel 1033
Hall, Clifton L. 243
Hall, D.D. 1334
Hall, E.W. 654
Hall, G. Stanley 128, 655, 2096, 2308
Hamilton, Andrew 1903
Hamilton, J.G. deRoulhac 1335, 2309
Hamilton, Malcolm C. 185

Author Index

Hamilton, Sinclair 2097
Hammond, Charles A. 2310
Hammond, William G. 1336
Hanawalt, Leslie I. 858
Handlin, Mary 656
Handlin, Oscar 656
Handschin, Charles H. 2098
Haney, John L. 2099
Hansen, Allen O. 437, 1034
Hansen, Carl F. 1904
Hansen, James E. 2311
Hanus, Paul H. 1646
Harding, Thomas S. 1337
Harding, Walter 1338
Hardy, Carrie A. 1647
Hargrell, Lester 1339
Harlan, Louis R. 46, 1340, 2312-13
Harms, Ernest 2314
Harrington, John H. 2315
Harris, Michael R. 1905, 2316
Harris, Seymour 657, 2317
Harris, William T. 1341, 1648-49,
    2100-2101
Harris, Wilmer C. 2102
Harrison, Lowell H. 1342
Hart, James D. 18
Hartshorne, E.Y. 859
Haskett, Richard C. 1035
Hasse, Adelaide R. 54
Hassenger, Robert 658, 1906
Hatch, Richard A. 1343, 1650
Haunton, Richard H. 1344
Havighurst, Robert J. 1907
Havighurst, Walter 860
Haviland, Virginia 2103
Hawkins, Hugh 659-60, 861-62,
    1651-52, 2318
Hayes, Cecil B. 1345
Headley, Leal A. 863
Heartman, Charles F. 2104
Heath, G. Louis 661
Hechinger, Fred 1908
Heerman, Barry 1909
Hefferlin, J.B. Lon 662
Heiges, Donald 586
Heimstra, William L. 1346
Henderson, Adin D. 2448
Henderson, John C. 316
Hendrick, Irving G. 438, 1036

Henry, David D. 663, 1910
Hepburn, William M. 664
Herbst, Jurgen 53, 130, 439-40,
    665-68, 864, 1037, 1911, 2105,
    2319-20
Hervery, Walter L. 2106
Herzog, John D. 441
Heslep, Robert D. 1348
Hewitt, John H. 1349
Hickerson, Frank R. 865-66
Hicks, John D. 46
Higham, John 381, 2321
Hill, Benjamin T. 1350
Hiller, Richard L. 2021
Hillesheim, James W. 227
Hills, E.C. 668
Hills, P.J. 1912
Hillson, Maurie 1913
Hillway, Tyrus 228
Hindle, Brooke 1038-40
Hiner, N. Ray 442
Hinsdale, Burke A. 229, 1351,
    1653
Hinsdale, Mary C. 1654
Hislop, Codman 1352, 2322
History of Education 443
Hobby, Selma Ann Plowman 1655
Hobson, Elsie G. 1353
Hodge, Frederick Webb 19
Hofstadter, Richard 230, 670, 2323
Hogan, Peter E. 867
Hogeland, Ronald W. 1656
Holden, Reuben A. 868
Holley, Howard L. 671
Hollingsworth, R.R. 1354, 1657
Hollingworth, Leta S. 2324
Hollis, Ernest V. 114, 634, 672
Holmes, Brian 2325
Holmes, Dwight O.W. 869
Holmes, Pauline 2326
Holsinger, M. Paul 444
Holsten, George H., Jr. 870
Holt, John 1879
Holt, W. Stull 2327
Honeywell, Roy J. 231, 1355-56
Hood, Bruce L. 284, 445
Hooker, Richard J. 1041
Hoover, Thomas N. 1357

249

Author Index

Author Index

Author Index

Smith, W.R. 2013
Smith, Willard W. 1185
Smith, Wilson 230, 270, 352, 518, 2451
Smythe, Donald 1713
Snedden, David 2159
Snow, M.S. 773
Snyder, Henry N. 774
Soderbergh, Peter A. 1535
Solberg, Winton U. 932-34
Soper, Wayne W. 166
Sorensen, Theodore C. 2452
Speare, Elizabeth G. 1186
Sperber, Robert I. 2453
Spieseke, Alice W. 2160
Spill, William A. 1537
Spivack, Robert G. 2014
Spring, Joel H. 455, 519-21, 1902, 2015
Spurlock, Clark 271
Stadtman, Verne A. 935, 2433
Stafford, Douglas K. 2454
Stambler, Moses 2016
Starr, Joseph R. 775
Stayer, George D., Jr. 167
Stearns, Raymond P. 1189
Steere, Geoffrey H. 2455
Steiner, Bernard C. 1190
Stephan, A. Stephen 776
Stephens, Clarence W. 1737
Stephens, Frank F. 936
Stephens, Roswell P. 1538
Stephenson, Martha 1191, 2456
Stephenson, Wendell H. 937
Stevens, Edward W., Jr. 2017
Stevens, Harry R. 46
Stinnett, T.M. 2457
Stock, Phyllis 522
Stocking, George W. 425, 523, 2458
Stone, Irving 938
Stone, James Champion 777
Stone, Lawrence 338, 384, 2383
Stone, Mason S. 1539, 2161
Storr, Richard J. 524-25, 778-79, 939
Story, Ronald 1540
Stout, Harry S. 1192
Stout, John E. 2459
Stoutemeyer, J.H. 526

Stover, John F. 46
Stowe, Harriet Beecher 1714
Straub, Jean S. 1193
Strayer, George D. 2162
Strickland, Charles E. 272, 1715, 2306
Stuart, George 1716
Studer, Gerald C. 1194
Studolsky, Susan S. 2018
Suarez, Raleigh A. 1717
Summerscales, William 2019
Sunderman, Lloyd F. 2163
Super, Donald E. 2020
Sutherland, Zena 2054
Sutton, W.S. 2460
Suzzallo, Henry 373
Swan, William O. 1541
Swem, Earl G. 1195
Swett, John 339
Swift, Fletcher H. 527-28
Swisher, Jacob 2461
Swont, Henry Lee 1718
Sykes, Frederick H. 781

T

Talbott, John E. 429, 529
Tanis, Norman E. 1196
Taopi, Cigala Wotamin 2462
Taylor, George Rogers 53
Taylor, Harold 782, 2463
Taylor, Howard C. 1719
Taylor, Hoy 1720
Taylor, Isaac 1542
Taylor, James M. 1543
Taylor, William R. 1544
Teaford, Jon 1197
Teitelbaum, Herbert 2021
Teller, James D. 313
Terrell, Mary C. 2464
Tewkesbury, Donald G. 783, 1546
Thayer, Vivian T. 340
Thelin, John R. 784, 2022
Thomas, Alan M., Jr. 530, 2023
Thomas, J.H. 1547
Thomas, Maurice J. 273
Thomas, Milton H. 168
Thomas, Russell 2465
Thomson, Robert P. 1198
Thorndike, Edward L. 2466

Author Index

Waring, Martha G. 1222
Warren, Charles 1564
Warren, Donald R. 342, 541, 1726
Waseman, Manfred J. 61
Watson, Goodwin 2478
Watson, Joseph S. 1565
Watson, Richard L. 381
Watson, Thomas S. 1566
Wayland, Francis 1371
Wayland, Sloan R. 2037
Weathersby, William H. 1567
Weaver, David A. 277
Weaver, Glenn 1223
Webb, Walter P. 794
Weber, Evelyn 1727
Webster, Noah 1504, 2171
Wechsler, Harold S. 795
Wechsler, Louis K. 1224
Weeks, Edward 542
Weeks, Stephen B. 1568
Wein, Roberta 1728
Weinberg, Meyer 177-78, 543, 2038
Weingart, John 698
Weinrich, R.C. 2039
Weiss, Harry B. 2172
Weiss, Robert M. 2479
Welch, d'Alte 2173
Wells, Guy F. 2174
Wells, Herman G. 1569
Welter, Rush 278, 343, 544
Wendt, Erhard F. 545, 2040
Wertenbaker, Thomas J. 945, 1225
Wesley, Charles H. 41
Wesley, Edgar B. 546, 1570
West, Earle H. 1571, 1729
West, H.F. 2480
Westerberg, Virginia 946
Wheat, Harry G. 2175
Whetzel, H.H. 947
Whitaker, A.P. 1572
White, Bruce 1730
White, Carl M. 62
White, Dana F. 1731
White, James C. 1573
White, Morton G. 2481
White, Ruth W. 1574
Whitehead, John S. 547, 796
Whitehead, Matthew J. 797
Whitehill, Walter Muir 42

Whitford, W.G. 2176
Whittaker, Rev. Nathaniel 1145
Whittemore, Richard 948-49, 2041
Whittenburg, Clarice 1575
Widen, Irwin 2042
Widmayer, Charles E. 950
Wiggin, Gladys A. 344
Wild, Payson S. 951
Wilkins, Burleigh T. 2482
Willard, H.K. 2483
Willcott, Paul 2177
Williams, Henry S. 1579
Williams, Jack E. 359
Williamson, E.G. 548, 2043
Williamson, Harold F. 951
Willingham, Warren W. 179
Willoughby, W.W. 2484
Wills, Elbert V. 1580
Wilson, Iris Higbie 929
Wilson, J. Ormond 2485
Wilson, John B. 1581
Wilson, Lawrence 1582
Wilson, Louis N. 180-82
Wilson, Louis R. 952
Wilson, Ruth D. 798
Winn, Ralph B. 279
Winship, Albert E. 345
Winsor, Charlotte 2044
Winter, Nathan H. 549
Winters, Elmer A. 2178
Winton, Ruth M. 2486
Wirth, Arthur G. 550, 1732, 2045-46, 2487
Wise, Arthur E. 551
Wish, Harvey 2488
Woerdehoff, Frank J. 2489
Wolcott, John D. 1583
Wolin, Sheldon S. 1949
Wollenberg, Charles M. 552
Wood, James E., Jr. 553
Woodburn, James A. 799
Woodbury, Marda A. 183
Woodrow Wilson Foundation 2490
Woodson, Carter G. 1584, 2491-92
Woody, Thomas 280-81, 346, 1228-29, 1734
Woolverton, John F. 1585
Wormeley, G. Smith 2493
Wright, Edith A. 184, 216
Wright, Frank W. 2179

TITLE INDEX

This index lists all titles of books cited in the text. Titles of essays are excluded. It is alphabetized letter by letter, and numbers refer to entry numbers.

Title Index

American Education: The Colonial Experience, 1607-1783 297, 993

American Education and Vocationalism 245

American Education in Foreign Perspectives 220

American Education through the Soviet Looking Glass 1837

American Heritage Pictorial Atlas of United States History, The 25

American Higher Education: A Documentary History 230

American Higher Education: Directions Old and New 571

American Higher Education, 1945-1970 1983

American Higher Education: Toward an Uncertain Future 650

American Humanism 2341

American Ideas about Adult Education, 1710-1951 224

American Ideas and Education 321

American Intervention 46

Americanization in the United States 1955

American Lawyers in a Changing Society 582

American Legacy of Learning, The 190

American Lyceum, Its History and Contribution to Education, The 1345

American Nonpublic Schools 320

American Population before the Federal Census of 1790 17

American Political Parties 43

American Primers, Indian Primers, Royal Primers 2104

American Public School, The 308

American Public Schools 339

American Revolution, The (Shy) 53

American Revolution, The: A Review of Changing Interpretations 46

American Road to Culture, The 1835

Americans, The 962

American School in Transition, The 306

American Science in the Age of Jackson 2262

American Social History before 1860 53

American Social History since 1860 53

American Spirit in Education, The 336

American University, The 566

American University in the Twentieth Century, The 622

American Writers on Education after 1865 1601

America's Educational Tradition 309

Analysis of the Specific References to Negroes in Selected Curricula for the Education of Teachers, An 1815

Analytical Index to Barnard's American Journal of Education 169

Ancients and Axioms 1105

Annals of Public Education in the State of New York from 1626 to 1746 259

Annotated Bibliography of the History of Education in Kansas, An 127

Annotated McGuffey, The 2118

Anti-Intellectualism in American Life 2323

Apprenticeship and Apprenticeship Education in Colonial New England and New York 1155

Articles in American Studies, 1954-1968 50

Augustana 807

Automation, Education, and Human Values 1772

Awarding College Credit for Non-College Learning 1959

B

Battlefield and Classroom 1701

Beginning of the Future, The 779

Beginnings of Public Education in North Carolina, The 202

Benjamin Franklin 1224

Benjamin Franklin and the University of Pennsylvania 1199

Benjamin Franklin on Education 189

Berkeley Student Revolt, The 1949

Better Than Rubies 522

Between Harvard and America 1652

Between Two Worlds 585

Title Index

T

SUBJECT INDEX

This index includes subject areas within the text. Underlined entries refer to main topic areas. It is alphabetized letter by letter, and numbers refer to entry numbers.

Subject Index

Alaska, University of 2415
Albemarle County, Va., Freedman's
      schools in 1558
Alcott, Bronson 1581
Alcott House 2186
Alexandria, Va.
  history of educational developments
      in 1011
  Lancasterian schools of 1421
Algebra, teaching of in the colonial
      period 1176, 1180
Allen, William F. 1495
Alma maters, colonial 1089
Almanacs
  classical elements in 1032
  educational theory expressed in
      1175
Alternative education 1893
Alton, Ill., boycotts of segregated
      schools in 1686
American Council of Learned Societies
      2362
American Education Society 1237
American Federation of Teachers 1859
American Indians
  bibliographies on 46, 55, 60
  education of 347, 2462
    in Catholic schools 513
    church-state conflict and 481,
      1690
    in the colonial period 1016,
      1026, 1145-46, 1196
    in the early national period
      (1783-1865) 1233, 1323,
      1401
    federal government and 2198
    in the period of educational ex-
      pansion (1865-1900) 1609,
      1638, 1690, 1701
  general reference works on 19,
      35
  image of in the colonial South
      1124
  See also names of Indian tribes
      (e.g. Choctaw Indians)
American Institute of Instruction 2395
American Journal of Education 403
American Missionary Association 1697
American studies
  bibliography on 50

periodicals on 75
Amherst College
  Nineteenth century student life
      at 1239, 1336
  plan for reading and study at
      803
Anderson, Alexander 2097
Anthropology, history of 2458
Antiintellectualism 2323
Antioch College 824, 897, 1360
Apprenticeship education 1155
Archaeology, periodicals on 75
Archives. See Manuscript and
      archival materials
Arithmetic. See Mathematics
Arkansas
  education in the national period
      (1783-1865) 1452
  of blacks 1697
  legal education in 697
  teacher's institutes in 1695
  See also Little Rock, Ark.
Art education 2176
Arts, rise of in higher education
      722
Atlanta, Ga., struggle for equal
      education in 2025,
      2469
Atlanta Medical College 1285
Atlanta University 2442
Augustana College 807
Autobiographies, bibliographies of
      56, 116
Aydelotte, Frank 810
Ayres, Leonard 2231

B

Babbitt, Irving 1905
Bagley, William Chandler 2335
Bailyn, Bernard 371, 470
Bank Street College of Education
      2044
Baptist Church, Southern higher
      education and 619
Barnard, F.A.P. 886, 1402, 1672
Barnard, Henry 196, 403, 1347,
      1392, 1433, 2109
  bibliography on 147
Barnum, P.T. 2059

Subject Index

Subject Index

Subject Index

Madison, James 991, 1284
Maine, education in 199
  higher education 654
Mann, Horace 249, 897, 1265,
        1309, 1317, 1341, 1360,
        1389-90, 1426, 1434,
        1439, 1441-42, 1460,
        1468, 2393
  bibliography on 115, 134, 138
Manual education. See Vocational
        education
Manuscript and archival materials
  bibliographies of and guides to
        38-39, 54
  periodicals on 75
  preservation and management of
        23
Manuscript and archival materials,
        educational 204
  bibliography on 176
Marsh, James 1574
Marwedel, Emma 1370
Maryland, education in
  the early national period (1763-
        1865) 1267
    blacks 1412
  the period of educational expansion
        (1865-1900) 1684
Massachusetts
  compulsory education in 2418
  education in the colonial period
        1050, 1197
  education in the early national
        period (1783-1865) 1243,
        1426
  higher education in 591
  history of education in 205
  licensing of schoolmasters in
        colonial 986
  Nineteenth century school reform
        in 458
  teacher training in early 256
  urban schools in 466
  See also Boston; Cambridge, Mass.;
        Lexington, Mass.; New
        Bedford, Mass.; Quincy,
        Mass.
Massachusetts, University of 822
Mathematics
  bibliography on 132

teaching of 2175
  in the colonial period 1062,
        1139, 1163
  textbooks 2095, 2157
  See also Algebra
Mather, Cotton 1100, 1122, 1152
Maxwell, William H. 2034
Mead, George H. 2270
Mechanical engineering 2232
  teaching of in the Nineteenth
        century 1310
Medical education 612, 638-39,
        780
  in Alabama 671
  in the colonial period 1112,
        1149
  in the early national period
        (1783-1865) 1377,
        1562
  in Europe (1750-1800) 957
  psychiatry in 728
  See also Atlanta Medical College
Meiklejohn, Alexander 1905, 2365
Menomonie Indians, education of
        2347
Mental health, education and 2146
Mental tests 2494
Methodist Episcopal Church, Nine-
        teenth century Indian
        mission schools of 1323
Michigan, education in 205
  the early national period (1783-
        1865) 1274, 1363
  higher education 625, 839,
        1363
  state control of 2331
  of teachers 2114
  See also Kalamazoo, Mich.
Michigan, University of 813, 830,
        908, 1518, 1537, 2275
  speaker ban at 688
Michigan State University 885
Microforms, guides to 8-9
Middlebury College, Nineteenth
        century student life at
        1239
Middle class
  in the creation of free schools
        1694
  higher education and 361, 580,
        1766

Nineteenth century Indian mission
schools of 1346, 1401
Presidential election (1892), Catholic
Indian education issues in
513
Presidents (U.S.), statements on edu-
cation 273. See also
College presidents; Ken-
nedy, John F.
Primers 2081, 2104, 2164. See also
NEW ENGLAND PRIMER,
THE
Princeton University 945
colonial period 1035, 1131, 1153
curriculum 970
influence on Southern education
987, 1297
Printers and publishers, of children's
books 2172
Private colleges 703, 2022
Private schools 320
in the colonial period 1159,
1163-64, 1212, 1222
in the early national period (1783-
1865) 1420, 1552
See also Catholic education
Professions 2228
Programmed learning 2350
Progressive Education Association 1896
Progressivism. See Education,
progressive
Project Focus 649
Protestantism, education and 1534
Psychiatry
of B. Rush 1523
in higher education 2282
in medical education 728
Psychoanalysis, curriculum theory and
2166
Psychology
origins of 2200
scientific 2071
teaching of in higher education
655
See also Child psychology and
guidance; Educational
psychology
Public Education Association of New
York City 392
Public School Society of New York
1398, 1417

Publishers. See Printers and
publishers
Puerto Ricans, education of 1820,
1824, 1827
bibliography of 105
Purdue University 1785
Puritans, education of 1141, 1169,
1172, 1184

Q

Quakers, educational activities of
237
in the colonial period 969,
1038, 1193, 1228
in New Jersey 280
Quincy, Josiah 2376
Quincy, Mass., education in (1873-
1881) 1664

R

Race and education 543, 2458
in the early national period
(1783-1865) 1320
instructional materials and 2080
in the Twentieth century 1857,
2038
See also Segregation
Rainey, Homer P. 917
Readers. See McGuffey readers
Reconstruction, education and 219,
1240, 1405, 1669
in Georgia 1354, 1657
in Little Rock, Ark. 1655
in New Orleans 1340
in Virginia 1387
See also Freedmen, education of
Reed College 824
Religion
bibliography on 46, 53
general reference works on 33
periodicals on the history of 75
science and in the colonial
period 1043
Religion and education 423, 487,
553, 2219
in the colonial period 1067,
1072, 1081, 1131, 1202
documentary history of 238